MY ANCESTOR WAS IN THE ROYAL NAVY

by Ian H Waller F

SOCIETY OF GENEALOGISTS ENTERPRISES LTD.

Published by
Society of Genealogists Enterprises Limited
14 Charterhouse Buildings, Goswell Road
London EC1M 7BA.

ISBN: 978-1-907199-24-0

British Library Cataloguing in Publication Data.
A CIP Catalogue record for this book is available from the British Library.

The Society of Genealogists Enterprises Limited is a wholly owned
subsidiary of the Society of Genealogists, a registered charity, no 233701.

About the Author

Ian Waller is a Fellow of the Society of Genealogists and a professional genealogist
specialising in English research. He is a council member and currently Chairman of AGRA
(The Association of Genealogists and Researchers in Archives). He has taught family history
to various U3A groups and at adult education establishments in Bedfordshire and
Hertfordshire as well as lecturing widely at the Society and to family and local history groups
around the Home Counties. He has also written many articles for the family history press and
is author of other Society publications in the 'My Ancestor...' series.

Cover Images - Foreground: Portrait of Captain Philip Beaver R.N (1766-1813) in naval full dress
uniform, c. 1805. Oil on canvas by John Opie. Public domain image (Wikimedia). Right: Compass, Toulon
Naval Museum. CC licence (Wikimedia). Background: Battle of Trafalgar by Auguste Mayer. Oil on
canvas, 1836. Public domain image (Wikimedia).

ii

CONTENTS

List of illustrations

INTRODUCTION

A s an island nation the sea has always played a great part in our defence and history. For over a century the Royal Navy as the 'senior service' numbered amongst one of the largest employers in the country. Besides examining the records and informing you how to find out about your ancestor's service this book also examines social aspects including what motivated your ancestors to sign up and enables you to gain an insight into the reality of a seaman's life.

To put this in context the following gives some idea of the numbers employed by the Royal Navy. In 1800 the strength was 128,000 men, in 1805 132,000 men and then in 1820 20,000 men. Each First Rate ship in the mid-1800s carried as many as 900 men. The strength obviously increased rapidly during war periods. In World War One over 430,000 men served with a further 30,000 in reserve forces. In World War Two over 50,000 Royal Navy members lost their lives, about 10% of the men. As such many families will have an ancestor who was connected with the service in some way be it a seaman, a dockyard worker, coastguard or a member of the reserves.

Why do we have a Royal Navy?

The Royal Navy's basic responsibilities included protecting and policing trade routes and our colonies, defending our coastline, imposing blockades on hostile powers, including the fighting of sea battles and the capture of enemy ships and crews. To do this the fleet had to be continuously battle ready and had to be larger than the next two largest navies put together.

Family historians are fortunate because there are masses of records detailing both the personnel of all ranks and the operational administration of the service. You may initially learn that your ancestor was a seaman from research not associated with the Navy such as a census return, civil registration certificate or from members of your family telling you that your ancestor had a Greenwich pension or was torpedoed in the First World War. Unlike Rodney and Del Boy's Uncle Albert in 'Only Fools and Horses' some seafarers' tales are worth listening to in order to get you started on the path to finding out more about your Navy ancestor and the work they actually did. All you may know is that your ancestor 'was in the Navy'.

Seaman or sailor

To identify your naval ancestor the occupational term of seaman or sailor was generally used. If your ancestor was a member of the Merchant Navy he was usually referred to as a mariner. Seaman was the preferred term of the Navy for its sailors. In many official documents members of the Royal Navy also frequently recorded the name of their ship as well as their rank or rating. The term 'sailor' as opposed to seaman was particularly common in the mid-Victorian period amongst crews of Portsmouth based ships.

This book covers all aspects of research for a Royal Navy ancestor whether a Commissioned Officer, Warrant Officer or a Rating. By necessity it is in two parts, the first part covering service, pension and other personnel records the second part covering administrative and operational records. To undertake research for your ancestor properly it is also necessary to have an understanding of the history and organisation of the Royal Navy, particularly around the reform and crossover period of the early to mid -1800s. Over the last few years it seems that the popular family history press has not published that many articles on Royal Navy research so this book aims to redress that balance and provide practical help to the family historian.

1. Fouled anchor is a naval symbol symbolising trials and tribulations.

The challenges of the record

Many of the records are very complex and sometimes heavily abbreviated and all too often it is necessary to look at various sets of records to build up a full and detailed picture of a person's career. If you are familiar with the records and know where to look and how to use them you will have a better chance of finding all the information about your Navy ancestor and what he (or she) did whilst in the service.

The mass of paperwork generated by the Admiralty can also present challenges to family historians. Many records are not indexed and as such it is sometimes difficult to identify individuals beyond name and rank, particularly for the period pre-1850 where perhaps only a ship's muster or description book gives genealogical and career details. There are a number of additional finding aids and resources available to help but to effectively search you need some basic information such as the name of at least one ship on which your ancestor may have served. It is generally easier to find information about a commissioned or Warrant Officer than a seaman before 1853. The other common challenge is in determining which of the different divisions of the Navy that your ancestor may have served in. Importantly you should try and confirm which branch he served in and whether he was a regular or a reservist as service records are different particularly in the early 20th century.

On a practical point it is recommended that you frequently check for new or additional online digitised records and material relating to Royal Navy ancestry.

An English man-o'war shortening sail entering Portsmouth harbour, by Dominic Serres (1719–1793). Public domain image.

4

CHAPTER ONE

Overview and history of the Royal Navy

The Early and Tudor Navy

England had no navy or fleet until the reign of King Alfred (871-901) whose first naval engagement was in 882 against the Danish in the Stour estuary, after which King Alfred had long ships designed and built which ultimately defeated the Danes around the Essex coast and the Thames estuary. It was these skirmishes which gave rise to the belief that King Alfred was considered to be the founder of the Navy.

During the reign of Edward the Confessor (1042-1066), the Cinque Ports were established - Dover, Hastings, Romney, Hythe and Sandwich, although Rye and Winchelsea later became Cinque Ports. Their purpose was to enable prompt mobilisation of mainly merchant vessels into a fighting navy in the event of enemy attacks or piracy.

In 1190, Richard I introduced maritime laws known as the Laws of Oleron which dealt with the rights and responsibilities of ships' captains in relation to discipline, pay, cargoes, sickness on board, mutiny and pilotage.

In 1415, Henry V's English invasion force was carried across the English Channel by around 1500 ships to fight at Agincourt. Henry V also built the first two purpose-built battleships of over 1,000 tons, namely 'Jesus' and 'Grace Dieu'.

Trinity House was inaugurated in 1514 to develop navigational aids including lighthouses, beacons and buoys. It was these beacons which signalled the impending invasion of the Spanish Armada in 1588.

The first naval dock in Britain at Portsmouth was built and commissioned in 1540 and in 1546 the Council of the Marine (later the Navy Board) was established, which remained virtually unchanged for 300 years. Later the Office of Admiralty was created which set up the administrative machinery for the control of the fleet.

2. Tudor navy.

The Royal Navy was, and still is, the only sea based service of the British armed forces and the 'modern' Navy traces its roots back to the time of the Spanish Armada in the late 16th century although Britain had been involved in sea warfare much earlier. Thus, the Royal Navy is the oldest branch of the military services in Britain and rightly earned the title of the 'Senior Service'. Certainly until the mid-20th century it was the most formidable navy in the world and was the key to the establishment of and maintaining and protecting the British Empire.

Tradition shows therefore that the 'modern' Navy was organised during the reign of Henry VIII with the establishment of the Council of the Marine, its secretariat, worldwide dockyards and purpose-built warships. Its successor, the Navy Board, then became responsible for administration until 1832 when it was amalgamated with the Admiralty.

Henry knew of the naval power of Scots King James IV who had amassed a large fleet to control the Western Isles and saw it as a direct threat to his prestige and more importantly a significant threat to England because Scotland was, at that time, closely allied to France.

To counter to this threat Henry established his own fleet and the 'Navy Royale' as it was then known began its long service. New purpose built battleships such as the *Mary Rose* were built alongside smaller galleons giving Henry an initial fleet of 58 ships partly funded by the huge financial resources from the dissolution of the monasteries. The *Mary Rose* was one of the larger ships of the fleet and was one of the first ships to carry heavy guns firing out of gun ports in the side of the hull. This is where the term 'port hole' originated.

When Elizabeth I came to the throne she inherited only 27 ships. England entered conflict with the Spanish who wanted to help restore Catholicism to England. Instead of building up the fleet again Elizabeth encouraged private enterprise in the fight against the Spanish. She used men including Sir Francis Drake to command her fleet and relied heavily on private merchant ships in attacks on the Spanish.

In 1588, the Spanish Armada sought to end the reign of Elizabeth I and thus restore Catholicism to England but it did not succeed because of our naval supremacy. The 80 English fighting ships at the time outnumbered the Spanish who, although having a fleet of around 130, only deployed around 20 fighting ships mainly as convoy escorts.

The Anthony Roll

The Anthony Roll is the earliest record of ships of the English Navy and dates from 1540. It is so named after Anthony Anthony its creator.

It consists of three parchment rolls giving information on 58 naval vessels including size, number of guns, crew and other equipment. The rolls were originally kept in the Royal Library. In 1680 Charles II gave two of the three rolls to diarist Samuel Pepys who had them bound as a single volume book which is currently deposited in the library of Magdalene College in Cambridge. The other roll remains intact and is deposited in the British Library.

This roll is the only known fully illustrated inventory of ships of the English Tudor navy. The inventories as listed have proven to be highly accurate although most of the ship illustrations are known to not be so because the detail of the ship design, particularly the flagging and rigging is thought to be illustrative only.

As the roll is the only known contemporary document detailing Tudor battleships it proved invaluable when the *Mary Rose* was salvaged in the 1980s. As she sank by accident in 1545 comparison between the information in the Roll and the physical evidence of the raised remains of the ship helped in the study of naval history of the period.

The first roll lists the carracks, a three - or four mast sailing ship developed in the 15th century for use on the high seas. The second roll lists galleons, oar-powered sailing vessels, and the third roll lists pinnaces, (light boats propelled by oars or small sails and used as a tender for warships and some merchant vessels) and row barges which are basically smaller versions of galleons.

The Navy in the Commonwealth period

The Navy Royale underwent little change from Elizabeth's death in 1603 to the accession of King Charles I in 1625. By 1633 his fleet numbered 50 ships but financial problems and poor administration meant that the number was reduced to 42 by 1642. Charles I levied 'ship money' from 1634 which was an unpopular tax which it is said contributed to the outbreak of the first Civil War in 1642. This tax was supposedly only applied to coastal towns during times of war. Charles I claimed that he owned the sea and as such taxed the people living within 15 miles of the coast. The collection of the tax inland during peacetime started in 1634 and provoked increasing resistance by 1636 although it was enforced by the Ships Money Act of 1640. There are few surviving records of this tax, held in local record offices, most of which relate to schedules of arrears, petitions and some lists of those liable to pay the tax.

At the start of the Civil War the Navy which had, despite the raising of ships money, been inadequately funded, declared in favour of Parliament. The Commonwealth administration built the most powerful and effectively run navy Britain has ever seen with a fleet of 102 ships. The fleet line was divided into three squadrons (red, white and blue) each with an admiral, vice-admiral and rear admiral which were the origins of today's Flag Officer ranks. The enlarged fleet proved its worth in fighting the Dutch War and against the Spanish. When King Charles II came to the throne he inherited a fleet of 154 ships at which time it became a permanent professional navy resulting in the establishment of the Royal Navy as we know it today.

To maintain the Royal Navy at its Commonwealth period strength and efficiency became a major problem until Samuel Pepys, the diarist, rose to the challenge firstly at the Navy Board and then going on to the Admiralty making both successful and efficient departments of government.

Wars against France and Spain

In 1688 a political revolution resulted in the fall of Pepys and started a series of wars against France and Spain which lasted until 1815. During this time Britain continually directed its main strength onto the world's oceans. The British Navy won a series of sea battles including Barfleur and La Hogue in 1692, Cape Finisterre in 1747, Quiberon Bay in 1759, the Glorious First of June in 1794, the Nile in 1798 and of course Trafalgar in 1805. Few sea battles have been fought since.

If your ancestor was in the Navy at the time of Trafalgar then there is an online database available through The National Archives website **www.nationalarchives. gov.uk/trafalgarancestors** which includes around 18,000 men and 1 woman. Most entries contain a brief biographical sketch including rank/rating, age and birthplace (in many instances).

Between 1689 and 1697 France defeated an Anglo-Dutch fleet off Beachy Head, Sussex, and carried out several campaigns against British merchant shipping. Part of the British fleet also had major naval success at Les Saintes in the West Indies in 1782. By 1793 there was a significant decline in the skills of the French Navy enabling the Royal Navy to gain victories in both the French Revolutionary and Napoleonic Wars.

During this time the Spanish Empire also remained a major target of British sea power. In 1704 the British captured Gibraltar which became our most important strategic base at the mouth of the Mediterranean. This attack was the first involving the Royal Marines (the naval infantry and artillery force) and was their only major battle honour although it has fought in many places since. Naval operations in the War of Spanish Succession were undertaken with our Dutch allies against both the Spanish and French. The war focused on the acquisition of a Mediterranean base and resulted in the capture of both Gibraltar and Port Mahon in Minorca. In addition both Newfoundland and Nova Scotia were obtained and victory was also achieved at St Vincent in 1797.

The war with France continued for around another ten years. The Navy's contribution during this time was that it prevented Napoleon rebuilding his fleet and in so doing encouraged enemies in Europe to rise up against him. In 1812 war broke out with America but Britain was able to deploy enough maritime strength along the eastern seaboard to bring peace in 1814.

During the 18th century the Royal Navy also carried out peaceful tasks amongst which was the scientific survey to find out more about the geography of the world. The Navy under Captain James Cook discovered Hawaii and mapped New Zealand and the east coast of Australia. It was also during these longer voyages that advances in health of crews at sea improved resulting in fewer debilitating diseases on board ships.

The Fleet

In order for the Navy to be successful in its various battles and blockades only larger ships were used in the main lines of battle and this led to the term 'battleship' being used. These were considered the most effective and powerful ships of the fleet. Throughout time ships needed more guns to be effective and to survive. In the mid-1700s a ship with 50 guns was needed but by the early 1800s that had increased to a minimum number of 74. This system of classifying ships became known as 'Rates' and was directly related to their size and gun power, which originally reflected on the amount of pay received by a captain. The larger the size of his ship the more he was paid.

The largest vessels with three decks and 100 guns were known as 'First Rates' and these tended to be the flagships such as *HMS Victory*. 'Second Rates' had three decks and 90 guns. 'Third Rates' had 74 guns and two decks. The largest number of ships of the fleet fell into the Third Rate class. 'Fourth Rates' originally had between 50 and 60 guns but by the mid-1700s most had 60 guns. For the family historian it is useful to be aware of the type and size of ship that your ancestor may have served on as this also affected the size of the crew and the number of Marines carried.

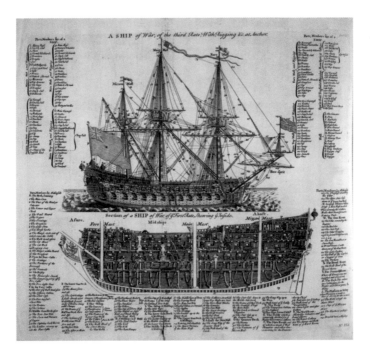

3. Third Rate Ship c. 1728. (1728 Cyclopaedia Vol 2).

A different type of warship emerged in the mid-1700s principally to protect merchant shipping. These were frigates of which there were two types both rated and both with upper deck guns; 'Fifth Rates' carried 32-36 guns and 'Sixth Rates' had 28 guns.

In the 1790s the Americans built large frigates with 44 guns spread over two decks. These were successful in the war of 1812 and this influenced Britain to subsequently commission frigates from around 1820 with 40-50 guns. They were all built to a similar design to the American frigates.

During the 1800s the Navy's main priority was in maintaining a fleet large enough to deal with any enemy offensives. Initially the fleet consisted of sailing ships which were more powerful than those at Nelson's disposal. The development of the screw propeller allowed later ships of the fleet from 1849 to become steam powered as opposed to relying on sail. It also meant that seamen had to develop new skills in order to man and sail the new ships.

Between the Crimean War and First World War

The Crimean War (1854-1856) gave Britain the opportunity to develop its ships even further with the introduction of iron built ships. *HMS Warrior* commissioned in 1861 was the first of a new breed of ships subsequently replacing the wooden ships used up to that time.

However until the late 1880s, confusion existed over ship design. Armour plating became thicker and subsequently guns were bigger, frequently mounted on surface deck swivel turrets, but it was difficult to combine these with sail vessels retained in some cases due to limited coal supplies and thus uneconomical steam engines. By the 1890s steel was widely used in ship construction. Steel armour also allowed the construction of large armoured cruisers which proved to be faster and more powerful than the earlier built steam battleships.

For almost a century between the Napoleonic and First World War the Navy's main thrust was in 'shore bombardment'. Perhaps the most notable was in the Gulf of Finland in 1855 where 3½ days of non-stop bombardment took place using mortar-vessels, gunboats and rocket-launches which destroyed the enemy positions with no British losses.

Mine warfare came to the fore during the Crimean War when the Navy suffered the losses of *HMS Merlin* and *HMS Firefly*. This led during the 1860s to the development of the 'locomotive torpedo', an air driven mechanical device capable of delivering an underwater charge. The first torpedo fired by the Navy was in 1877. In the 1880s

Britain built heavily armed torpedo boat destroyers; the first entering service in 1894. Torpedoes and the development of internal combustion engines and batteries gave the Navy its first submarines and in the first ten years of the 20th century more than 70 submarines were built. British torpedoes in this period covered around 4,500 metres running at speeds of up to 35 knots.

A major reform of the Navy took place over a six year period starting in 1904 following the appointment of Sir John Fisher as First Sea Lord. He thought that by exploiting revolutionary technology Britain could maintain maritime security and *HMS Dreadnought* was the result. He also ordered the scrapping of older ships and those ships which were in reserve were made ready for war. Most of the fleet was concentrated in home waters in order to meet the impending German threat. Fisher's foresight was paramount in allowing Britain to obtain naval supremacy leading up to the First World War.

The First World War

From the naval point of view, The First World War was the time for the fleet to prove themselves having undergone major reforms. However the Royal Navy was only involved in a few minor engagements at sea. During the war it was mainly deployed at home in an effort to blockade Germany and to draw the German 'High Seas Fleet' into engagements where decisive victory could be gained. The Battle of Jutland was probably the best-known First World War battle where the Royal Navy suffered heavy losses but succeeded in its strategic goal of making sure the German Navy never put to sea again and subsequently scuttled itself in Scapa Flow.

At the start of the war Germany had armed cruisers stationed around the world and some were used to attack British merchant shipping. The Royal Navy systematically hunted them down and the German East Asia Squadron was defeated near the Falkland Islands at the end of 1914.

Early on in the war the British initiated a naval blockade of Germany which was effective in preventing supplies from reaching its ports. At the same time international waters were mined restricting ship movements in entire sections of the oceans. Germany began an operation using unrestricted submarine warfare in an attempt to sever supply lines to Britain. At the start of the war Germany had 29 U-boats and in the first ten weeks of conflict five British cruisers had been lost to them. In retaliation the Royal Navy employed anti-submarine measures in the form of Q-ships, increased patrols, use of depth charges and hydrophones. Notwithstanding these measures too many merchant ships were lost as a result of enemy action resulting in the widespread introduction of convoys which reduced losses significantly. In May 1917, Britain introduced its convoy system. Convoy of between 10 to 50 merchant ships were frequently escorted by a cruiser, six destroyers, 11 armed trawlers and a pair of torpedo boats, together with aerial reconnaissance that could detect the movement of enemy submarines. Convoy gathering points were established along the Atlantic coast of both North and South America, to transport men, arms, food and horses, in other words the basic supplies of the war effort. The convoy system resulted in a sharp decline in German submarine damage to British shipping.

The Royal Navy was also heavily committed in the Dardanelles Campaign against the Turks and instigated its land force known as the Royal Naval Division.

During the period of the First World War personnel numbers increased from around 250,000 in 1914 to around 450,000 at the end of the war. Similar increases took place in the numbers of Royal Marine personnel whose strength in 1918 numbered 55,000. The Women's Royal Naval Service 'WRNS' was established in 1917 and numbered around 7,000, their prime role being to release men to crew the ships and for the women to take over communications, logistics and general administration. They were disbanded at the end of the war but reinstituted in 1939.

The Royal Naval Air Service was established in 1914 to have a mainly reconnaissance role. Converted ships were used to launch aircraft with but the planes landed in the sea. It was not until 1918 that the Navy commissioned its first purpose built aircraft carrier, *HMS Argus*.

Between the two World Wars

In the inter-war period the Royal Navy was affected by the signing of various treaties which restricted its power. The Washington Naval Treaty signed in 1922, together with the financial conditions which existed in post war Britain meant that the Admiralty had no choice but to scrap many of its ships and cancel a progressive shipbuilding programme. It also converted three ships to become aircraft carriers, *HMS Courageous, Furious* and *Glorious*. There were few new additions to the fleet throughout the 1920s and early 1930s aggravated by the 1930 London Naval Treaty. By 1938 when most of the limits were being ignored, and because of the developments in the arms race, new ships were commissioned including *Illustrious* class aircraft carriers, such as *Ark Royal*, and more cruisers and destroyers.

The Second World War

Although the Royal Navy had the world's largest fleet when it entered the Second World War logistically it could not fight Germany, Italy and Japan simultaneously.

When the war commenced it was only against Germany which was totally unprepared for war.

Success against the Germans began with the sinking of *Graf Spee* in the Battle of the River Plate in December 1939. The most successful German ship was *Bismarck* which sank *HMS Hood*, in the Atlantic in 1941. In retaliation *Bismarck* was crippled by bombers from *HMS Ark Royal* and then wrecked by *HMS King George V* and *Rodney*.

During the war and the Battle of the Atlantic, France's defeat gave German U-boats strategic Atlantic bases so they could effectively attack the convoys from North America which kept Britain supplied. The Battle of the Atlantic was the longest continuous naval campaign running from mid-1940 to the end of 1943.

The defeat of France created problems in the Mediterranean. A new British fleet was created which replaced the French fleet, up to that time an allied navy, and to attack it at Mers El Kebir. Italy also entered the war at this point so the Mediterranean Fleet asserted its superiority over the Italians disabling half of their battleships in the attack on Taranto. The Germans ultimately joined with Italy giving them renewed air and submarine power and caused a fair amount of damage to the British fleet. The Mediterranean campaign centred on Malta, because the British used the island as a base for ships, submarines and aircraft allowing them to disrupt enemy supplies destined for enemy forces in North Africa. The British Navy mounted major convoy operations to sustain Malta. After concerted efforts by the British the Mediterranean finally re-opened as a shipping route. The Italians changed allegiance after the successful invasion first of Sicily then of Italy.

Fleets of new ships were developed for operations that became fully fledged invasions. The most notable operation was 'Neptune', the maritime aspect of Operation 'Overlord', during the landings in Normandy began in June 1944.

Being heavily involved in the war against Germany and Italy, the Royal Navy was almost powerless to halt the Japanese onslaught that began in December 1941. Two ships were sent to Singapore but these were sunk by Japanese Navy torpedo bombers leading to the fall of Singapore and at the time the end of Royal Navy involvement in South East Asia. However, this was short-lived as later in the war the Royal Navy reappeared in Asia in strength. In 1945 a large British fleet based around a powerful carrier force fought alongside the Americans in Japanese waters.

The Royal Navy seemed to fare better in World War Two than it did in World War One but still suffered heavy losses both in ships and personnel. 1,525 vessels including 224 warships were lost and well over 50,000 naval personnel lost their lives, some 20,000 more than in the First World War.

Details of the deaths of over 125,000 Navy officers and ratings from both world wars are available on both the Commonwealth Wargrave Commission website: **www.cwgc.org** and **www.naval-history.net**

Social change in the 20th century

After the end of the Victorian period ship-board conditions became more humane; after all, seamen were members of a second-to-none permanent uniformed military service. Both officers and men became highly trained in the use of new technologies. New establishments were founded to teach gunnery and torpedo work and officer training and education began to be carried out at both Dartmouth and Greenwich. The RN Museum at Portsmouth holds a series of Gunnery manuals mainly associated with *HMS Excellent* (Portsmouth training unit and headquarters) for the period 1817-1860.

Life at sea was transformed when communal eating and sleeping was replaced by a system of 'centralised messing', where sailors slept and ate in separate areas and where bunks replaced hammocks. The Navy also realised that it needed better qualified men to master advancing technology and if it was to attract the right type of personnel then conditions at sea had to significantly improve.

The only 20th century mutiny took place in 1931 (Invergordon Mutiny) as a result of significant cuts in wages of seamen which had happened throughout the 1920s. Crews of various warships refused to sail on exercises but on a positive note this led to prescribed pay rates being restored in 1934.

During the mid-1950s the officer entry age was increased to 18. It also became much easier for ratings to achieve officer rank. Members of the Women's Royal Naval Service (WRNS) served at sea for the first time in the 1990s and today there is no distinction between men and women in the Royal Navy.

Board Room of the Admiralty, 1808, from Microcosm of London. Public domain image.

CHAPTER TWO

Administrative organisation of the Navy

In order to understand where your ancestor fitted into the Royal Navy it is necessary to know of how the Royal Navy was organised and controlled by the various bodies as each had specific responsibilities.

The records in the ADM series at The National Archives are divided into 29 specific divisions reflecting Navy organisation and generally you will need to know in which department your ancestor's records are likely to appear.

The Admiralty

The Board of Admiralty which is traditionally comprised of up of seven members, first came into existence in the reign of Charles I. It has however not had a continuous role and was re-commissioned between 1689 and 1701 and then from 1709. The Board which acted on the advice of the Navy Board (see below) was in effect the government quango or political arm of the Navy made up of members of Parliament and responsible to the electorate for procuring and distributing supplies and finding enough men to maintain this fighting force. As the Admiralty was not a permanent establishment its role was basically supervisory.

4. The old Admiralty Building c.1830.

The Admiralty had no direct responsibility for the day to day operation of the Navy or for the appointment of its senior officers. Operations were handled by the Secretary of State and senior appointments were discussed in Cabinet and with the Monarch, It is interesting to note that all regulations, orders and instructions were issued through rather than by the Admiralty. Three boards were set up to administer the Navy:

The Navy Board

The Navy Board was established in 1546 to organise the administration of the Navy and advise the Lord Admiral. Until the mid-1600s it looked after all aspects of naval administration but after this period other boards took on responsibility for other specific areas thus leaving the Navy Board to concentrate on building and maintaining the vast fleet of ships and also advising the Board of Admiralty. Originally members of the Navy Board were drawn from the professional men of the Navy which included shipwrights as well as commissioned officers. With a review of naval administration in 1832 the duties previously undertaken by the Board were integrated with the Admiralty.

Much of the background material that you would need to flesh out the bones of your ancestor's naval career can be found in the vast records of the Navy Board at both

The National Archives and importantly at the National Maritime Museum including financial matters (including budgets, naval estimates etc.), naval medicine (including the administration of hospitals at Haslar and Stonehouse), transport, shipbuilding (including repair surveys and cost estimates of ships), disciplinary matters, and research and development in matters such as improvements to the health of seamen and shipbuilding techniques.

The Victualling Board

Before 1684 all food and drink for Navy ships was supplied by private contractors, however the quality was generally poor and varied so the Victualling Commissioners took over the central responsibility to bring a degree of uniformity to all naval supplies. The office of Assistant Controller of Victualling Accounts was created in 1691 but was relatively short-lived, being abolished in 1731.

From 1793, the Victualling Board was responsible for feeding the Navy in Britain and overseas which was a mammoth task as it was estimated that around 400,000 men were scattered around the world in such places as India, the Americas and Australia. Every week each man required 7lb. of biscuits, seven gallons of beer, 6lb. of meat, two pints of pease, three pints of oatmeal, 6oz. butter and 12oz. cheese. In context to feed the crew of a 74-gun ship for a week required two tons of biscuit, a ton of salt beef, a quarter of a ton of cheese and 4,480 gallons of beer.

To facilitate logistics victualling yards were established in various parts of the world to supply Navy ships whilst on their voyages (see later) as it was not possible to procure everything that was needed all the time and on all stations and that it was customary that ships in port received fresh unsalted beef and fresh vegetables. Provision also had to be made to supply fresh water in places where this was not readily available. Contractors still supplied provisions to the Victualling Board's yards in London, Portsmouth, Plymouth, Chatham and Dover as well as overseas yards at Gibraltar and Port Mahon. This administration continued until 1832 at which point the responsibility was integrated into the Board of Admiralty.

The Sick and Hurt Board

During war times from around 1653 the Sick and Hurt commissioners dealt with wounds and medical matters but in peacetime such responsibilities rested with the Navy Board. Until the Seven Years War the Navy did not have a permanent medical organisation and sick and injured men were cared for outside of the Navy administration. The commissioners were responsible for the relief of sick and wounded seamen. The only establishment within Navy control was the Royal

Greenwich Hospital which was a home for pensioner seamen and which had only limited space for invalids. It was not until the mid-1700s that the naval hospitals at Haslar and Stonehouse were developed, enabling the Navy Board to exercise control over its medical requirements. Hospital ships were sometimes used from the mid-1600s which carried warranted surgeons. Surgeons were examined by the Sick and Hurt Board from 1796 whereas before that time a surgeon's appointment was subject to approval and licensing by the Barber Surgeons Livery Company. Surgeons carried a Warrant Officer rank until 1844.

In 1740 the Sick and Hurt Board also became responsible for prisoners of war but this responsibility passed to the Transport Board in 1796. This signalled the demise of the board because in 1806 its medical responsibility was also transferred. The Transport Board was then abolished in 1817 and its responsibilities became part of the Victualling Board.

In 1832 when the Victualling Board was abolished naval medicine became the responsibility of the Physician General of the Navy (later the Inspector-General of Naval Hospitals and Fleets). In 1844 ships' surgeons were given commissioned status instead of being of warranted rank.

Transport Department

The transport department had a chequered history and was abolished and reformed on several occasions. Their prime responsibilities were the transportation of troops overseas, prisoners of war from 1796 and the Navy medical service from 1806. On amalgamation some of the former Commissioners of the Sick and Hurt Board became the medical committee which operated within, but independently to, the Transport Board.

When abolished in 1817 the duties of the Transport Board were divided between the Navy Board, (Transport branch) and the Victualling Board, which just to confuse matters also had a medical commissioner and a transport organisation! At the same time the business of the Prisoner-of-War Department became part of the Victualling Board's medical department.

Beyond 1832 when both the Navy and Victualling Boards were abolished transport was under the control of the Comptroller of Victualling and Transport Services, later (1862) to become the responsibility of the Director of Transports.

During the First World War transport matters were dealt with by the Ministry of Shipping but in 1921 the function became the sole responsibility of the Board of

Trade Marine Department transferring for the duration of the Second World war to the Ministry of War Transport.

Works Department

In 1796 an Inspector General of Naval Works was appointed as part of the Navy Board with specific responsibility for dockyard civil engineering. By 1813 the role also included buildings and architectural works. After re-organisation changes which took place in the 1830s the Admiralty controlled the department as the Architectural and Engineering Works Department under which it remained until the end of the First World War.

Surveyors Department

Up to 1832 all matters relating to the building and fitting out of ships was under the direct control of the Surveyor of the Navy which was initially part of the responsibility of the Navy Board, but from 1832 the Surveyor became responsible to the Board of Admiralty where he served as a permanent member. In 1872 he was no longer a member of the Board but had the right to attend meetings when the business of his department was conducted. He later (in 1862) became the controller of the Survey Department and his role included overseeing the work of Scientific Service, Naval Construction, Engineering, Naval Ordnance, Dockyards and Hydrography. During the Second World War he was also responsible for the supply of equipment to Combined Operations Headquarters.

Ordnance Department

The Ordnance Board had sole responsibility for the supply of guns and ammunition to the Navy up to 1855 but when the Ordnance Board (which also supplied the army) was abolished the War Office had direct responsibility although a serving naval officer was appointed as Director-General of Naval Artillery. In 1868 he had additional responsibilities placed upon him relating to the stores generally of the War Office. A Director of Naval Ordnance of the Admiralty took over the role in 1888 shortly before the new Naval Ordnance Department was established at the Admiralty in 1891.

During the First World War a separate Directorate of Torpedoes and Mining was established leaving the Directorate of Naval Ordnance responsible only for guns and ammunition. Both departments existed until after the Second World War combining together in 1958. A Naval Ordnance Inspection Department was established in 1922 controlling the manufacture and testing of weapons and ammunition for the fleet.

Staff Department including Naval Intelligence

The Naval Staff divisions have sole responsibility for the Fleet's effectiveness in the event of war directing strategy, tactics, operations and intelligence, reporting directly to the First Sea Lord.

They also direct other departments in order that manpower, training, weapons and materials are adequate for the operational effectiveness of the Navy. The department was established in 1912 initially serving three distinct roles, operations, mobilisation and intelligence, but it was not really organised to be effective throughout the First World War. However although the organisation changed from time to time, the Operations Division functioned effectively during both world wars. The department consisted of various divisions with specific responsibilities.

The Trade Division was responsible for the protection of maritime trade primarily operation of the wartime convoys and escorts and the arming of merchant shipping. The Naval Air Division was also responsible for the direction and organisation of the Fleet Air Arm and during the later years of World War Two the Signals Division. The Local Defence Division was responsible for naval defences worldwide and for minesweeping until the start of the Second World War when it became the responsibility of its own division. There was also a Historical Section which compiled the official histories.

Perhaps the most important division, certainly during the Second World War, was the Naval Intelligence Division. This was originally established in 1886 and was concerned with the collection of intelligence on foreign navies and war planning. In July 1917 it absorbed 'Room 40' (the room used at the Admiralty) which was manned by civilian experts who spent their time deciphering enemy wireless signals. During both World Wars the Naval Intelligence Division also produced illustrated handbooks on different parts of the world, detailing geographical and historical factors. 'Room 40' became the Government Code and Cipher School in 1919 but by 1922 was part of the Foreign Office. During the Second World War it had a branch based at Bletchley Park as well as a section of the Naval Intelligence Division based in Oxford.

Further information on the records of the Naval Intelligence Department are given in the Operational Record section of this book.

Pay Department

Before the 1832 reorganisation of the Navy accounting was the responsibility of several different officials. The history of the department can be traced to the days of

Henry VIII when there was a Treasurer of the Navy who was the senior member of the Navy Board and controlled all Navy accounts. Ultimately the Navy Pay Office became a separate entity until absorbed into the Paymaster General's Office in 1835. Several subordinate offices then came into existence including the Office of Seamen's Wages, the Allotment Office and the Ticket Office, where tickets for the wages of disabled, discharged or deceased seamen were examined. Between 1715 and 1830, three sets of pay books were maintained for each ship in commission, recording the names of all officers and men aboard each vessel. They were kept by the Pay Office, the Comptroller of the Navy and at the Ticket Office. This is why there are three series of records in the ships' pay lists and musters (see later).

In the 1832 re-organisation accounting and pay departments became a single department directed by the Accountant General whose responsibility covered all naval accounts. The records of this department are particularly important to family historians and the records which the department encompassed will be dealt with separately later. The key records which form part of Admiralty Division 14 include various departmental ledgers and accounts including records of ships' establishments, pay and pensions, services of petty offices and seamen, medals, wills and personal effects in the event of death and the distribution of bounty and prize money.

1780 caricature of a press gang, from Vaisseau de Ligne. Public domain Image.

CHAPTER THREE
Naval Recruitment

The fleet more than quadrupled in size during the 1700s and by 1805 had around 850 vessels. The larger size fleet required more seamen. From the 17th to 19th centuries the Royal Navy figured amongst Britain's largest employers. At its height in the days of the Napoleonic Wars there were over 150,000 men employed in the various branches of the Navy. In peacetime the numbers employed varied from 12,000 to 20,000 men during the 18th century.

This was the time of the press gang, as there was no statutory alternative to its use and the Royal Navy had always encountered recruiting problems because there were never enough sailors to adequately crew the ships particularly in times of war. The Navy used three types of recruitment - voluntary enlistment, recruitment under the Quota Acts or Impressment.

Voluntary Recruitment

Volunteers received conduct money and two months' salary on enlistment but were required to purchase their clothes, hammock and equipment (known as slops) from the Purser of their allocated ship.

Quota Recruits

In times of war, and particularly during the French Revolutionary War, William Pitt, the then Prime Minister introduced legislation in the form of Quota Acts to supplement recruitment to the Navy. Each county in Britain had to provide a quota of men for naval service and numbers depended upon the size of that county's population. London had to provide 5,704 men for naval service in 1794. As an incentive to recruitment a bounty was normally offered but this did not always have the desired effect and frequently counties had to resort to other means of recruitment to meet their quotas. Petty criminals were offered the choice of going to prison or joining up for naval service which potentially had the offer of a pension at the end of their service. However whilst satisfying an immediate need, this type of recruitment frequently brought with it other problems relating to discipline and health. Like impressment quota recruitment was a short-term measure.

As an alternative to impressment men were encouraged to volunteer for Navy service which was to be paid for locally by a special poor rate and for which a bounty was offered. Two Acts of Parliament were passed one in 1795 and one a year later for 'raising a certain number of men in the several counties in England'. The number of men required from each county was based upon the number of households required to pay land tax. In Rutland for example (an inland county) 23 men were required but in Middlesex the number was 451. The administration of the system in each county was down to the Quarter Sessions and at parish level was the responsibility of the churchwarden and overseer. There was however some inequality in the amount of bounty as that was also fixed locally. This was paid in two parts, when they enlisted and then when they boarded their ship.

The overseers had to return to the Quarter Sessions a list of the men enrolled which included their name, parish from which they served, their parish of birth, their occupation, age and the bounty they were to receive. The same information had to be forwarded to the Admiralty. The overseers returns are held locally and some of the Admiralty lists are available at The National Archives although there are many gaps. Those which have survived are in series ADM 7 and ADM 30. The returns from the Quarter Sessions were slightly more detailed as they also gave the physical description, enlistment date, date of the commitment to service and it was from these that notices of desertion were compiled (see later).

In many cases the counties did not achieve their quota, the exceptions being the City of London and Lincolnshire. Desertion was also a problem as many men disappeared between receiving their bounty and actually boarding their ship. Hence the listing for those men, with vivid physical descriptions appeared in the local newspapers.

The quota system attracted mainly young men around the ages of 23-25 years who had come from a variety of occupations although few of these men had experience gained at sea.

Pressed Men

For a significant period impressment had been a standing authority from the state for the recruitment to naval service. The Impress Service (the press gang), served to seize men in British seaports for employment at sea. Impressment originated in Elizabethan times and later under the Vagrancy Act 1597, men of disrepute could be drafted into service.

By the Commissioners for Executing the Office.
of Lord High Admiral of the United Kingdom
of *Great Britain* & *Ireland*, &c and of all
His Majesty's Plantations, &c.

IN pursuance of His Majesty's Order in the Council, dated the Sixteenth Day of *November*, 1804, We do hereby Impower and Direct you to impress, cause to be impressed, so many Seamen, Seafaring Men and Persons whose Occupations and Callings are to work in Vessels and Boats upon Rivers, as shall be necessary either to Man His Majesty's Ship under your Command or any other of His Majesty's Ships, giving unto each Man so impressed One Shilling for Prest Money. And in the execution hereof, you are to take care that neither yourself nor any Officer authorised by you do demand or receive any Money, Gratuity, Reward or other Consideration whatsoever, for the sparing Exchanging, or Discharging any Person or Persons impressed or to be impressed as you will answer to it at your Peril. You are not to intrust any Person with the execution of this Warrant, but a Commission Officer and to insert his Name and Office in the Deputation on the other side hereof, and set Your Hand and Seal thereto. — This Warrant to continue in Force till the Thirty First Day of December 1809, and in the due execution thereof, all Mayors, Sheriffs, Justices of the Peace, Bailiffs, Constables Headboroughs, and all other His Majesty's Officers and Subjects whom it may concern, are hereby required To be aiding and assisting unto you, and those employed by you, As they tender His Majesty's Service, and will answer the contrary At their Perils

Given under our Hands and the Seal of the Office of Admiralty, the   1809.

Captain
Commander of His Majesty's
the

By Command of their Lordships,

5. Transcript of the warrant issued by the Admiralty Commissioners to Press Gang officers.

There was an organisation at the ports charged with obtaining seamen by seizure. The Impress Service as it was known, was limited to seizing men who were seamen and the age limits were set at between 18 years (set in 1703) and 55 years of age (set by 1740). These limits were frequently ignored, and apprentices were exempt. Any man who was paid the King's Shilling to enlist became known as a 'Prest man'. Prest is derived from the French word meaning subject to loan or advance.

The Impress Service covered every port in Britain and in the majority of cases the senior officer was a Captain within the Royal Navy. Some of the smaller ports were under the charge of a Lieutenant. In both cases serving in this capacity was a recognised alternative to being on half-pay. The men who actually went out to secure men to serve were known as 'gangers' hence the nickname 'Press gang' and were not usually serving seamen.

The gang were paid per recruit which would be anything up to 10 shillings and it was not unusual for men to bribe their way out of being pressed by offering the gangers money. The more well-to-do were known to pay around £10 for their continued freedom. Merchant ships were the obvious place to seek seamen and as long as the gang left enough men on board to 'navigate the ship' that was all they were required to do. There was no formal interpretation of this, so merchant captains often stowed away important men and officers so they could not be found as the press gang searched their ships. The gang also recruited from boatyards on the rivers as these people often had the trade skills which could be utilised on board a Navy vessel such as carpenter, sail maker, etc.

Foreigners could not be impressed but were not prevented from volunteering for service. There were exceptions. If a foreigner married an English woman or had crewed on a British merchant ship for at least two years they lost their exemption and could be impressed. It is thought that the ignoring of this rule and the impressment of many Americans into the British Navy was one of the causes of the American War of 1812.

Once a man had been seized by the press gang he could either sign on voluntarily receiving all the volunteer benefits, or he could remain pressed with no benefits. The Admiralty and Trinity House issued protection certificates for specific types of employment and these had to be carried by such persons and shown to the press gang on demand to prevent the holder being impressed.

Desertion amongst pressed men was rife and was worse in the West Indies' stations than anywhere else. Merchant ships paid an impressive £46 to tempt men to work their passage home to England which many of course did. As the problem was so common the Admiralty took some steps to try and stem desertion. They did not allow shore leave, they kept the sick on board ship instead of transferring them to shore, and they withheld pay and above all gave pardons if the deserters voluntarily re-joined the service after a period of absence. To put this in perspective of the complement of 175,000 pressed men in 1780 around 42,000 actually deserted and had 'run' against their names on ship's musters.

Impressment has not been used in Britain since the end of the Napoleonic wars (1815) although the right did not become extinct until around 1853 when continuous service was introduced. In 1835 legislation was passed exempting impressed sailors who had served for five years in the Navy from any further terms of impressment. The introduction of continuous service for seamen who wished to make a career in the Navy meant that, after a fixed number of years, they would receive a pension.

Until 1853, Navy ratings signed up for service on a particular ship and were only employed for the duration of the voyage and this is why it was not unusual for a sailor to jump between Royal and Merchant Navy service. Before 1853 there were no individual service records kept on a sailor. After Continuous Service was introduced centralised records were kept on individuals and a form of Continuous Service Engagement was introduced with a pension granted after a fixed number of years. Modifications to the system took place in 1870, which was used for recruitment until 1956 and later for apprentices. All recruits entering the Navy were thereafter given a continuous service (CS) number which remained the same throughout their careers.

Captain Edward Vernon (1723-1794), by Francis Hayman. Public domain image.

CHAPTER FOUR

Officers and Ratings in the Royal Navy

Officers and ratings within the Royal Navy fall into four basic categories:

- Flag Officers.
- Commissioned Officers.
- Warrant Officers.
- Ratings.

The Naval Hierarchy

Flag Officers:
Admiral of the Fleet, Admiral, Vice Admiral, Rear Admiral, Commodore.

Commissioned Officers:
Captain, Commander, Lieutenant Commander, Lieutenant, Sub Lieutenant, Midshipman.

Warrant Officers:

Senior Rates:
Chief Petty Officer, Petty Officer (titles usually include their specialism).

Junior Rates:
Leading Seamen, Leading Hands, Able Seaman (titles usually include their specialism).

Flag Officers

Admiral of the Fleet - was the highest naval flag rank and was in overall charge of the fleet. The first Admiral of the Fleet was appointed in 1688 by King James II. The title was given to the most senior of Admirals. Originally there was only one officer of this rank but this changed to three in the 1870s and in 1898 to four to correspond with equivalent ranks in the army. Regulations made it compulsory for Admirals of the Fleet to retire at age 70. In 1940, all retired rank-holders were placed on the active list for life in the same way that army Field Marshalls held their rank for life. Since the 1990s this rank no longer exists.

Admiral - the ranks of Admiral, Vice Admiral, and Rear Admiral originated when the fleet was organised in 1620. The ranks were organised into three squadrons, red, white and blue.

6. Admiral c.1805.

These colours were introduced by Elizabeth I when the fleet was divided into its three squadrons and each was headed by the Admiral who used a red flag, the Vice Admiral who used the white flag and the Rear Admiral who used a blue flag. As fleets grew in size during the 17th century, the squadrons became too large for one Admiral so three Admirals existed in each squadron and this is where the rank hierarchy came into existence with an Admiral in command and a Vice Admiral second in command and a Rear Admiral third in command. This resulted in the ranks of Admiral White and Blue (there was no Admiral Red as this was the Admiral of the Fleet), Vice Admiral of the Red and Rear-Admiral of the Red, with the same ranking system (Admiral, Vice Admiral and Rear Admiral) existing in the blue and white squadrons. The squadrons ranked in the order Red, White, Blue, and Admirals took seniority according to the colour of their squadron.

Once in the red squadron promotion could not go any further but there was a hierarchy of lower ranked Admirals. A Rear Admiral (Blue) on promotion became a Rear Admiral (White). Once he had reached Rear Admiral (Red) he would then become a Vice Admiral (Blue) and move up through the squadrons ultimately becoming an Admiral (White). It was only in the Red squadron that the hierarchy was not followed. The situation changed slightly in 1805 after the battle of Trafalgar when the rank of Admiral of the Red was introduced and was in effect a reward for successes at Trafalgar. It was the highest rank an Admiral could attain until 1862.

With the changing face of the Royal Navy the coloured squadrons were discarded in 1864, mainly because they had no relevance in the age of steam warships. The Red Ensign was allocated to the Merchant Navy of Britain, the Royal Navy adopted the White Ensign, and the Blue Ensign was used by naval auxiliary vessels. Admirals of the Fleet flew the Union Flag, Admirals flew the St. George Flag, Vice Admirals the St George Flag with a red sphere in the top left quarter, and Rear Admirals flew the same but with a red sphere in the top and lower left quarters of the flag.

Commodore - the lowest flag rank was Commodore. In 1690 the title of Commodore was endowed on the senior Captain of a squadron or a Commander in Chief of a small station when no flag officer was assigned to it. It was a temporary rank which at the end of the specific command meant reversion to Captain. Advancement to Commodore did not affect a man's seniority position in the Captain's list. In 1747, equivalent ranks between Army and Navy proposed that Commodores were the equivalent of army Brigadiers.

Commissioned Officers

These officers were firstly appointed to a ship for particular commissions and were ranked according to seniority.

Captain - the title of Captain was universal to the senior officer commanding a ship irrespective of his actual rank. On promotion from Lieutenant, officers were appointed to a small ship and after gaining experience were allowed to take command of a rated ship. In most cases a Captain's duties on board ship were to prepare the ship for sailing, make inventories of stores and write reports for the Admiralty on work being done on the ship. He was also responsible to recruit the ship's company and maintain the muster book. During a voyage, he was responsible for the condition of the ship and the well-being of the crew. He was also responsible for directing the ship's involvement in naval engagements.

Post-Captain - Sometimes your ancestor may be referred to as a Post-Captain. The term Post-Captain was used by those given the substantive rank. Once an officer had been promoted to Post-Captain, his further promotion was strictly by seniority. It was regarded as a major milestone in his career. An officer who was promoted from Commander was a captain, but when he was given a command, his name was 'posted' in the *London Gazette*. He 'took post' and usually commanded a rated vessel which was a ship that could not be commanded by a Commander or Lieutenant (Post ship).

A junior Post-Captain would usually command a frigate or a large sloop, while more senior Post-Captains would command larger ships. In 1795 epaulettes were introduced to distinguish between a Post-Captain's seniority. A Post-Captain with less than three years' seniority wore a single epaulette on the right shoulder, and a Post-Captain with three or more years' seniority wore an epaulette on each shoulder.

Commander - the rank of Commander was instituted in 1794 and was only obtainable by being commissioned to command a vessel. After 1794 Post-Captains were only appointed from the Commanders list. In the 1820s a Commander became the Captain's second in command.

Lieutenant-Commander - this rank applied to Lieutenants who were commanding small vessels, who would be known as a Commander if in a bigger ship. The rank changed when the rank of Commander became the Captain's second-in-command. In recognition of being senior lieutenants, they were given a distinction which differentiated between senior and junior lieutenants including a slightly different uniform. Lieutenants with eight years' of service were given this distinction. At the start of the First World War the rank of Lieutenant-Commander was established giving automatic promotion to Lieutenants who had completed eight years' service.

Lieutenant - the rank of Lieutenant was originally a temporary rank established in 1580 as an understudy to the Captain in case he suffered an accident or illness. Samuel Pepys, as part of his reforms, introduced an examination to test their abilities and made a lieutenant's job permanent and with direct responsibilities not just merely an understudy. The First Lieutenant became responsible for the organisation and administration of his ship under the direction of the Captain and it was this position that ultimately became Commander. He was responsible for all navigation and for maintaining discipline amongst the crew. The 'junior lieutenants' were responsible for ensuring the crew carried out their duties. Lieutenants received their commissions only for specific ships. They were required to have at least six years sea service before passing the promotion examinations.

7. First Lieutenant 1909.

Sub-Lieutenants and/or Mates - any person who satisfied the age and service conditions and passed the examination could be commissioned to this rank. It was normal for candidates to commissioned ranks to progress through a number of different ratings including that of Master's Mate which was technically a senior petty officer rank. A mate assisted the Master who taught him navigation skills amongst other things. This rank was the only ratings rank allowed to command any sort of vessel. They could pass examinations qualifying them to act as Second Master of vessels which did not have a warranted Master. In 1824 the ranking structure changed and would be Lieutenants were Master's Mates. In 1840 the rank of Mate was established below the rank of Lieutenant and in 1860 were renamed Sub-Lieutenants becoming the lowest junior commissioned rank and the only way to progress to Lieutenant.

Warrant Officers

Warrant Officers reported directly to the Captain and were in charge of specific branches of the ship's company. For administration purposes they reported to the different boards which were in charge of naval affairs including the Victualling, Ordnance and Navy Boards. They frequently held a warrant rank having served an apprenticeship and were usually examined before being granted a warrant. In the 18th century, there were two types of Warrant Officer, those classed as sea officers and those classed as inferior officers. Five Warrant Officers, classed as standing officers, were warranted to a ship. If they were warranted to a ship which was not in commission at any time then they were assigned to the dockyard (as part of the Ordinary) and were usually employed in maintenance work. In the 19th century some warrant ranks were transferred to commissioned rank and with the advent of steam the Engineers branch was introduced.

Master - was the senior warrant rank equivalent to that of Lieutenant and was usually held by men who were well educated. Masters were professionally examined by Trinity House and had to re-qualified if appointed to a larger rated ship. Masters could command ships in non-combatant duties. In the mid-19th century Masters attained and were fully integrated into the commissioned rank structure but the navigation branch of officers was gradually phased out. The Master's main duty was navigation. He had a direct supervisory role for Midshipmen and Mates in navigation and particular responsibility for the ship's compass. He was also responsible for the maintenance of the rigging and sails, stowing of the hold, reporting any fabric defects to the Captain, the issue of rum and other alcohol and entered information about weather and expenditure in the ship's official log book.

Surgeon - All surgeons were warranted by the Navy Board. Up to 1832 their examinations were normally conducted by the City of London based Barber-Surgeons Company or the Victualling Board. After that date the Admiralty supervised the examination process. There was only one surgeon appointed to each ship irrespective of size but he was assisted by one or more Surgeon's Mates who held the class/rank of an inferior Warrant Officers. The rank of surgeon became a fully commissioned rank in the 19th century. They were responsible for the treatment of the sick and injured (whether crew, passenger or convict), the dispensing of medicine and carrying out surgical operations. They also kept a medical journal detailing treatments and were responsible on board ship for all health matters.

Purser - warranted by the Admiralty but did not require any examination or professional qualifications. In exchange for their warrant a financial surety was deposited. They were to oversee supply and issue of victuals, clothing and consumables. In the 19th century the rank was commissioned and had the responsibility for payment of victuals and wages to the crew. Thus he became responsible for the compilation of the pay lists and musters. The Purser was one of the five standing officers of the ship.

Boatswain - was one of the oldest ranks dating back to medieval times, appointed by the Admiralty and initially responsible to the Navy Board. He had responsibility for the rigging, sails, boats, anchors and all cabling. In most cases they were less educated than the senior Warrant Officers, and the rank did not achieve commissioned status. The ships sail maker and boatswain mate were under the direct command of the boatswain. Again this rank was one of the five standing officers appointed to a ship.

Carpenter - was responsible for the maintenance of the hull and masts of the ship. Many qualified as civilian rather than naval employees of the Navy Board working mainly in the dockyards and only periodically as officers on ships. Most carpenters actually served apprenticeships and qualified as shipwrights in the dockyards before going to sea. In 1918, they were renamed Warrant Shipwrights when they ceased to work solely with timber. They were one of the five standing officers appointed to a ship.

Gunner - this rank can be traced back to the 15th century and as the name suggests were responsible for the maintenance of guns, their equipment and ammunition which meant they had to adhere to strict rules. They were examined and appointed by and were responsible to the Ordnance Board. They made tackle and breeches for guns. They had to ensure that gunpowder on board and in magazines were kept dry. They remained a warranted rank. In the 1880s other specialities were added such as torpedo gunners and those involved with mines.

Engineers - In the early days the naval engineer was employed by the firms that built the ships engines. Engineers were first introduced in 1837 but it was not until 1847 that they became warranted or commissioned. As advances were made the ranking system for engineers developed. Seniority in the division was undertaken in the same way as elsewhere in the Navy.

Petty Officers and Inferior Warrant Officers

Midshipmen - a senior Petty Officer, usually held by men wanting to become commissioned officers. This rank itself was never of commissioned status. The rating of the ship determined the number of Midshipmen on the crew. There was a problem created by the large number of men seeking to obtain a Lieutenants commission that, to enable men to be given a chance, various supernumerary posts, paid as Able Seamen were created. The number of men in this position taken on board a ship was totally at the discretion of the Captain. During their period as Midshipmen, they undertook instruction in seamanship and were able to wear a uniform, something that other Petty Officers were not able to do until general uniform introduction.

8. Midshipman of the early 20th century.

The rank of Midshipman originated during the Tudor period, however the first use of the term Midshipman was in 1662. The term Midshipman originates from an area of a ship where Midshipmen worked or were berthed.

By the 18th century four classes of Midshipman existed based upon the ordinary or the extraordinary. Most were officer candidates who failed the Lieutenant examination or were passed over for promotion. By 1794, all Midshipmen were considered officer candidates, and the original rating was phased out.

By 1661, young men who wanted to become officers were sent by their families to serve on ships with a 'letter of service' from the crown. The main context of the letter was to instruct captains that the bearer was to be shown 'such kindness as you shall judge fit for a gentleman, both in accommodating him in your ship and in furthering his improvement'. They were often referred to as 'King's Letter Boys' to distinguish their higher social class from the original Midshipman rating.

From 1677 those promoted to Lieutenant had to have served as a Midshipman which required compulsory sea service of at least six years.

In 1729, the Royal Naval Academy was established, which in 1806 became the Royal Naval College. The academy intake was 40 students between 13 and 16 years of age who studied for three years and would earn two years of sea time as part of their studies. The rating of Midshipman Ordinary was used by graduates of the Royal Naval College to distinguish them from Midshipmen who had served aboard ship.

Around half of the Midshipmen were the sons of other naval officers or of professional men. Some were even of the landed gentry and the family connections became an obvious advantage for prospective officers. Therefore some were considered to have a considerable influence on the Royal Navy. The remainder, who became Midshipmen, were of artisan or working class backgrounds who, to some degree, suffered because their chances of promotion to Lieutenant were slim due to competition from the upper classes.

Since many Midshipmen were from the gentry or had naval connections some exploited their connections and had their names included on ships musters without actually serving on the ships, a practice known as 'false muster' which enabled them to be promoted to Midshipmen, or even Lieutenant, without having completed the requisite time at sea.

Classes of Petty Officer

The rating of a Petty Officer is indicated by which class he belonged to as determined by his title:

Chief Petty Officer - Master at Arms, Chief Gunner's Mate, Chief Boatswain's Mate, Chief Captain of the Forecastle, Admiral's Coxswain, Chief Quartermaster, Chief Carpenters Mate, Schoolmaster, Steward, Cook.

Petty Officer 1st Class - Ship's Corporal, Gunner's Mate, Boatswain's Mate, Captain's Coxswain, Corporal of the Forecastle, Quartermaster, Yeoman of Signals, Coxswain of the Launch, Captain of Main and Fore Tops, Sail maker, Rope maker, Carpenters Mate, Caulker, Block maker, Armourer, Leading Stoker, Sick Berth Steward.

Petty Officer 2nd Class - Coxswain of the Barge, Coxswain of the Pinnace, Corporal of the mast, Sail maker's Mate, Coxswain of the Cutter, Cooper, Caulkers Mate, Sick Berth Attendant.

Master-At-Arms - This was a warranted rank with appointment by the Admiralty. He was responsible for training Petty Officers in the use of small arms (a role which diminished with the establishment of the Royal Marines) and also in generally policing the ship. Many who became a Master-At-Arms had an army background. In the early 19th century the rank became that of a Petty Officer.

Chaplains - In 1626 chaplains were placed on each ship under a decree from Charles I. No person could be appointed a Chaplain unless they were 35 years of age and ordained in the Church of England ministry. Chaplains were examined by the Bishop of London and appointed by the Admiralty. Up to 1843 they were warranted but from then on they became a commissioned rank which from 1859 included four classes of chaplain. Later chaplains were appointed from all denominations.

Cooks - From 1838 onwards cooks were ranked as Petty Officers but up to 1703 were a warranted rank. They were often disabled seamen and in many cases had no formal training or apprenticeship. From around 1740 their main responsibility was to ensure that meat was stored properly and also to prepare food for the ships company. There was usually more than one on board ship depending upon the ships rate.

Schoolmasters and Instructors - This rank was established in 1702 and was frequently given to those holding the rank of Midshipman. Initially qualification was by examination through Trinity House but in 1819 the responsibility for qualification came under the Royal Naval College. Schoolmasters and Instructors became a warranted rank in 1836 and later in 1861 became a commissioned rank subject to seniority. The rank temporarily vanished in the early 20th century but was reinstated after the First World War as an executive officer known as 'instructor'

Ratings

The word rating is used in the Royal Navy to describe a seaman's status, skills and ability based upon the type of work they were involved in. There are 60-plus different types of rating.

The most common ratings are Ordinary and Able Seaman.

Ordinary Seaman - This was the lowest rating on a ship and was introduced into the Navy in 1652. The Ordinary Seaman was generally one who was not experienced as a sailor. Most seamen gained their experience through working on board a ship and could then specialise and progress up the rating ladder. Ordinary Seamen were expected to 'know the ropes' hence the popular saying. Ships had rigging and miles of other ropes which Ordinary Seamen were expected to know how to use, work and locate. They were also required to row boats, load guns, work the anchor and generally learn to cope with life at sea. In most cases they progressed to Able Seaman in their early 20s.

Able Seaman - Again this rating was introduced in 1652 and, as the name suggests, they were to be able seamen, i.e. those who had become competent in their job and gained their knowledge through experience. Most able seamen had around five years of experience before advancing to the rating and were appointed by the Captain of the ship on which they served. Once they became able they did not lose that rating.

Other types of Ratings

Chiefs - Chief shipwright, Chief stoker, Chief mechanician, Chief Ordnance Artificer, Chief engine room artificer, Chief Air artificer, Chief armourer, Chief electrician engineer, Chief yeoman of signals.

Mates - Boatswain's mate, Steward's mate, Sail maker's mate, Cooper's mate, Gunner's mate. Caulker's mate, Cook's mate.

Captains -These were men assigned to certain parts of a ship and were always ratings despite a somewhat superior title. Captain of the foretop, Captain of the mizentop, Captain of the forecastle, Captain of the hold, Captain of the head, Captain of the mast, Captain of the maintop.

Quarter Master - responsible for all supplies on the ship and their distribution and loading.

Stewards - Steward, Ward steward, Purser's steward, Gunroom steward, Captain's steward.

Coxwains - Coxswain of the launch, Coxswain of the pinnace.

Yeoman - Yeoman of the powder room, Yeoman of signals, Boatswain's yeoman, Carpenter's yeoman, Gunner's yeoman, Purser's yeoman.

Others - Wardmaster, Wardroom cook, Tailor, Barber, Poulterer, Cooper, Engine room artificer, Stoker, Corporal, Gunner, Gunroom cook, Telegrapher, Leading seaman, Leading telegrapher, Storekeeper, Quarter gunner, Sail maker, Writer (sometimes of Chief Petty Officer rank).

Boys - Boys were rated first, second or third class depending upon age. Boys who joined the Navy under the age of 15 years were rated third class, between 15 and 17 years as second class (unless they joined from a training ship). A first class boy was one who was training to become an officer or who had graduated from a training ship.

Training ships - The earliest naval training ships were run by the Marine Society. The Society recruited boys and young men for the Royal Navy at the beginning of the Seven Years War against France with the object of training boys before they were sent to sea. In 1876, the Society acquired '*Warspite*' and throughout its 40 year life sent over 28,500 trained boys into the Royal Navy with many more entering the Merchant Navy.

The Royal Navy's first training ships were *HMS Implacable* based at Plymouth and *HMS Illustrious* based at Portsmouth. They gave teenage boys training in naval life, skills and discipline and provided a source of recruits for the service. From their establishment in 1855 the various ships (ran by the Navy as well as asylum boards, societies, etc.) catered for boys from differing backgrounds, including fee-paying prospective officers to those from Poor Law workhouses or other institutional care including reformatories. Having completed training on the ships they were guaranteed a position in the Royal Navy from the age of 16 years upwards.

Landsman - This was a rate given to those serving on board ship but who lacked experience at sea. In many cases during the 17th and 18th centuries the rate related to men who were recruited as a result of the press gangs. Most of the landsmen performed menial tasks as it took the best part of two years to train them in the art of seamanship. The rating was discontinued in 1862 and all landsmen became ordinary seaman (2nd class).

Boatswain uniform, c.1820. Public domain image.

CHAPTER FIVE

Identifying Royal Navy personnel by their uniform and insignia

Uniforms

It is more than probable that you will have a photograph of your ancestor in a Navy uniform. This could either be an exhibition photograph, posed in a studio or perhaps the 'snap' taken in some foreign clime. Either way the identification of rank and/or rating can be ascertained either from uniform identification or from the badges or insignia within the uniform. Although badges of rank have not changed significantly over the period of the Royal Navy's existence, the uniforms have. In fact early on there was no uniform. It is more than likely that the photograph may well have been taken in the late 19th or early 20th century or during the First World War.

Since the 1740s Royal Navy personnel, whether officers or ratings, have worn a uniform. It is therefore possible to identify from photographs or even earlier portraits what rank they held and even the type of job that they did. Uniforms changed style and were subject to a series of official Royal Naval Uniform Regulations. The Royal Naval Uniform regulations are published in detail within the Navy Lists. To help identify a uniform period it is worthwhile looking at the relevant section and year in the Navy Lists. Not only will the style of uniform help with identification but also knowledge of the various badges, insignia and buttons will provide the clues.

Before the 1740s the Royal Navy had no established uniforms, but many officers particularly of the more senior ranks wore clothing and sometimes wigs which denoted their social class.

Over a fairly short period of time the Navy introduced uniforms for its officer positions when the commissioned officer structure was initially that of a Captain and a Lieutenant, together with a sailing master, the first Warrant Officer position. Uniforms for Midshipmen were then introduced in 1758 and for the rank of 'master and commander' in the 1760s and were given, albeit temporarily, to Lieutenants in command of vessels who did not have a Captain's commission. By the early 1790s, this rank simply became Commander and uniforms became more standardised.

Royal Naval Uniform regulations were first instigated in 1748 in response to the naval officers wishing for an established uniform indicating their seniority and service. From the outset two different uniforms were provided. This philosophy has remained with all ranks throughout naval history. The 'best uniform' originally consisted of a blue coat with embroidery and white facings which was worn with white breeches. The 'working uniform' was a plainer uniform for day-to-day use. In 1758 Midshipman's uniforms had a distinctive white patch on the collar which remains insignia for the rank today. The higher ranked petty officers, such as the boatswain and gunner had been allocated blue uniforms as well. The standard means of determining rank in these early days of Royal Navy uniforms was the arrangement of buttons and well as gold facing on the buttons and cuff bands. As a general rule, the more buttons and gold facing a person wore, the higher was their rank and position.

9. Examples of uniforms worn by various Navy officers shortly after regulation.

In the 1760s Lieutenants' uniforms consisted of an open faced blue jacket with white waistcoats. Captains wore a similar jacket usually closed by gold laced buttons. By the 1770s, most warrant and petty officers had some type of uniform as well.

By 1767 the term 'best' uniform was replaced by 'dress' and the 'working uniform' became known as 'undress' uniform. In 1795 epaulettes were introduced and this style of uniform and associated insignia evolved until the final style was introduced in 1846. Epaulettes were used to determine a commissioned officer's rank. Warrant and petty officers wore various blue coats with piping and buttons to determine their various positions. This was deemed impractical for the changing face of the Navy and in 1856 sleeve stripes were used to denote an officer's ranking and these are still in current use. Sleeve stripes evolved from stripes of lace woven into the cuffs of Admirals' uniforms as early as 1795.

In 1825 white breeches were replaced by ordinary blue trousers for officers although the wearing of white trousers continued to be part of the uniform for officers serving in the West Indies and the Far East until the outbreak of the Second World War when shorts were introduced. A white tunic was also introduced for tropical service in 1877. Throughout the 19th century the Uniform regulations were not as prescriptive as they are today and as such there was a considerable variation in uniform styles. Blue caps were also introduced which had to have white tops. During the Second World War a battledress type working uniform became the norm.

Ratings' blue uniforms were first established in 1857 and this gave rise to the nickname of 'bluejackets'. Prior to this seamen usually wore 'slops', or clothing sold to the ship's crew by a nominated contractor. Until this time many captains established general standards of appearance for the seamen on their vessel, but there was often little uniformity between ships.

In the 17th century, a 'slop-chest' was in use on board ships from which sailors could buy articles of kit with the cost thereof being debited against their pay, normally the equivalent of about two months pay. There are abbreviations for these transactions included in pay lists (see later). By the early 1800s the 'slop-chest' contained more sophisticated articles of clothing including blue coats, waistcoats, trousers, standard checked shirts and hats. For the first few months at sea, sailors wore more or less what they wanted, but after this initial period they needed a change of clothing. The first ratings 'uniform' was borne out of necessity and not by profound wisdom. In the days of the press gang when sailors were forced into service the Navy clothed them from the 'slop-chest' in an attempt to standardise their dress. However when peace came at the end of the Napoleonic Wars a uniform for ratings was introduced. The system of making the men pay for their own uniforms lasted until the introduction of Continuous Service Engagement in 1853. In 1853 there was also a major reorganisation when training services were introduced particularly boys entering training-ship and these were the first people in the Navy to receive their kit and bedding on enlistment.

Another factor was connected with the social status of the 18th century seaman. Most had no social standing and after the American Revolution the Royal Navy frequently impressed American seamen on vessels taken at sea. There was also constant desertion particularly when a ship was in a port and this factor alone meant that the Admiralty was reluctant to invest in uniforms.

The establishment of a standard uniform more or less corresponded with the continuous service engagement. However a number of changes were introduced the most significant being the removal of the original blue jacket in 1890. Bell-bottom trousers are synonymous with naval ratings but these were deemed obsolete by the mid-1970s. Bell-bottoms were the icon of the square rig uniforms and were originally introduced so they could be rolled up and secured clear of the feet and ankles when sailors were working on the rigging. They were kept inside out when not worn to prevent fluff and shine when ironed. They were replaced by flared trousers in the 1970s.

10. Examples of uniforms worn by seamen in the 'Victorian Navy'.

The first broad collar was worn as part of the uniform from the 1830s. Early collars were round because they were fashionable ashore and for no other reason. Modern square cut collars existed from the 1860s and included two or three ornamental white tapes around the edge. The square collar was also easier for men to sew than the round collars. The part of the ratings uniform that hangs from the back of the neck is known as the bib. In the days of sail most sailors had long hair that was blown about and could easily be caught in rigging or machinery. Sailors at sea would braid their hair and dip it in tar. When ashore they would cut a bib out of sack cloth and tie it around their neck to stop shirts being soiled with tar.

11. 1860 uniform for seamen illustrating the bib, braids and hair dipped in tar.

The adoption of the blue uniform was because of relatively cheap indigo imported from India - a tropical plant from which blue dye was extracted. Indigo based dyes were the only ones that could remain fast in the constant exposure to sunlight. The British established large indigo plantations in both the East and West Indies with the principal object of providing dye to the Admiralty for uniforms.

Before 1870 boots and shoes were only worn as part of a uniform when ashore or as part of ceremonial dress when aboard a ship. Being bare foot was considered more suitable when working on rigging or on deck. The tradition continues in tropical climes to this day albeit at the discretion of the individual seaman. Footwear used for ceremonial purposes had to be highly polished in a manner prescribed by the uniform regulations.

12. Seaman in early 'uniform' usually determined by the ship's captain.

Headdress

The headdress worn by Navy personnel can also help identify the era of service. Originally the officers wore cocked hats with rank insignia. The cocked hat was ornamented with a gold braided loop running from the top to a button. The rank insignia was used from about 1825 and applied to both the Executive and Civil Branch officers. Flag officers had twisted braid of three loops, Captains and Commanders had two loops and Lieutenants had one loop.

From 1832 to 1856 the Civil branch of the Navy wore the same cocked hats but the centre braid was not twisted. The civil branch included all non-executive officers not in the Military Branch such as engineers, medical and paymaster staff.

13. Royal Navy officer wearing a cocked hat - insignia denotes rank (private collection).

Cocked hats were replaced in 1856 by peaked caps with badges and a variety of braiding to the peaks denoting rank and status. Generally speaking the cap badges were of an anchor (gold for executive officers and silver for civil offices) surmounted by a crown and surrounded by laurel leaves in gold embroidery. After 1870 the anchor was surrounded by oval gilding. Up until 1891 the crown was detached but after 1891 the crown of the cap badge was incorporated into the badge.

Sennet hats which were a straw boater style of hat were introduced as part of the uniform in 1857 although they did have their origin in the Napoleonic Wars. A black sennet was worn in home waters and a white one in the tropics. If it went out of shape it was painted with gelatine and dried in the sun which seemed to restore its original shape. After 1921 a blue replacement cap was worn in winter and a white one in the summer.

By way of uniformity the RNVR had the same cap badge from 1901 with engineer officers receiving the same in 1915 and other civil branch officers in 1918 thus the officer's badge became standard. It was not until 1940 that RN Chaplains were given a cap badge. WRNS officers have the same style badge but this is blue instead of gold. Over a period of time the design of the crown also changed.

14. Cap badge worn by the RNR officer's c. 1898.

In 1856 the peaks of caps were embroidered in gold. Flag officer's peaks were braided all round, Captains and Commanders were braided on the front edge only and for other officers the peaks were left plain. In 1860 the embroidery on an executive officers cap peak was changed to an oak leaf design but for civil branches this was left plain.

Engine room artificers were the first ratings to be given a cap badge in 1868 and this was the same style as those for civil branch officers but with a purple background. In 1879 Chief Petty Officers were given a peaked cap with a badge of a crown above a oval containing an anchor on a black background. It wasn't until just after the First World War that all Petty Officers wore the same badge.

In 1890 the junior rates of non-executive branches were also given peaked caps and long jackets. They were given a badge similar in design to that of a Chief Petty Officer but they were woven in red instead of gold and silver.

For the seamen the familiar cap with the name band of the ship on which they currently served was introduced as part of the 'blue uniform' from the start of continuous service in 1853/4. When the 'pork-pie hat' was introduced in 1859 it was customary for a band to be worn indicating the name of the ship where the sailor was currently serving. This identification system has never been replaced although today it is restricted to ceremonial dress. Each time a rating changed ship a new hatband would be supplied. If you are lucky enough to have your ancestor's hatbands don't be surprised if there are many different bands amongst the collection. Over the years there has been a variety of headdress which basically evolved to fit conditions. Different branches of the Navy also wore different style hats including berets.

Uniform Buttons

Alongside badges and cap regalia, buttons are another way of identifying a Royal Navy ancestor. From 1748 when official uniforms came into existence flag officers had four types of buttons. Their dress uniform buttons were covered in embroidery and their undress uniform buttons were gilt. For the rank of Captain and below the buttons were smooth domed although Lieutenants for some reason had a different type of button on their undress uniform, that of a less domed design incorporating a 'Tudor rose'.

In 1774 flat button was used incorporating a foul anchor. The foul anchor as naval insignia originated as the seal of Lord Howard who was the Lord Admiral of England at the time of the Spanish Armada subsequently adopted to this day as the seal of office. When this office became part of the Board of Admiralty the symbol was retained on buttons, official seals and cap badges.

When the new style button was introduced it was worn only by Captains and Commanders but by 1787 Midshipmen and Warrant Officers uniforms incorporated the same style of button. The foul anchor was also adopted in the Admiralty seal. For admirals their buttons took a similar form from 1787 but with a laurel wreath. From around 1805 special buttons were introduced for medical officers and masters and pursers. Surgeons' buttons had an anchor on and if they were serving in a hospital as opposed to on board ship the buttons incorporated an H & S, one letter each side of the anchor. Masters buttons were a large anchor with two small ones and Pursers had two anchors crossed.

15. Various styles of buttons used on Royal Navy uniforms.

Because the Merchant Navy also adopted the foul anchor emblem a crown was added to the buttons of all naval officers in 1812. Several alterations to the style of buttons were made in 1827 notably the doming and surrounding with a rim in the form of a rope and by 1832 the civil branches had lost their special designs so all wore the same type of button which are essentially the same design and styling as used today.

The civil branches of the Navy also had distinguishing collar badges on their full dress uniforms.

Good Conduct, Sea Service, Wound and Watch Badges

Good conduct badges were introduced in the Royal Navy in 1840 and were in the form of chevrons worn on the left sleeve below the rating badges. The badges were of gold lace and had the appearance of being promotion rankings which of course they were not. Each badge was awarded after a certain period of service as a result of good character and behaviour.

Before the advent of continuous service in 1853 a man's Merchant Navy service would also have counted towards his good conduct entitlement.

When the badges were first introduced one badge was awarded after five years, the second after ten years and the third after 15 years but in 1860 there was an alteration to the qualifying period. From that date the first was awarded after three years making the second awarded after eight years and the third after 13 years.

Further adjustments were made between 1946 and 1950 when the qualifying terms were respectively four, eight and 12 years for the badges.

Sea service chevrons were awarded to denote service overseas after 5 August 1914 and in sea-going ships of war, auxiliaries, minesweepers and armed merchant ships. Service chevrons were awarded for service in 1915, 1916 and 1917. They were worn inverted above the cuffs of the right arm on all uniforms. For ratings they are normally blue or red and for officers they are gold and silver. Petty Officers are classed as ratings for the purpose of the award.

Watch badges were inverted chevron stripes, either red for a starboard watch worn on the right arm or blue for a port watch worn on the left arm. It is believed that these were originally 'unofficial' as they do not form part of the uniform regulations until 1888 and sometimes vary from ship to ship. There origin is unknown but as they frequently appear in photographs of ratings need explanation.

As a mark of recognition a badge was also introduced in July 1916 denoting each occasion a sailor had been wounded during the war. The badge was a stripe of gold braid sewn vertically on the left sleeve of the uniform jacket. For practical reasons no more than three braids could be worn.

In 1922 the Admiralty ordered that service chevrons and wound stripes were no longer to be worn on the uniform so none existed in the Second World War.

Non Substantive Badges (Rating Badges)

A series of badges worn on the left arm had been used by the Navy from the earliest times to indicate what a man's job was on board a ship and more importantly so that the officers and other ratings also knew what they were required to do. They were in effect 'trade badges'. They also affected how a man was graded and paid. In the early 1800s there were 48 different ratings but by the time of continuous service in 1853 there were 79. During the period some of the original badges had become obsolete and some new ones were added. Before 1830 the various ratings could be extended or removed at the discretion of the captain of the ship on which they served. Generally the badges were gold for wearing on the best uniform (commonly known as the No. 1 uniform), were red for wearing on the standard blue uniform although some were blue to wear on the white uniforms. WRNS badges of rate were always blue.

All this changed with the introduction of Gunnery Schools, the first being in Portsmouth in 1830. They introduced the first permanent rating, that of a seaman gunner, but it was not until 1860 that a badge was given to a gunnery rating depicting obviously a gun. In 1885 torpedoes were used by the Navy and men were thereafter trained in both gunnery and weaponry (torpedoes). A new set of badges was introduced with torpedoes or guns.

In 1885 badges were also introduced for sick berth attendants and by 1890 there were additional badges for artisans, stokers, police signallers, physical training instructors and in the early 20th century there were further badges which took into account advancements in wireless telegraphy, cooks, stewards, divers, photographers, electricians, anti-aircraft and submariners. Even more were added in the Second World War.

Many of these badges incorporated stars and crowns to indicate class of rating such as leading rating, coxswain or 1st 2nd or 3rd class but they were by no means standardised in position or meaning as each branch developed its own style of rating badges. Some attempt at standardisation occurred after the Second World War but even by 1956 frequent changes in non-substantive badges were still occurring.

From an identification aspect it is important to find out when badges were introduced and ended being used although some badges continued to be used on uniforms after the date when it ceased to be recognised. Very often this occurred when a seaman was approaching the end of his service and he did not convert to a new one.

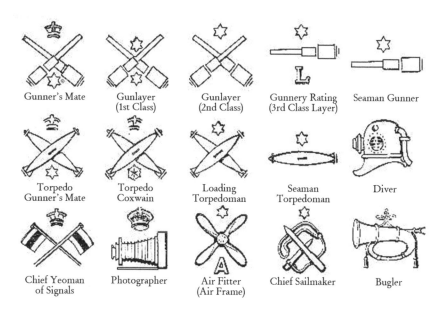

16. Selection of rating badges.

The following indicate the commencement of the various categories of badges up to and including the Second World War:

- Gun over a rifle and cutlass - gunnery instructor - 1860.
- Gun - seaman gunner - 1860.
- Gun over a torpedo -1885.
- Torpedo over a gun - 1885.
- Anchor with intertwined cable - 1890.
- Red Cross -1885.
- Crossed rifles - marksman - 1890.
- Single rifle - 3rd class marksman - 1890.
- Star - schoolmaster or ship steward - 1890.
- Crown - 1890.
- Crown with letters N & P - Navy police - 1890.
- Crossed hammer and axe - mechanic/engineer 1890.

- Torpedo crossed over a hammer and axe - 1890.
- Gun crossed over hammer and axe - 1891.
- Crossed guns - 1903.
- Torpedo - 1903.
- Clubs - physical training instructor - 1904.
- Crossed Flags -1909.
- Crossed torpedoes - 1909.
- Bird wings crossed by a flash - telegraphist - 1909.
- Ships propeller - 1914.
- Letters OC - officers' cook -1916.
- Letters OS - officers' steward 1916.
- Spoked steering wheel (RNAS) - 1918.
- Trident with or without a crown - 1918.
- Rangefinder (as in gun) - 1918.
- Divers helmet - 1919.
- Sextant - 1921.
- Two blade propeller - 1923.
- Coiled rope with harpoon and lightning crossing over - submarines - 1930.
- Camera - 1931.
- Marlinspike and crossed fid - sail maker - 1932.
- Straight winged aircraft - observer - 1934/5.
- Aircraft with a swept wing - 1939.
- Airscrew with two blades - aircraft mechanic - 1939.
- Bomb pointing down - bomb disposal - 1941.
- Marlin Spike inside a shackle - Rigger - 1941.
- Crown topped by an eagle with a tommy gun across - 1942.
- Spiders web crossed by lightning - radio operator - 1944.
- Compass/dividers (geometric) - navigator - 1944.
- Ships wheel - coxswain/quartermaster - 1948.
- Lightning flash with letters in centre - 1948.

Naval Swords

Swords and personal weaponry were as much a part of the 'uniform' and these were also controlled by regulations. It is possible that family historians will have a naval sword as part of their family archive. The principal weapons were the Dirk, Cutlass and Sword and some were ceremonial or dress whilst others were for weapons.

Dirk - The wearing of a dirk was primarily the domain of the Midshipman. The weapon was a short sword around 8" to 17" in length very often a straight double edged tapering blade although some of the longer ones were slightly curved.

Cutlass - This was the fighting weapon of the Navy and the whole ship's company were issued with a cutlass alongside boarding axes and pikes. The blade of a cutlass has varied over time but was usually 25"-30" in length and usually a curved blade. It had either brass, iron or leather grips and knuckle guards.

Sword - Up to around a century and a half ago no standard pattern existed for an officers' sword. Like early uniforms it was a matter of personal choice. From 1700-1740 an officer's sword tended to have a curved blade but from the late 1700s it was not unusual to have two swords as part of the uniform, one for ceremonial purposes and the other a more formidable sword which could inflict wounds or even kill.

As the start of the 19th century an official sword was established by the Admiralty and the swords were used to denote rank with various shaped hilts, grips and pommels, each type of sword being used to denote different ranks. Most blades were straight and grooved and the standard length of 32" became the norm. In 1827 a sword with a half-basket hilt was introduced which has been in use ever since. By 1846 Wilkinson blades were fitted to all swords.

Medals and Awards

It is more than probable that medals and some honour awards may well exist within your family archive and as such will aid in the identification of any Navy ancestor. As such it is useful to know where the medal rolls can be found and also what the various medal may have been awarded for. The most effective way of identifying the medals is by the actual design of the medal and the colour of the ribbons (if still attached) or by using one of the many published medal guide books. Clarification of the award can also be established by referring to the medal rolls. All medals irrespective of time period in which they were issued are subject to an 'orders of wear' i.e. have to be worn in a certain order according to official regulations which apply mainly to honours, awards and gallantry medals. Campaign medals need to be worn in the order of the date of the campaign from left to right.

Before the first official campaign medal for the China wars in 1842 men were rewarded in different ways. Prize money was one of the oldest forms which was distributed amongst ships' crews when they captured an enemy vessel. These captured vessels were frequently used by the Navy rather than the Navy building new ships.

Prize Money

Surviving prize money lists are found in series ADM 128 and cover the period from 1803 to about 1937. They are however far from complete. Those that do survive give moderate information including name, rank or rating (depending whether the ancestor was an officer or rating) and the date of payment. Many of our ancestors would have considered both the prize money and the prospect of promotion a serious incentive for a naval career. Prize money was often supplemented by the award of medals which were privately minted (see below) and in the case of officers the award of presentation swords which may exist within your family archive.

Medals

There are many references to colour and style/design of medals that identification is normally straightforward particularly if the ribbons are still attached. Medals denoting naval service are worn on the left breast in line with the bottom edge of the lapel of the square collar. Ribbons only are worn on all but ceremonial dress when actual medals were displayed. After 1922 the Admiralty ordered that war medals were no longer part of the uniform.

Fortunately the medal rolls contained within series ADM 171 (Navy Department Medal Rolls) can be accessed online using Ancestry.

UK Navy Medal and Award Rolls online at Ancestry.co.uk

The database contains lists of Royal Navy officers, ratings and civil staff entitled to medals and awards in relation to their service. The database covers the period between 1793 and 1972 and include medals awarded for British and worldwide campaigns including both world wars.

Although most medal rolls do not provide a significant amount of detail they are a good starting point to access the service records. The medal rolls include the recipient's name, the naval division and the service number. Most rolls are arranged by campaign or action, then ship, rank and name.

The database enables flexible searches to be made by the recipient's name, medal or award, campaign or service, service date, ship name and service number. It is also often useful to browse the various medal rolls as the early pages of each roll often give explanations and other information which can be useful in research. All the volumes can be browsed.

ADM 171

Navy Department: Medal Rolls

Rolls and lists of officers and men of the Royal Navy who were awarded or claimed medals and clasps issued to commemorate actions and campaigns. The series also includes Royal Marines.

The series contains medal rolls for the First World War for awards of the British War Medal, Victory Medal and the 1914-1915 Star as awarded to men serving in the Mercantile Marine Reserve and to the officers and men of the Royal Naval Reserve who so qualified. Also included are the rolls relating to the Arctic Medal, 1875-1876; the Sea Transport Medal, 1899-1902; and the Delhi Durbar Medal, 1911.

Although you should commence your search using the online website Ancestry.co.uk, it is sometimes necessary to search the original rolls by visiting The National Archives or to browse search the images online when you are unable be easily identify the name of the recipient as there are always errors or omissions within human compiled indexes.

Service Medals

Naval General Service Medal 1793-1840 and 1915-1962

17. 1793-1840 medal ribbon.   *18. 1915-1962 medal ribbon.*

The Naval General Service Medal (NGSM) was approved in 1847, for issue to officers and men of the Royal Navy although a few awards were made to officers and men of the army who were on board ships at qualifying actions. The ribbon was white with narrow blue edges.

The issue of the medal and clasps was originally restricted under Admiralty order of June 1847 to participants in those actions for which gold medals had previously been conferred on Flag Officers and Captains. The order of June 1848 extended the award to all 'gold medal' actions or operations, all actions in which the First Lieutenants or Commanders were promoted, all boat actions in which the officer commanding was promoted and co-operation with land forces in sieges and landings for which the Army had awarded gold medals.

The NGSM was retrospectively awarded for naval actions which occurred from 1793 to 1840 such as the Napoleonic Wars and the French Revolutionary Wars. A clasp on the ribbon was given for each battle or action covered by the medal and as such the medal was never issued without a clasp. There are 231 clasps covering a variety of actions.

In order to receive the medal claimants had to have survived until 1847 and then had to apply for it (see claimants books in ADM 171) and it is clear from the number of men serving and the number of medals minted that there were men who did not apply for it. Claims were time limited and had to be submitted by May 1851. Next of kin could not apply for a medal on behalf of a deceased relative. The medal was however still awarded to next of kin if the claimants died between the date of their application and the date of presentation.

This medal and the Military General Service Medal, the army counterpart, were the first British campaign medals, issued to all ranks just for 'being there'.

The second issue of the General Service medal covers the period 1915-1962 and the ribbon was white with a broad crimson edge and two parallel red stripes inside.

There is a small but useful finding aid at The National Archives in piece ADM 73/94 which is an alphabetical index of Greenwich Hospital in-pensioners who claimed the Naval General Service Medal for the period 1848-1849.

The Royal Navy Long Service and Good Conduct Medal

19. RNLS & GC.

This medal was introduced in August 1831 and had an anchor surmounted by a crown and enclosed in an oak wreath on one side and on the other was engraved the recipient's details.

Over its life the medal changed dimensions and ribbon colour. The original medal was 34mm in diameter and had a dark blue ribbon. In 1848 the medal became 36mm in diameter with a dark blue ribbon flanked with narrow white edges. Other minor amendments to the way the medal was hung were introduced in 1874.

Today's Long Service & Good Conduct Medal is based on the 1848 issue. One side shows the reigning monarch, whilst the other side has an image of a three-masted man-of-war surrounded by a rope tied at the foot with a reef knot and the words 'For Long Service and Good Conduct' engraved around the circumference. The recipient's name is no longer included.

A rating who completed 15 years of service from the date of his or her attestation or from the age of 17½ years, whichever is later and who also holds all three good conduct badges is eligible to receive the medal. However, awards were only made after a thorough check of a sailor's record of service as there were a number of minor offences which could normally preclude a rating receiving the award.

A clasp to the medal was introduced during the reign of King George V and could be awarded for an additional 15 years of service. This clasp has a laurel leaf design. When the ribbon was worn alone a silver rosette in the centre denotes award of the clasp.

Various branches of the Navy (Royal Naval Reserve, Royal Naval Volunteer Reserve, Royal Fleet Auxiliary and Coastguard) also had long service and good conduct medals denoted by different coloured ribbons.

Campaign Medals

There were a number of other medals awarded specifically for Royal Navy involvement. Some elements relate to the award of clasps or bars as opposed to separate medals. The medal rolls in series ADM 171 provides a record including:

Arctic Medal 1818-1855

The medal is unusual in that it is octagonal in shape as opposed to being round. The medal was awarded to those involved in polar expeditions between the two dates provided they served at least six months. The ribbon is watered white. The medal was not inscribed but it is known that some were privately engraved with the names of the recipient.

20. Burma Medal 1824-1826.

This medal was awarded to those men who took part in the subjugation of Burma in 1824-1826. Originally intended for East India Company officers and men it was extended to the men of the Royal Navy and fitted with a bar. The ribbon is maroon with edge stripes in deep blue.

China Medal 1840-1842

21. China Medal.

This medal was issued in 1843 to members of the Royal Navy who participated in the First Anglo-Chinese War (1839-1942). It was originally intended to be awarded exclusively to all ranks of the East India Company's forces but under the direction of Queen Victoria the British Government awarded it to all members of the Royal Navy who served between 5 July 1840 and 29 August 1842 in the various actions, namely: Canton River 1841, the capture of Chusan 1840-1841 and various actions in the Yangtze River and the assault of Chinkiang. This campaign became known as the First Opium War opening five far eastern ports to trade, and vesting Hong Kong to Great Britain.

Those in receipt of this medal and who also served in the Second China War of 1861 were supposed to receive clasps which were issued with the second medal but this was not always the case because of differences in design specifications and inadequate fixings. It may not always be possible to determine without reference to the medal rolls who was a bona-fide recipient of the second medal as the clasp may not exist if your ancestor's medal still survives.

St Jean D'Acre Medal 1840

This medal was awarded for action in the Syria Campaign of 1840 by the Sultan of Turkey. A clasp titled 'Syria' was also attached to the Naval General Service Medal for recipients. The ribbon is red with white edges. If your ancestor was an officer there is a small but useful finding aid in piece ADM 105/38 which lists all those officers who served at the siege.

New Zealand Medal 1845-1866

22. NZ Medal.

This was a campaign medal awarded to naval personnel who took part in the New Zealand (Maori and Land) Wars of 1845-1847 and 1860-1866. The medal was authorised in 1869 and it is thought recipients had to participate in both wars to qualify. The ribbon is blue with a central red stripe.

South Africa (Cape of Good Hope) Medal 1850-1853

23. Cape of Good Hope Medal.

This medal was awarded for service in the South African campaigns. The ribbon is gold with one broad and one narrow deep blue stripe at each end.

Crimea Medal 1854-1855

24. Crimea Medal.

This medal was issued to officers and men of Royal Navy units that fought against Russia at Crimea. The medal had very ornate clasps in the form of an oak leaf with an acorn at each edge, one of several unique features of the medal. The Azoff clasp was only issued to Naval and Marine personnel. The other clasps were for Balalaika, Inkerman and Sebastopol, The medal without any clasps was issued to those who were present in the Crimea, but not present at any of the qualifying actions. The ribbon is pale blue with yellow edges.

Baltic Medal 1854-1855

25. Baltic Medal.

This campaign medal was issued to officers and men of the Royal Navy who served in Baltic Sea operations against Russia in the 'Baltic' theatre of the Crimean War. The medal primarily covered naval actions but it was also awarded to the Sappers and Miners involved in the demolition of Russian fortifications. The ribbon is yellow with light blue edges (reverse to the Crimea medal).

India Mutiny Medal 1857-1858

26. India Mutiny Medal.

This medal was awarded to members of the Royal Navy and the Naval Brigades who saw action in the Sepoy wars and uprisings. The ribbon is white with two red stripes equally spaced.

China Medal 1856-1860

Awarded to all Navy personnel involved in the 2nd China War. The ribbon is maroon with yellow edges.

Canada General Service Medal 1866-1870

27. Canada Gen Service.

This medal was not minted until 1899 and was awarded primarily to Navy officers and men who were involved with the Red River Rebellion. The ribbon is three equal stripes of orange, white and orange.

Abyssinia Medal 1867-1868

28. Abyssinia Medal.

This medal was awarded to crews of ships and members of the Naval Brigade who took part in the Ethiopian Wars of 1867-1868. The ribbon is red with broad white stripes.

Ashanti Medal 1873-1874

29. Ashanti Medal.

The first Ashanti Medal was instituted on the 1 June 1874 for award to members of the Naval Brigade deployed during the Third Anglo-Ashanti War. The ribbon is yellow with black edges and two narrow black central stripes.

Arctic Medal 1875-1876

This medal was awarded to those men who took part in the British Arctic Expeditions and served on *HMS Alert* and *HMS Discovery*. The ribbon is a fawn colour with no stripes.

India Medal 1854

30. India Medal.

This medal was awarded for various minor campaigns which took place on the Indian subcontinent commencing in 1852 and was extended to become the East India General Service Medal. Each action was supported by a clasp. The ribbon is divided into five stripes three red (edge and centre and two blue/green.

South Africa Medal 1877-1879

31. SA Medal.

The South Africa Medal was instituted in 1879 and was awarded to members of the Royal Naval Brigade involved in a series of tribal wars between 1877 and 1879; the ribbon is gold with broad and narrow deep blue stripes towards each edge.

Egyptian Medal

32. Egypt Medal.

This medal was awarded for service in the Egyptian campaigns between 1882 and 1889. The ribbon is three blue and two white wide stripes in the middle. In the same campaign the *Khedive Star* 1891 was conferred by Khedive Tewfie of Egypt to Navy personnel. The ribbon is solid deep blue with two central white stripes.

Ashanti Medal 1887-1900

33. Ashanti Medal.

Awarded to naval and marine personnel who were employed in expeditions or engaged in operations against natives on the African coast. The ribbon is three black stripes with two green inner stripes.

Khedive's Sudan Medal 1896-1908

34. Khedive's Sudan Medal

This medal was awarded for service in the Sudan between 1896 and 1908. The ribbon was a broad deep blue stripe with narrow green stripes and red edges.

Sea Transport Medal 1899-1902

35. Sea Transport Medal.

The Sea Transport Medal was a campaign medal awarded to masters and officers of merchant ships that were used to ship both men and equipment to South Africa during the South African War or China during the Boxer Rebellion. It was also awarded by the Admiralty to some Royal Navy personnel and was originally intended for issue in later actions but it never survived. The ribbon was red with a blue stripe near to each edge.

China Medal 1900

The China War Medal 1900 was a campaign medal for issue to British sea troops who fought during the Boxer Rebellion of 1900.

Queen's & King's South Africa Medal 1899-1902

36. Queen's SA Medal (so captioned). *37. King's SA Medal (so captioned).*

Most Royal Navy personnel only qualified for the Queen's South Africa Medal as naval action in the Boer War was almost complete when the King's Medal was instituted after 1 January 1902. Different clasps were awarded for different actions.

The ribbon of the Queen's South Africa Medal consists of five stripes: red on each edge, narrow dark blue inner stripes and a wider central orange stripe.

Naval Good Shooting Medal

38. Naval Good Shooting Medal.

This was awarded to seamen who achieved good hits at target practice during exercises. Whilst not a campaign medal as such the medal rolls are included within AD 171. Entry in the medal roll includes name, official number, number of the medal, rank or rating, type of gun used, ship and to whom the medal was delivered. The ribbon consists of five stripes, the outer two being blue followed by white inner stripes and a central red stripe.

Some medals in the early period were awarded privately and do not form part of the medal rolls.

Louisberg Medal 1758

This medal was awarded to members of the Royal Navy for acts of bravery or distinguished service during the capture of Louisberg. The ribbon is half blue and half yellow.

Davidson Nile Medal 1798

This medal was awarded to Navy personnel for their participation in the Battle of the Nile. There is no ribbon attached to this medal.

Earl Of Vincent Medal 1800

Awarded by the Earl of Vincent and privately struck. Medal awarded to the ratings of Ville de Paris.

Boultons Trafalgar Medal 1805

Matthew Boulton privately awarded the medal to those Royal Navy survivors of Trafalgar.

Davison Trafalgar Medal 1805

This was awarded specifically to those ratings as members of the crew of *HMS Victory*. The medal roll can be seen at Portsmouth on the Victory archive.

Bagur Medal 1811

39. Bagur Medal.

This was a special medal awarded by the Spanish Government for action in the Peninsular War of 1810. It was specific to the crews of Ajax, Cambria and Kent who landed at both Bagur and Palamos. The medal was amongst the first to be accompanied by a ribbon which was red with gold edges.

Naval Gold Medal 1795

40. Naval Gold Medal.

Minted in two sizes, the larger was awarded to Admirals the smaller to Captains for various naval actions from 1795-1815. The ribbon was white with blue edges.

Royal Navy WW1 Medals

The medals awarded to Royal Navy personnel of all divisions for service during the First World War are the same as those awarded to other armed forces.

Five different campaign medals were awarded, the 1914 Star, the 1914/15 Star, British War Medal and Victory Medal. The Silver War Badge was awarded to members of the naval forces who retired or were discharged due to sickness or injuries sustained as a direct result of conflict.

Records of the award of medals are also contained in ADM 171 and can be searched for by name on Ancestry.

Gallantry Medals and Awards

There are several medals awarded for gallantry not always unique to the Royal Navy. Besides being in possession of a medal it is important to try and locate the citation as this will give an insight into the circumstances of the award. In many cases the citation does not survive and it may be necessary to search the *London, Belfast* or *Edinburgh Gazettes*. The gazettes can be searched online at **www.thegazette.co.uk**. The Navy Lists or the Admiralty Fleet Orders may also carry some notification about recipients depending upon circumstances and the medal awarded.

If the citation has not survived it will be necessary to search operational records to try and find details of the circumstances of the award (see later). Very often local newspapers also carried a report or at least some mention of those awarded gallantry medals. Many awards are recorded in ADM 171 so can be accessed online.

The Albert Medal

41. Albert Medal.

This medal was instituted in 1866 and initially awarded for saving life at sea but this was extended to land in 1867. Those who received the award were listed in the *London Gazette*. The award could be gained by both Royal Navy and Merchant Navy personnel. In series BT 97 there is a list of recipients between 1866 and 1913 together with photographs of all recipients in the period 1866-1879. ADM 171 covers the awards to 1948. There were various classes of the medal and the ribbon was either a series of red and white stripes for land awards or blue and white stripes for sea awards. In context only about 250 sea awards were ever made. The award has been superseded by the George Cross.

Conspicuous Gallantry Medal

42. Conspicuous Gallantry Medal.

This award was for petty officers and seamen and was first introduced for the Crimean War and again for the Ashanti war of 1873-1874. It is one of the medal awards that is recorded in the Navy List. There are no notices of award in the *London Gazette* after 1874. The recipients of the medal during the First World War are recorded in ADM 171 so are available on Ancestry. The roll for the First World War and later includes the name, service number, medal number, rank or rating and ship's pay number together with a brief comment on reason the medal was awarded. The ribbon for the naval version of the medal was changed after the First World War from one of two stripes of dark blue flanking a central white stripe to a white ribbon with narrow dark blue edge stripes.

Conspicuous Service Cross (Later Distinguished Service Cross)

43. DSC.

The award was originally created in 1901 as the Conspicuous Service Cross, for award to warrant and junior officers of the Royal Navy. It was renamed the Distinguished Service Cross in October 1914, eligibility being extended to all naval officers (commissioned and warrant) below the rank of Lieutenant Commander. The ribbon has three equal stripes of dark blue, white and dark blue. Since 1933 the DSC serves as the award for gallantry at sea for all ranks.

The medal roll for Royal Naval Reserve officers is in series BT 164/23 (name indexed) covering the period of the Second World War.

Distinguished Service Medal

44. DSM.

The Distinguished Service Medal was until 1993 a decoration awarded to Royal Navy personnel. The medal was established in 1914 and was the equivalent to the DSC for ratings. The ribbon consists of three equal stripes: dark blue, white, and dark blue, with a thin dark blue stripe down the centre of the white. For the First World War period all recipients were recorded in the Navy List.

Meritorious Service Medal

45. MSM.

The Royal Navy's Medal was established in 1919 although it had been in existence from 1845. It was awarded to petty officers and senior Navy ratings for gallantry not in the face of the enemy and for meritorious service The MSM was superseded as a gallantry award in 1928 by the Empire Gallantry Medal, but resumed in 1977. It is now awarded to senior Warrant Officers in the Royal Navy, the Women's Royal Naval Service and the Royal Naval Nursing service. The Royal Navy ribbon is crimson with white edges and a white centre stripe.

Military Medal

46. MM.

The Military Medal was introduced during the First World War in 1916. Navy personnel who received the Military Medal appear in the ADM 171 medal rolls for the period 1917-1921 and again for 1942-1972. The ribbon is dark blue with five equal centre stripes of white, red, white, red, and white.

Mentioned in Despatches

Being 'Mentioned in Despatches' was a way of bringing to the attention of senior Admiralty officers the deserving service of both officers and men. There is an index of Royal Navy personnel Mentioned in Despatches for the First World War period held at The National Archives but there is no listing of Naval despatches in the *London Gazette* before the end of 1916. There is also a roll listing Royal Naval Reserve officers in the Second World War in BT 164/23 as many of these were merchant seamen by profession.

Of interest is the list of officers Mentioned in Despatches between 1884 and 1885 relating to the actions in Egypt and Burma. The list can be found in series ADM 7/914.

MIDs (Mentioned in Despatches) for Navy personnel were only recognised by certificates and gave an entitlement to wear a multi-leaved emblem up to 1910 after which the emblem was a single leaf.

Foreign Awards

Many British Royal Navy personnel received awards from foreign governments. Some very early records of awards from 1745 can be found amongst the Foreign Office Correspondence for which the card index at The National Archives is useful to identify individuals, although it may not be complete. This index is the subject of digitisation and will shortly be searchable using The National Archives' online catalogue called Discovery.

From the First World War onwards records exist in ADM 171 for awards from France, Belgium, Netherlands, USA, Norway, Russia, Denmark and Greece given to both officers and ratings from all branches of the Navy including the reserves.

CHAPTER SIX

*Basic genealogical sources for
Royal Navy personnel*

As the Navy travelled throughout the world events such as birth, baptism, marriage, death and burial have been recorded at the various establishments. Many of these records have been deposited at The National Archives and as such will be valuable though perhaps not initial sources for research. As the Royal Navy had many foreign stations it is also possible that some events may be recorded in the ecclesiastical or civil registry systems in the foreign country in which the stations were located. This is particularly true of the late 19th and 20th century events. Many records relating to the post 1950s baptisms are still retained by the Naval Chaplaincy Service.

Naval Baptism Registers - United Kingdom

Chatham Dockyard - Baptisms 1867-1974 - ADM 338/17-18.
Chatham Navy Barracks - Baptisms 1907-1983 - ADM 338/19-20.
Chatham RN Hospital - Baptisms 1907-1961 - ADM 338/22.
Portsmouth Haslar Hospital - Baptisms 1829-1862 - ADM 305/86.
Portland Naval Hospital - Baptisms 1913-1977 - ADM 338/59.
Greenwich RN Asylum - Baptisms 1822-1856 - RG 4/1678 Shotley Training
    Est. - Baptisms 1905-1965 - ADM 338/37-41.
Sheerness Dockyard - Baptisms 1688-1960 - ADM 6/430, 432, 438.
Greenwich - Baptisms 1720-1864 - RG 4/1669, 1670, 1677, RG*/16-18.

Naval Burials Registers - United Kingdom

Sheerness Dockyard - Burials 1730-1826 - ADM 6/430, 431.
Portsmouth Haslar Hospital - Burials 1826-1954 - ADM 305/103-115.
Londonderry - Burials 1914-1946 - ADM 338/50.
Greenwich - Burials 1705-1966 - RG 4/1669-1676, ADM 73/460-465.
Greenwich RN Hospital School - Burials 1807-1856 - RG 4/1679.

The records with an RG prefix are also available to search and download on the BMD Registers and TheGenealogist websites.

Naval Baptism Registers - European Stations

Malta Dockyard - Baptisms - ADM 338/51.
Malta RN Hospital - Baptisms 1924-1977 - ADM 338/52.

Naval Burial Registers - European Stations

Greece - Burials 1894-1925 - ADM 121/102.
Italy - Burials 1915-1918 - ADM 121/102.

Naval Baptism Registers - rest of the world

Boaz Bermuda - Baptisms 1918 - ADM 6/439
Bermuda Ireland Island - Baptisms 1824-1954 - ADM 6/434, 435, ADM 338/11.
Mauritius - baptisms 1915-1976 - ADM 338/55.

Naval Burial Registers - rest of the world

Alexandria, British cemetery - Burials 1822-1916 - ADM 121/102.
Bermuda Ireland Island - Burials 1824-1946 - ADM 6/435, 436.

Naval Chronicle Index to Births, Marriages and Deaths

The Naval Chronicle was a monthly publication running from 1799 to 1818 and containing records of births, marriages and deaths principally of officers and their families. Publication ceased at the end of 1818 and was re-established (initially as the Sailors Home Journal) running between 1853 and 1863.

An index of the events in the earlier run of the publication was published in 1989 and is available in The National Archives library and the Society of Genealogists' library.

It is particularly useful where an officer is not included in the published biographical material. The index is alphabetical and then chronological within each section. Event reports within the *Chronicle* vary in length and detail, some being amazingly short and other providing useful biographical and family history information. Some volumes are available as e-books using the internet but a full set does not seem to be available. However the major copyright libraries have the volumes. Many editions of the Naval *Chronicle* can be viewed online using: **www.historicalnavalfiction.com** (Don't be put off by the name of the website!)

In the birth section the index gives:

• The name of the naval officer.
• His rank.
• The volume and page number within the *Chronicle*.
• An indication of whether the birth was of a son or daughter.
• Sometimes indicating where and if stillborn.

In the marriage section:

• The name of the RN officer or daughters are given together with rank.
• Volume and page number.
• In some instances, where the marriage took place.

For deaths the index gives:

• The name of the person and includes wives, widows etc. of the naval officer.
• The rank of the officer.
• The volume and page number within the *Chronicle*.
• Sometimes location of death and relationship.

In all cases it is therefore possible to search the actual *Chronicle* using the index information and in many cases clues enable the parish registers also to be searched.

Naval Census Returns 1851-1911

From 1861, and for subsequent censuses, returns were submitted for every Navy vessel in British waters and worldwide. Commanding Officers were required to compile returns whether their ships were in port or on the high seas. It is however known that some returns were never submitted or have been lost, for example about 40 ships mainly overseas did not submit a return for the 1901 census.

47. Crew details of a ship included on the 1861 census returns.

Seamen's wills and effects papers

The Prerogative Court of Canterbury prior to 1858 had the responsibility for proving the wills of both ratings and officers who died abroad. Up to 1815 it also had the responsibility for those who died in service where more than £20 was owed to them in wages. The indexes will often indicate the name of the ship on which the testator was serving when the will was made. In some cases the abbreviation PTS is used indicating 'foreign parts'. PCC records are held at The National Archives and searchable through TNA Discovery website.

After 1858 naval wills were under the jurisdiction of the Principal Probate Registry although the wills of seamen and Warrant Officers for the period 1786-1882 were the responsibility of the Navy Inspector of Wills.

The type of work undertaken by Navy personnel particularly ratings was considered to be dangerous and it was also not unusual on long voyages for men to become sick or be killed as a result of accident or war. This was a concern for both the Admiralty and the seamen. Many seamen made wills to be effected upon death irrespective of jurisdiction.

In many cases there was a problem of impersonation of deceased seamen by others who wanted to cash in on the value of the deceased's effects. After a fairly long battle a Navy Inspector of Wills was established in 1786 to stop the criminal practices which had existed up to that time.

The Inspector of Wills had the responsibility to make sure all naval personnel wills were properly registered and above all that records were kept of the registered wills. The administration under this Navy department provides the family historian with a good number of documents the main series being seamen's wills.

Inspector of seamen's wills

These indexed records are held by the National Maritime Museum and relate to Ratings, Officers and some civilians in Navy employ who died in service between 1910 and 1959. The records are in separate lists depending upon status. Recorded information includes the number of the case and certificate, the date registered, name of the ship on which the death took place and the date of death, name and the name and address of who the administration was awarded to.

The later registers for the Second World War and aftermath also record official number, branch of the service, date and place of birth, cause of death and gallantry awards or decorations.

On the death of either a rating or officer a document/correspondence file was opened which was forwarded to the Naval Historical section once the work was concluded. It is sometimes possible to access the original file subject to privacy restrictions as procedures followed by the Navy are in accordance with the Seamen and Mariners Property Act 1865.

Seamen's wills

The original wills deposited with the Navy Pay Office and numbering around 20,000 are in series ADM 48 and these can be searched and downloaded using 'Discovery' for the period 1786-1882. Original wills where validated by the Admiralty were in most cases on printed forms. If the original wills were not validated they were, in most cases, returned to the executors and a direction to that effect was noted in the register.

The registers of wills form series ADM 142 and are part of The National Archives Digital Microfilm project so can be freely downloaded. The registers are arranged alphabetically in two series covering 1786 to 1861, and 1862 to 1909. Several of the earlier volumes within the register record the name, address and relationship of the executor or administrator of the will.

Most of the wills begin with the words 'In the Name of God, Amen' and were usually printed forms with main details filled in by hand. Some however were written out by hand rather than using the pre-printed form. In some cases there is additional or supporting correspondence.

The wills usually provide:

- The seaman's name.
- Date the will was made.
- Rank or rating.
- The name of the last ship on which he served.
- Details of his effects.
- The name (and sometimes the address) of the person who was to receive the effects in the event of his death which was normally the nominated next of kin.

As well as being signed and dated by the testator the, will was usually witnessed (or authenticated) by both the master and captain of the ship that the seaman was serving on when the will was made.

Registers of deceased ratings

These registers in series ADM 154 cover the period 1859-1878 and list the ratings who died in service. The register includes the name of the ship on which death occurred, whether there was a will and details about his next of kin. The relationship of the next of kin is denoted by a series of abbreviations: F, M, W, B, S relating to father, mother, wife, brother, sister.

Seaman's effects papers

The effects papers are in different classes for different branches. They basically relate to the applications by the next of kin of a deceased seaman for unpaid wages or pensions due. Depending upon the series some papers are supported by birth or marriage certificates or wills.

Effects papers fall into three classes:

- Officers and civilian effects papers 1830-1860 in series ADM 45 (Next of kin claims for unpaid Royal Navy pensions).
- Seaman's effects papers 1787-1834 in series ADM 80 with miscellaneous papers in series ADM 304.
- Seaman's effects papers 1800-1860 in series ADM 44 indexed in ADM 141.

ADM 44

These are applications from the next of kin of deceased ratings arranged under the first letter of the name of the seaman and importantly they include the name and address of the claimant. The letter in the piece number is the initial letter of the surname. There are separate certificate numbers for each letter of the alphabet.

ADM 141

Indexes to Registers of Seamen's Effects Papers arranged alphabetically in three series covering 1802 to 1824, 1825 to 1848 and 1849 to 1861.

These volumes are slightly unusual in the way the index works. Names are in alphabetical order by the initial letter followed by the vowel but unlike usual indexes they in turn then take the first consonant after the initial letter, whether before or after the vowel.

The details in pieces ADM 141/4-9 which relate to 1825 onwards, include date, name, CS number, ship and date of death.

ADM 45

Officers' and Civilians' Effects Papers 1830-1860. The applications relate to commissioned and Warrant Officers as well as members of the civilian branches such as surgeons etc. They normally provide rank, date of death, the name and address of claimant, the date that the claim was processed and the total value of the remaining effects. These records are indexed within Discovery. A small cost is payable to download the document or they can be downloaded for free (except for print cost only) at The National Archives.

ADM 80/4 and 5

Register of dead seamen's wages for the period 1787-1809 arranged alphabetically by initial letter of the surname and providing basic information such as name, rating and ship's name of men who served in the Royal Navy. Electronic images of these records can be searched online through Discovery.

There are also similar records in series ADM 80 which relate to merchant seamen who may have had some service with the Royal Navy.

ADM 304

Within this series there are effects entry books specific to particular establishments. Those for the Royal Naval Hospital in Malta covering the period 1845-1855 are in piece ADM 304/28 and in ADM 304/32 for the period 1851-1860. The effects details are the same as for other classes.

For the period during and immediately following the Second World War 1941-1957 there are similar records for deceased casualties who died at Haslar Hospital in series ADM 305/116

There are also classes of document that provide information relating to the sales of deceased seamen's effects when they deserted.

Other records of wills and letters of administration

Records exist in series ADM 80 of the probates for Greenwich Hospital in-pensioners and staff for the period 1732-1767 and also between 1861 and 1869. Many of these records are indexed and provide the names of both the testator and executors.

Similar records exist for those who made wills whilst in the Gibraltar Naval Hospital between 1809 and 1815 in ADM 105/40. These records include the date that the will was sent to the Inspector of Wills office and detail the doctor who certified the sanity of the seaman.

If there was no will the next of kin were required to send a certificate of kinship to the Navy Bill office in order to obtain letters of administration. These documents exist for only a short period between 1795 and c.1807. The information that these records contain relate mainly to the applicant not the seaman. They include applicants name, relationship to the deceased, the name, rank and date of death of the deceased seaman. Such applications were dealt with by the Admiralty Courts and are contained in series HCA 30/455-458.

There may be some information more particularly for officers in the Inland Revenue Death Duty Registers at The National Archives.

CHAPTER SEVEN

Divisions and branches of the Royal Navy

The Royal Navy, as early as the Napoleonic Wars, and particularly for the duration of the two world wars, established other divisions and reserve forces to enhance and supplement the work of the full time professional Navy. Although some of these only existed for the duration of wars others have become well established and still exist. It is more than possible that your ancestors served in one of these divisions rather than in the 'Royal Navy' itself, and as such, their uniform may be slightly different. Also they could have been merchant seamen in which case additional records will need to be researched. If all you know about your ancestor was that 'they were in the Navy' then research needs to include the records of the other divisions if you are unsuccessful in locating information about them in the main service records. Each division generated its own records although in some cases the service/pension records could be integrated within the established Navy records.

Sea Fencibles

The Sea Fencibles were the brainchild of Rear Admiral Sir Home Riggs Popham who organised a part-time coastal militia recruited from local fishermen and boatmen, under the command of Royal Naval officers. Their prime purpose was to form a local defence corps that could be mobilised in case of invasion or emergency.

In March 1798, five post-captains were appointed to command and superintend the enrolment of men locally raised in five coastal districts running around the south east coast from Emsworth on the Hampshire/Sussex border, to Great Yarmouth. Five further districts were created soon afterwards covering the area from the Isle of Wight to Land's End, with an 11th district from Saltfleet to Flamborough Head on the east coast. The post-captains and their subordinate officers in the 11 districts were under the jurisdiction of the Admiralty and were stood down in October 1801.

In 1801 after agreement with Admiral Nelson a member of the crew of each fencible smack could volunteer for service on Navy ships to defend the Thames estuary.

In July 1803 the Sea Fencibles re-emerged with a much larger establishment devolved into around 40 districts covering the United Kingdom and a further 20 districts covering Ireland. The whole service in Ireland, alongside that of signal stations and the Impress Service, was superintended by an admiral. The Sea Fencibles were again stood down in October 1810 at which point their strength numbered around 23,000 men.

Each member of the Sea Fencibles was eligible to receive a 1s. per day when required for service, but the main incentive appears to have been the immunity from service in the militia and from the press gang. Many of the officers within the Sea Fencibles were those who otherwise would have been on half-pay but they received full pay whilst attached to the Sea Fencibles.

When recruiting for the Sea Fencibles recommenced in July 1803, local newspapers carried advertisements asking those willing to serve to attend a meeting to enrol. The following instructions with two major incentives were frequently published with the adverts in some districts:

'That all who shall voluntarily enroll themselves as Sea Fencibles, for the defence of the coast, will be exercised one day in every week, and be paid on such days, and at all times, when called out to perform any service, one shilling each man, but none shall be enrolled who are not settled inhabitants of the District.

As the situation of the country requires the service of every person on the sea coast, no seafaring man, fisherman, or other person, whose occupation or calling may be, or has been, to work in vessels, or boats, or otherwise, nor any of those who have received regular protections, such as pilots, fishermen, masters of barges, or who are protected, by being in the service of the Excise, Customs, or Post Office, will be exempted from the Impress, unless enrolled to serve in the Sea Fencibles.

And those who shall enroll themselves, and perform properly, the services required, will be protected from being impressed'.

The recruiting campaign was overly successful as many who attempted to avoid impressment into the Royal Navy or Militia service joined the Sea Fencibles thus making it difficult for the full time Royal Navy to recruit men. In addition some of the commanding officers were more than happy to have fit and mature men capable of fulfilling their roles in the Fencibles. The Admiralty was fully aware of the situation and tried various methods, mainly unsuccessfully, to reduce the numbers of Fencibles in order that they could be pressed into the Royal Navy.

The Sea Fencibles initial duties included guarding the Martello towers and patrolling the beaches adjacent to where it was thought the French might invade. In addition they were trained to use the cannon and pike and in the handling of armed coastal craft which were usually provided by local owners under contract to the Admiralty.

In addition to defending the coastline the Sea Fencibles were also involved in other activities. A report in the *London Gazette* of 12 January 1799 reports shows that on the 9 January 1799 the brig Susannah sailed from Dartmouth only to be taken later the same day by the French privateer L'Heureux Speculator. This was observed by the Brixham Sea Fencibles who went off in a boat armed with pikes and muskets and recaptured the Susannah and the French crew who were attempting to make their escape. On their return to port two boats were prepared with a view to capturing the privateer, but this was unsuccessful. On the 8 January a small cutter was observed taking two brigs off the North Foreland, whereupon the local Sea Fencibles pushed off in three boats and re-captured the two brigs.

The Sea Fencibles also undertook ceremonial duties and were often given a relatively high profile in the local newspapers. When the Royal Family sailed into Portland Roads on board *HMS Cambrian* in 1800, the Portland Sea Fencibles fired the appropriate salutes.

According to an Admiralty circular dated August 1803, one of their tasks was to survey the coastline within their Division and to inform the Admiralty which areas in each Division might be most exposed for the landing of the enemy and also to note the tides most suitable for that purpose.

Sea Fencible Divisions around the United Kingdom and Ireland

The coast of England, Scotland and Wales was divided into about 36 sections, each supervised by up to three Royal Navy Captains. A section was sub-divided into areas of the coastline which were the responsibility of a Royal Navy Lieutenant, The coast of Ireland was similarly divided into about 21 sections.

The original divisions running from 1798 to 1801:

Emsworth to Beachy Head

Beachy Head to Deal

Deal to Faversham

Leigh to Harwich

Harwich to Yarmouth

Isle of Wight

Coast of Hampshire

Coast of Dorset

Coast of Devon

Plymouth to Land's End

Saltfleet to Flamborough Head

The divisions existing between 1803 and 1810:

Emsworth to Beachy Head

Emsworth to Calshott Castle

Beachy Head to Dungeness

Dungeness to Sandgate

Sandgate to Sandown

Chatham to Sheerness

Sandown to the North Foreland

North Foreland to East Swale

Along the Medway from Maidstone

Lower Hope to Blackwater

Blackwater to the Stour

The Stour to Southwold

Southwold to Cromer

Cromer to Fosdyke Wash (up to 6 Feb 1806)

Hunstanton to Fosdyke Wash (after 6 Feb 1806)

Cromer to Hunstanton (after 6 Feb 1806)

Fosdyke Wash to the Mouth of the Humber

Mouth of the Humber to the River Ouse

River Ouse to Flamborough Head

Flamborough Head to the River Tees

River Tees to North Shields

North Shields to St Abb's Head

Firth of Forth

River Tay to Dundee

Coast of Angus

Shetland Islands

Isle of Wight

Calshot Castle to St Alban's Head

St Alban's Head to Puncknowle

Puncknowle to Teignmouth

Teignmouth to the Rame Head

Rame Head to the Dodman

Dodman to Land's End

Scilly Islands

Chepstow to the Mouth of the Bristol Channel

Bristol to Gloucester

Kidwelly to Cardigan

Hartland Point to Kingroad

Upper part of the River Severn

Holyhead and Anglesey

Liverpool and its neighbourhood

Lancashire Coast

Workington to Whitehaven

Land's End to Hartland Point

Irish Sea fencible districts, 1803 to 1810:

Malin Head to Horn Head

Horn Head to Teeling Head

Teeling Head to Donegal

Ballyshannon to Killala

Killala to Blacksod Bay

Blacksod Bay to Killery Harbour

Killery Harbour to Greatman's Bay

Greatman's Bay to Black Head

Loop Head to Kerry Head

Kerry Head to Blasket Island

Blasket Island to Valencia	Hook Tower to Arklow
Valencia to Dursey Island	Arklow to Killney
Dursey Island to Mizen Head	Sligo
Mizen Head to Galley Head	Donaghadee to Larne
Galley Head to Cork Island	Howth to Ballriggan
Cork Island to Youghal	Dublin - Gun boats
Youghal to Waterford	

Equipment and ship/boats for the Sea Fencibles

Each sea-port had to equip, at their own expense, a number of armed vessels and hulks, to be stationed and in the charge of and exercised by the Sea Fencibles. In cases where the proportion of Sea Fencibles was greater than the port could find ships for, vessels were provided by Government to meet the need.

Each port had to allocate a place for assembling ships which was initially determined by the respective commanders of Sea Fencibles. The Admiralty determined a general rendezvous in the locality for the whole fleet to assemble when required for action. It was deemed that coastal vessels such as colliers of about 150 tons, would make the best gun-vessels, and merchants and ship owners in every port had to fit all their vessels to carry two guns forward and two aft. To accommodate the guns all vessels had to be fitted with ring and eye bolts for guns, and that all smaller vessels had to be prepared to receive large oars to act against the enemy if necessary.

When the vessels had been modified to Admiralty guidelines guns and ammunition were put on board by Government at no cost to the owners but the masters had to give an undertaking (and sometimes enter into a surety or licence) to return them when demanded and to keep a regular account of the expenditure in operating them.

All the vessels and boats employed in this service received a letter of marque, in order to entitle their crews to benefit from the prize money that they may have made.

Records of Sea Fencibles

The following records are held by The National Archives at Kew:

Sea Fencible Pay Lists

Series ADM 28 comprises Sea Fencibles Pay Lists for the period 1798-1810 which contains musters and receipted pay lists arranged by district with each having a separate piece number. The musters and pay lists consist of the names of men acknowledging receipt of pay. They also contain information relating to the appointments of serving naval officers to the Sea Fencibles. A list of districts and the officers who served in them can be found in ADM 28/145 which is a working notebook and may contain other snippets of information.

The pay lists detail:

- Name of individual (not alphabetical).
- Dates on which they exercised.
- No of days entitled to pay.
- Sum paid for the days exercised.
- Date payment was made.
- Who received the pay.

48. Sea Fencibles pay list (TNA, document reference ADM 28/14).

Sea Fencible Entry Books

Series ADM 11/14-16 comprises Entry Books for the period 1804-1813 which contain orders appointing officers to Sea Fencibles, tenders, cutters signal stations, Impress Service and other shore appointments. Series ADM 6/55 contains similar information of officer appointments.

Sea Fencible Irish Establishment

Series ADM 1/621 relates to the Irish Establishment for the period 1806-1809 and contains the monthly consolidated returns made to the Government of Ireland and the Admiralty.

Navy Board Out-letters

Series ADM 354 comprises Navy Board Out-Letters. Throughout this series and in relation to the appropriate dates there is correspondence between officers and the Admiralty relating to the operation of various districts of Sea Fencibles. To locate the documents search Discovery using the terms 'Sea Fencibles, ADM 354'.

Certificates of Service

Series ADM 29 contains Certificates of Service. There are a few records for men who served with the Sea Fencibles within this series. If you have a name it is worth undertaking a search for a possible record.

Some County Record Offices hold papers relating to Sea Fencibles and private papers, accounts, diaries etc. of naval officers superintending the Fencibles. Various interest groups host internet websites for specific stations or districts which give background information relating to both individuals and operations. Details of individuals will supplement information found in official records.

Royal Naval Artillery Volunteers

The Royal Naval Artillery Volunteers were established as a force for coastal defence protecting dockyards and commercially important ports. They were established throughout the country under the RNAV Act of 1873. In order to qualify for service the volunteers had to be of good character, physically fit, over 17 years of age and were required to attend at least two drills per month. Whilst on board ships they were required to perform all regular duties of a sailor. Boys of 14 years of age and upwards could be enrolled and trained as buglers. Men who belonged to any other volunteer force who were liable to be called out for service in case of war were not enrolled. Apprentices could not be enrolled without the consent of their masters. Any persons dismissed from any other service for misconduct could not be enrolled without Admiralty approval. In many cases the volunteers were recruited from local rowing and sailing clubs and this was particularly true of the Thames area. All the men were trained in two aspects of Navy life: the Navy gun drill and the skills on the use of boats and oarsmanship. In the London area the volunteers main training ship was '*Rainbow*' moored on the Thames embankment close to Somerset House.

Men were not required to serve on ocean-going vessels as their work was restricted to serving on coastal patrol vessels. They were formed into brigades of between 60 and 80 men each designated by a local name and split into four batteries. When serving on board the ships they were paid in exactly the same way and at the same rate as full time seamen, received a pension entitlement and were entitled to the provision of victuals.

Each brigade was under the control of a permanent Officer Instructor, who was commissioned to the equivalent rank of Lieutenant and a Petty Officer. The Officer Instructor was responsible to the Admiralty for the administration and performance of the unit and had to keep muster rolls when the brigade was not in service. As soon as they became active on board a vessel then they were recorded on the muster of that vessel. Only some ships' musters for the early years up to 1878 exist.

The uniform worn by all members, whether officer status or rating, was basically the same as that for their equivalent rank in the full-time Navy. The cap badge and uniform buttons had the letters RNAV divided by an anchor and the officers' stripes were in the same order as regular officers except they were set in wavy lines as opposed to straight lines.

Records of Royal Navy Artillery Volunteers

Because brigades were locally raised, the records which they generated, if they have survived, can be found in local record offices. There are various returns (mainly statistical) held at the Parliamentary Archives and local newspapers often contained reports of the local brigade activities.

Royal Naval Reserve

Ever since the establishment of a fighting Navy, the Merchant Navy has always acted as its reserve, providing both additional personnel and materials.

During the 17th Century the Navy relied on recruiting from the whole 'maritime community', including merchant ships, colliers and fishing vessels. The peacetime service required up to 4,000 men and could usually meet this number from volunteers. But in war time over 20,000 men were needed. During the 18th Century the Royal Navy had access to the largest reserve of seamen.

The methods of recruiting seamen in the Merchant Navy relied upon the payment of higher wages than a seaman could earn in the Royal Navy. Consequently the Royal Navy was forced to rely on impressment with men usually pressed from incoming as opposed to outgoing merchant vessels. Hence, some foreign seamen also served in the Royal Navy as no differential was used by the press gang for 'recruitment'.

The first seagoing Naval Reserve was the Royal Trinity House Volunteer Artillery, created in 1803, based in London and numbering about 1,200 officers and men paid for by Trinity House. It was large enough to man ten frigates on the Thames below Gravesend, and served to act as a deterrent against invasion. The Artillery only lasted a couple of years and was disbanded after the Battle of Trafalgar in 1805.

During the Crimean War from 1854, the Navy was forced to maintain a fleet in the Black Sea and one in the Baltic. In order to service the fleets at this time men had to be recruited from every available resource. In June 1858 a Royal Commission was set up to look at the manning of the Navy generally which initially recommended more training ships for boy seamen, free uniform, bedding and mess utensils for new recruits, improved victuals, improved pay for seamen and gunners, and the formation of a Royal Naval Reserve.

The Royal Naval Reserve (RNR) was therefore founded in 1859 to meet this need as a reserve of professional Merchant Navy seamen and fishermen with the purpose of assisting or serving the Royal Navy in times of war. Although the RNR was originally a reserve of seamen it was extended in 1862 to include officers.

Drill ships were established at the main ports around the coast of Britain and Ireland where recruits underwent gunnery training for one month each year that they served in the reserve. Thereafter members of the reserve, usually the officers embarked on battleships or battle cruisers, were to receive further training within both gunnery and Navy operations.. The RNR was administered by the Registrar General of Shipping and Seamen jointly with the Admiralty.

At the start of the First World War the RNR consisted of around 30,000 officers and men. A number of RNR officers qualified as pilots and flew aircraft and airships with the Royal Naval Air Service (RNAS) and many reserve seamen became part of the Royal Naval Division serving on the Western Front. Merchant Navy officers and men serving for the duration of the war also undertook duties on hospital ships, fleet auxiliary vessels and on armed merchant cruisers.

During the Second World War the RNR were involved from the outset. RNR officers took command of destroyers, frigates and submarines as well as working as specialist navigation officers in aircraft carriers. The RNR came to the fore in convoy work where the escort commander was frequently drawn from the officers of the RNR.

In 1890, the Royal Navy was in urgent need of 100 more Lieutenants and The Admiralty decided to recruit 100 officers from the Merchant Navy, 90 of whom were Royal Naval Reserve officers, who accepted permanent commissions as Lieutenants in the Royal Navy. These men never progressed beyond that rank and were nicknamed the 'hungry hundred' stemming from the fact that most Merchant Navy officers had to sign on for each new voyage while Royal Navy officers were engaged on a continuous service and thus had a regular salary. By the late 1890s and with the continued shortage of Royal Navy Lieutenants a further 50 RNR Officers were given permanent commissions. These too had a nickname and were known as the 'famishing fifty'.

In 1902, the Admiralty established a unit of 600 men, of the Royal Naval Reserve at St John's Newfoundland on board *HMS Calypso*. These men were local fishermen and seamen some of whom served with the North Atlantic and West Indian Squadrons and who continued to serve with the regular Navy in World War One.

Members of the RNR were as professional as their Royal Navy counterparts. Up until 1903 there had been no specific medals for campaigns awarded to RNR men so King Edward VII approved a special medal for their services in South Africa and China. In 1907 a 'Long Service and Good Conduct' medal for ratings of the RNR and the Royal Naval Volunteer Reserve was instigated and awarded after 15 years' service. Similarly a RNR Officers' Decoration was established in 1909 for 15 years' service. In 1910, the Trawler Section was formed to recruit and train fishermen for service in minesweepers and other smaller vessels in times of war and skippers were known as 'Skipper RNR(T)'. Initial enlistment took place from 1911 at the ports of Aberdeen and Grimsby where the country's largest fishing fleets were based. This service evolved into the Royal Naval Patrol Service.

The Trawler Section (later the Royal Naval Patrol Service)

The Royal Naval Reserve Trawler Section was set up in 1911. It was abolished in 1921 after the end of World War One hostilities. It had always remained quite distinct from the RNR as it only employed fishermen. In both world wars a large number of trawlers were built or requisitioned by the Royal Navy complete with their crews, who were engaged to serve with and on a named vessel for the duration of the war only.

On the outbreak of war almost 200 trawlers and their normal crews were immediately mobilised and began minesweeping. By the end of the war the section had over 700 vessels employed in minesweeping employing around 39,000 officers and men.

A naval trawler was built in a similar way to an ordinary fishing trawler with special fittings for naval purposes. Existing fishing trawlers were ideally suited because they were robust boats designed to work with heavy trawls in all types of weather and had large clear working decks. Trawlers were easily adapted to minesweepers by replacing the trawl with a mine sweep and by adding depth charge racking and a gun on the bow of the trawler.

Shipyards such as Smiths, based at North Shields and on the River Tees, were used to build naval versions of trawlers as they were already building civilian trawlers before the outbreak of the war. The Admiralty sold the surviving trawlers to commercial fishing interests when the war ended. During the First World War a massive programme to purchase trawlers to provide a cheap anti-submarine and minesweeping patrol service was implemented. The Admiralty settled on three standard classes of trawler known as Mersey, Castle and the Strath.

The minesweeping technique used was fairly revolutionary and involved two trawlers towing between them a sweep, held taught and at the right depth. This process required the trawlerman's skill to maintain the correct depth as the tide changed, and to cover all the ground without gaps, the object being to secure mine free passages along the East Coast. The swept mines were then destroyed by gunfire. In the early part of the war he majority of mines were laid by German surface ships but by 1915 the Germans began using mine laying submarines making detection less easy.

Life on board minesweepers had a degree of monotony with up to 12 days at sea in all weathers followed by four in harbour. The prospect of death and mutilation was ever present in the minds of the crews. For the duration of the war trawlers, in many cases kept their small crews intact throughout, continuously swept our coastal waters. If they were hit then in no more than a few seconds after striking a mine, there would be no trace of the trawler and in many cases the crew were also lost because of contamination of the water by explosives.

The Royal Naval Patrol Service was active during World War Two and operated mainly auxiliary ships such as trawlers, minesweepers and anti-submarine vessels to protect convoys and the coastal areas around the United Kingdom. The service also employed men outside maritime occupations.

In the summer of 1939 the Admiralty built 20 new naval trawlers and acquisitioned a further 67 from Britain's fishing fleet. At the outbreak of World War Two every available minesweeper of the Royal Navy and Royal Naval Patrol Service was located at the central headquarters of the RNPS located at Sparrow's Nest in Lowestoft. Here, throughout the war was the headquarters for more than 70,000 men and their 6,000 boats including motor fishing vessels, minesweepers and launches. However Grimsby, as it had in the First World War, became the largest minesweeper base in Britain and was responsible for the clearance of nearly 35,000 mines from coastal waters. The war was not without cost to the service which lost over 250 vessels. Nearly 15,000 men of the service were killed in action with a fair number having no known grave.

Because it used poorly armed and mostly outdated vessels the RNPS became known as the Navy within the Navy or more so 'Harry Tate's Navy' or 'Sparrows'.

The phrase 'Harry Tate's Navy' dates back to the First World War and depicted anything amateurish. Harry Tate was an old music hall entertainer whose act showed him as a clumsy comic with a car that gradually fell apart around him. By the start of World War Two the name became synonymous with the Royal Navy and was used to poke fun at the trawlers and drifters of the Royal Naval Patrol Service who proudly adopted the name Harry Tate's Navy. Men who served for longer than six months in the RNPS were honoured for their service by being able to wear a unique silver badge on the sleeve of their uniform.

Service records of the Royal Navy Reserve Trawler Division

Service records of ratings who served in the RNR (T) can be found in BT 377/7. Their service numbers were prefixed with the letters DA, ES, SA, SB, or TS. The records of ratings whose service numbers begin with SBC have not survived.

The Royal Naval Reserve and the Royal Naval Volunteer Reserve (see below) amalgamated in 1958 and were thereafter known as the 'Royal Naval Reserve'.

Records of the Royal Naval Reserve

Officers

Navy Lists

Information about Royal Naval Reserve officers is included in the Navy Lists from 1862. During the two world wars much of the usual information was confined to confidential editions which were for service use only. The Confidential Navy Lists (ADM 177) as well as a complete set of the published Navy Lists are available on open access at The National Archives. There are also good runs of the Navy List at the Society of Genealogists and the National Maritime Museum.The information contained within both sets of Navy Lists gives name, rank, date of commission and seniority. It also indicates the names of the ships on which the officers served.

Service Records

Officers' service records for the period 1862-1964 are in series ADM 240 and are organised by rank and seniority. Around the outbreak of the First World War, a record-of-service card was introduced for officers in the Royal Naval Reserve. Before then details of all naval officers' service had traditionally been recorded in books or registers. As the use of cards became the normal system of recording officers service the records of officer from all branches of the service become intermingled. There is an alphabetical index for this series in ADM 240/84-88. These records of service include those of engineers and paymasters.

For officers who served in the First World War their service record may be in either book/register or card form or even in both forms. If not found in ADM 240 it will be necessary to look at the other series of officers' service records in ADM 340 (see later). It is highly improbable that records in series ADM 240 will relate to officers who were born too late to have served in the First World War.

Ratings

Service Records

Both of the following sections records (BT 164 and BT 377) are name indexed using Discovery. Digital images of the service records can be downloaded for a small cost at home or available free of charge whilst researching at TNA or in the Library of the Society of Genealogists.

Serving between 1860-1908 (BT 164)

Only a selection rather than the complete series of records have been retained in series BT 164 for the above period. These records can be searched by name, date or place of birth and service number using the 'Online Collections' section of Discovery. These service records give a seaman's personal details together with a record of service and any training given. They also show details of retained pay. The records are contained in either book volumes or on cards each covering five years' service in the RNR. As such there may be more than one page or card relevant to each individual denoted by consecutive alphabet lettering.

Serving between 1908-1958 (BT 377)

These records are arranged by service number with online name indexes via Discovery.

The information available from the records irrespective of format (book entries cover two pages and card entries have a front and back) includes:

- Name.
- Date of birth.
- Address.
- Names of parents.
- Physical description.
- Date of enrolment, training.
- Names of and duration of service for ships on which he served.
- Full period of service and details of any engagements not completed together with the stated reason.

On the service cards dating from 1908 to 1955 a man's previous or subsequent service numbers may be recorded on the cards. It should be noted that as enrolment was for five years a different service number will be allocated to each five year period. They did not keep the same number throughout.

It is important to note that as the medal rolls also provide a man's service number. It is sometimes easier and quicker to look for his medals before looking for a service record.

As many men in the RNR had a Merchant Seaman background it is also worthwhile checking the Merchant Navy service records of Merchant Seamen particularly the section including the 1918-1921 records. As an alternative the Fleet Air Arm Museum holds the original records for RNR ratings up to c.1927 as well as some record cards for officers of the executive, engineers and telegraphic departments.

If you cannot locate a record it could be that the record is in an index entry only as in some cases names appear in indexes but not records. It is possible that the record did not survive, which is particularly true of the 1860-1908 period, if the record is not among the selected sample. The record may also be in another series, if for example he changed division or if his record is amongst Merchant Navy service records. (See *My Ancestor was a Merchant Seaman*.)

Medal entitlement

In some instances medal entitlement is noted on the individual's service record.

The Royal Naval Medal Rolls contained within series ADM 171 can all be searched by name using **www.ancestry.co.uk** and relate to the RNR as well as the Royal Navy.

The original records of the recipients of the RNR Long Service medal are recorded in classes ADM 171/70-72. Honours and Awards for the RNR during the First World War are in ADM 171/77. In both cases each volume is arranged in generally alphabetical order by surname. Correspondence and papers relating to awards specifically to RNR officers serving in World War Two are in series BT 164/23.

The Campaign Medal Rolls for all Navy personnel including the RNR are in ADM 171 with officers rolls in ADM 171/92-93 and rolls relating to ratings in ADM 171/120-124.

Mercantile Marine Reserve

As there was an overlap between the RNR and the Merchant Navy it is possible that some RNR members also served in the Mercantile Marine Reserve and it is necessary to follow up this possibility by checking the medal records of the Mercantile Marine Reserves in series BT 351/1/1-2. The cards record the issue of the British War Medal and the Mercantile Marine Medal in the First World War and provide the name, place of birth, year of birth, date of issue of medals, ribbons and clasps, discharge/RS2 number and can be searched using Discovery.

Royal Naval Volunteer Reserve

The Royal Naval Volunteer Reserve (RNVR) was established in 1903 and was formed using civilian volunteers. Up until this time the Royal Navy relied upon professional seamen drawn from the Merchant Navy or from fishing fleets but because of the rapid expansion of the Navy at the turn of the century it needed to look wider for volunteers to serve. The men of the RNVR served both on land and at sea. Five divisions were established in London, Liverpool, Bristol and covering the rivers Tyne and Clyde and this is where most of their training took place.

The RNVR earned the nickname of 'wavy navy' presumably after the wavy gold lace incorporated into their uniforms.

One of the most important jobs carried out by the RNVR was the administration of the Mine Clearance Service which was established in 1919 to clear all sea mines. Volunteers agreed to serve 'either ashore or afloat' when required, and as such performed a wide range of naval duties. With the outbreak of the First World War in August 1914, they were assigned to ships and many were ordered to join the Royal Naval Division (see below).

Records of the Royal Naval Volunteer Reserve

Ratings Service Records

Unfortunately not all Royal Naval Volunteer Reserve records have survived.

The records which have survived are held in series ADM 337 which have been digitised and are available through Discovery. Records exist for ratings who joined between 1903 and 1919 and officers who signed up between 1914 and 1922. If a RNVR man served with the Royal Naval Division then his records may well be with that set of records (see below).

The digitised documents (found in ADM 337) provide a range of information on each individual, including:

- Name.
- Division.
- Service number.
- Date of birth.
- Former occupation.
- Physical description.
- Ships and units served in, and period of service.

Some records provide remarks about character and ability and may contain details of the place of birth.

Ratings' records are arranged by division. When a rating joined they were allocated to divisions and their service numbers were prefixed by a distinguishing letters. If a man joined after the outbreak of the First World War then they may have a Z after the distinguishing letter.

The Fleet Air Arm Museum at Yeovil hold some engagement papers for men who joined some divisions and these can be useful if you are unable to locate a service record because they have not survived or to supplement information given in service records.

Additional Officers' Service Records

These form part of the general Royal Navy officers' records in series ADM 340. The officers' records include, name, rank, details of appointments and promotions, honours and awards from World War One and importantly the name and address of the next of kin. It is also useful to trace the officers using the Navy Lists.

Medal Records

First World War Campaign Medal entitlement can also be established using the medal rolls which are available on both Findmypast and Ancestry. The medal rolls include the following information: name, service number, rank, medals awarded, how the medals were issued, other awards for gallantry and distinguished or meritorious service, service details, date and cause of death.

Medal Rolls for RNVR Petty Officers and ratings are held at The National Archives in the series ADM /171/125-129 and ADM /171/139.

Division Letters

AA	Anti-Aircraft Division
B	Bristol
C	Clyde
E	Birmingham Electrical Division
K	Crystal Palace - entry for the army
L	London
M	Mersey
MB	Motor Boat Service
MC	Mine Clearance
P	Crystal Palace - entry as a civilian
R	Royal Naval Division
S	Sussex Division (sometimes ST)
SWS	Shore Wireless Service
T	Tyne
W	Wales
Y	Possible the men did not serve

Royal Navy Motor Boat Reserve

This reserve was formed in 1914 with three different ratings all wearing special caps and badges and with the officers being part of the Royal Navy Volunteer Reserve. The members of this reserve force were identified from cap badges which incorporated the letters RNMBR as well as collar badges. The reserve existed only for the duration of the First World War. The records associated with the Motor Boat Reserve are included with the RNVR series.

Naval Brigade

As a forerunner of the Royal Naval Division a Naval Brigade was formed on a temporary basis from both Seamen and the Royal Marines to undertake operations on shore predominantly during the mid-to-late 19th century. Seamen were trained in gunnery and land-based warfare at Portsmouth.

Interestingly, between 1850 and the start of the First World War the Royal Navy only fought one ship-to-ship action (in 1877) and its only war service was carried out on shore through Naval Brigades with the men taken from aboard its vessels. Naval Brigades were engaged on land in some of 'Queen Victoria's Wars' including the Crimean War, Second Opium War, The Indian Mutiny, Ashanti Wars, Zulu War, Boer War and the China Boxer rebellion.

Those who remember the Royal Tournament Field Gun Competition may be interested to know that this commemorates the Naval Brigade and their involvement with the Relief of Ladysmith in the Boer War when 12-pounder guns from two ships *HMS Powerful* and *Terrible* were dragged across almost 200 miles of rough terrain from Durban in 1899.

Service Records

The service records of those men who served as part of the Naval Brigade can be found amongst the general Royal Navy service records.

The Naval Brigade evolved into the Royal Naval Division formed during the First World War.

Royal Naval Division

The division was formed in August 1914 from surplus naval reserve forces when warships were fully crewed. The Royal Naval Division filled a shortfall in infantry divisions of the army but remained under Admiralty control until 1916 even though they were fighting on land alongside the army. In 1916 the control passed to the War Office and the Army supplied the shortfall in battalions and brigades to the establishment of the Division from July 1916 onwards.

The Royal Naval Division was assembled at Crystal Palace from men drawn from the Royal Navy itself and from the Royal Naval Reserve, Royal Naval Volunteer Reserve, Royal Marines (Light Infantry, Artillery and Band), The Royal Naval Auxiliary Sick Berth Reserve and the Royal Fleet Reserve.

ROYAL NAVAL DIVISION
HANDYMEN TO FIGHT ON LAND & SEA

1ˢᵗ BRIGADE

BATTALIONS:
"BENBOW"
"COLLINGWOOD"
"HAWKE"
"DRAKE"

RECRUITS
WANTED

2ⁿᵈ BRIGADE

BATTALIONS:
"HOWE"
"HOOD"
"ANSON"
"NELSON"

RECRUITS
WANTED

VACANCIES ғᴏʀ RECRUITS BETWEEN THE AGES ᴏғ **18** ᴀɴᴅ **38**
CHEST MEASUREMENT. 34   HEIGHT. 5 FT. 3½ IN.
PAYMENT from 1/3 per day. · FAMILY ALLOWANCES
Besides serving in the above Battalions and for the Transport
and Engineer Sections attached.
MEN WANTED
who are suitable for Training as Wireless Operators. Signalmen
and other Service with the Fleet.

49. Royal Naval Division recruitment poster.

Throughout its existence the Royal Naval Division retained naval traditions such as flying the White Ensign, using bells to signal time, used naval language and continued to use naval ranks. Attempts to convert the Royal Naval Division to army practices were generally unsuccessful. It was disbanded in 1919.

The Royal Naval Division was very active participating first in the defence of Antwerp in late 1914. But 1,500 sailors of the division fled to the Netherlands where they were interned. The division was then posted to Egypt prior to serving in the Ottoman Empire principally at the Battle of Gallipoli where it suffered heavy losses, so much so that it no longer contained a significant number of naval servicemen. In July 1916 it was re-designated the 63rd Division and was reposted to the Western Front for the remainder of the war.

Besides the Antwerp and Gallipoli campaigns the RND were also involved in other campaigns at Ancre valley in 1916 and at Passchendaele, Welsh Ridge and Gavrelle on the Western Front in 1917. The RND (as the 63rd Division) played an active role at the Hindenberg Line in 1918 and continued until the end of the war at Cambrai, Canal du Nord, St Quentin Canal and Mons.

The battalions of the Division were named after famous Admirals, Anson, Benbow, Collingwood, Drake, Hawke, Hood, Howe and Nelson. The Division originally consisted of two Navy and one Royal Marines Infantry brigades split into 12 battalions but with heavy casualties and few recruits the naval establishment was steadily reduced. Two naval battalions were disbanded in June 1915, and in August of that same year the whole Royal Marine Brigade was also disbanded. In February 1918 two more naval battalions were disbanded. By the end of the war the strength consisted of only two brigades of five battalions. Each battalion had its own badge.

As in the army the Royal Naval Division battalions were organised into brigades:

- 1st Brigade: Benbow, Collingwood, Drake, Hawke.
- 2nd Brigade: Anson, Hood, Howe, Nelson.
- The 3rd Brigade was made up of Royal Marines designated as battalions from their bases - Chatham, Deal, Plymouth and Portsmouth.

50. Badges for various RND battalions.

After designation as the 63rd (RN) Division they were supplemented with additional army battalions:

- 188th Brigade: Anson, Howe (also two battalions of Royal Marines).
- 189th Brigade: Drake, Hawke, Hood, Nelson.
- 190th Brigade: Hon. Artillery Co., Royal Fusiliers (7th Bttn.). Royal Dublin Fusiliers (10th Bttn.) and the Bedfordshire Regt. (4th Bttn.).

Many of the men from Benbow, Collingwood and Hawke battalions were interred very early in the war in Holland and the battalions were replenished from surplus army enlisted men, mainly Durham miners. The type of Navy discipline which prevailed at the time was said to be appreciated by the mining communities who staffed them perhaps because of the family type atmosphere which prevailed.

Records of the Royal Naval Division

War Diaries

The War Diaries of the RND and later the 63rd RN Division are to be found in ADM 137 primarily ADM 137/3063-3088 and these cover other operational records and casualty lists etc. After the army assumed responsibility for the RND the War Diaries became the responsibility of the War Office. The main diaries are found in WO 95/3118-3119 and WO 95/4290-4291 but it is also worth noting that other diaries also exist for specific campaigns. A search on Discovery using the search term 'RND War Diaries' will provide a full listing many relating to individual and named battalions.

Service Records

Service records cover the period 1914-1922 and are contained in series ADM 339 for both officers and ratings. These can be searched and downloaded using Discovery. Many of the records hold significant details about the men who served including:

- Name.
- Branch of service.
- Rank (with dates of commission if applicable).
- Residence.
- Occupation.
- Religious affiliation.
- Details of next of kin.
- Activity within the RND and details of where they served.
- Honours and awards.

- Wounds and illnesses/disabilities and where they were treated.
- Ratings' records also give date and place of birth and a physical description which includes an indication on their swimming ability.

Most of the records were typed as opposed to being hand written but include some obvious as well as less obvious abbreviations many of which are administrative. In some cases the records include death information including burial place. Sometimes copies of actual newspaper obituaries are attached. Men who died whilst in service were described as 'discharged dead' (DD) a familiar naval term dating from the early ships' musters.

Royal Naval Division casualty ledgers for the First World War are held by the Imperial War Museum, London.

The Jack Clegg Memorial Database of Royal Naval Division

Casualties of The Great War

This database which is available online at both ancestry.co.uk and Findmypast is a register of the deaths of servicemen who served in the Royal Naval Division (RND) in the First World War and was compiled from the original service records and other sources listing Royal Naval Division casualties. The database is named after Private John Clegg of the 1st Royal Marine Battalion, Royal Naval Division, who was 'wounded and missing' at the Battle of the Ancre in 1916 and compiled by Jack Marshall his great nephew.

The information in the database includes:

- All RND servicemen who died in service in the period 1914-1919.
- All RND servicemen who died after leaving the service generally up to 1926 but there are some cases recording deaths as late as 1942.
- Army troops who died while serving in a naval battalion or unit.
- Ex RND personnel who transferred from service in the Army or Air Force and Army officers seconded to RND service specifically with naval and Royal Marine battalions.

Royal Navy Submarine Service

The Royal Navy Submarine Service, the '*Silent Service*', began in 1901 at *HMS Dolphin* in Hampshire. The Royal Navy was thought to be the last maritime power to instigate the use of submarines because of Admiralty objections to using them.

The first submarine known as 'Holland 1' was brought into service in 1901 and certainly proved its worth during World War One. The fleet had 100 craft but unfortunately lost just over half of them to enemy action. It was not until World War Two when the fleet was replenished to a further 100 craft, that the country really reaped the benefits of submarine warfare operating mainly in the Mediterranean, the Far East and in Norwegian waters. However losses were high and over 50% of the crews were lost at sea.

Service Records

Records of service are amongst the general service records of Royal Navy personnel

The Royal Navy Submarine Service archive is essentially original documents and papers transferred from *Flag Officer Submarines Historic Document Section* and drafting records covering both world wars. The archive collections also include many personal diaries and documents deposited by men of the service. The archive is part of the submarine museum situated in Haslar Road, Gosport. An appointment is needed for personal visits.

Fishery Protection

The fishery protection role of the Royal Navy can be traced back to the early 1480s or even earlier as fishermen had for years fought skirmishes with foreign fishermen to protect their rights to fish in home waters.

From the reign of Edward IV, English fishermen were fishing in the waters around Iceland and Greenland. Protection was provided by the Navy of the time paid for by levies from the fishing industry. Sometimes protection was not afforded or was under strength particularly in times of war. Many fishermen were killed in the actions and by the 16th century it was clear that a proper protection force was needed. The first Fishery Protection ships, patrolled the British fishing grounds but did so only in the herring fishing season.

The rivalries between the U.S. and Britain in North America meant that fishery protection in that area became very important so much so that a fishery protection squadron was based in Newfoundland. Throughout Navy history specific, often purpose built ships have been assigned to the fishery protection squadron.

Service Records

Records for those who served in fishery protection are amongst normal naval service records.

Royal Naval Air Service

In the early part of the 20th century the Royal Navy used airships and balloons for reconnaissance. The first thought given to an aerial service for the Royal Navy was in 1908 when it was decided to provide the Navy with an airship. However in 1911 the Royal Navy lost its 'Mayfly' airship and this was deemed to be the start of a dedicated naval air service using aircraft.

By 1910 some Royal Navy officers were already training to fly aircraft but this was outside formal naval training. Officers were using the facilities of the Royal Aero Club based at the time on the Isle of Sheppey. Civilian instructors as members of the club were the people training the Navy officers.

In 1912 the Royal Flying Corp was under the administration of the Army but the Royal Navy, besides having airships, was given 12 aircraft. The first flight from a moving ship took place in May 1912 and in 1913 the first seaplane carrier, *Hermes*, was commissioned and the Navy built its coastal air stations. The first Naval Air Service seaplane base was established on the Isle of Grain, Kent and in 1913 aircraft from the Naval Air Service took part in naval exercises for the first time.

The Naval Air Service became the Royal Naval Air Service in 1914 and became the naval wing of the Royal Flying Corps. Within a few months the RNAS had 217 pilots and 55 seaplanes as well as 40 other planes. One of the most successful seaplanes used by the RNAS was actually built by the Americans. The Royal Naval Air service became independent of the Royal Flying Corp in August 1915 when the Admiralty assumed operational responsibility.

By the outbreak of the First World War the RNAS had more aircraft than the Royal Flying Corp. The main role of the RNAS was patrolling British coasts for enemy ships and submarines, attacking enemy coastal territory mainly in Belgium and defending Britain, particularly London, from enemy bombers and Zeppelins. There were also two RNAS Squadrons fighting on the Western Front. In 1916 the RNAS lost its responsibility for Zeppelin patrols when this was transferred to the RFC but the Naval Air service continued to bomb the Zeppelins on the ground in Germany.

The growth of the RNAS during World War One made it a formidable fighting force. When it merged with the Royal Flying Corp in April 1918 to form the Royal Air Force its strength included 67,000 officers and men, 2,949 aircraft, 103 airships; and 126 coastal stations.

On 1 April 1924, the Fleet Air Arm of the Royal Air Force was formed consisting of those RAF units that were embarked on aircraft carriers and fighting ships. Only weeks before the formation of the Fleet Air Arm, the Royal Navy had commissioned *HMS Hermes*, their first purpose built aircraft carrier. It was the planes of the Fleet Air Arm which flew trials from the deck of *Hermes*.

RAF control was short-lived as in May 1939 the Fleet Air Arm was returned to Admiralty control and renamed the Air Branch of the Royal Navy. At the onset of the Second World War, the Fleet Air Arm consisted of 20 squadrons with 232 aircraft. By the end of the war the strength of the Fleet Air Arm was: 59 aircraft carriers; 3,700 aircraft; 72,000 officers and men; and 56 naval air stations.

During the Second World War the Fleet Air Arm took a leading role in operating fighters, torpedo bombers and reconnaissance aircraft. At the start of the Battle of Britain, the Royal Air Force was short of fighter pilots so the Fleet Air Arm formed a major part of the sky defences where whole Squadrons of Navy aircraft were 'loaned' to the RAF. By the time of the Battle of Britain, the aircraft carrier had replaced the battleship as the Fleet's main ship and its aircraft were now a formidable fighting force working alongside the RAF.

In 1938 an Air Branch of the Royal Naval Reserve was established. At the start of the war there were no qualified pilots because those who originally volunteered had not completed their pilot training. However at the end of the Second World War the division had over 8,000 aircrew and post war consisted of 12 reserve air squadrons, grouped regionally into Air Divisions. In 1980 the RNR Air Branch became the modern RNAS based at Yeovilton and Culdrose.

Records of the Royal Naval Air Service

Officers Service Records

The records of RNAS Officers serving between 1914 and 1918 are in series ADM 273 which consists of the records of around 7,500 men. They are available to search online using Discovery. They are in indexed volumes arranged in service number order more or less in order of date of entry, rather than alphabetically. Some individuals appear to have more than one entry in the registers. The reason for this is unclear.

Many officers transferred into the RNAS from the Royal Navy so their earlier record will be in the Royal Navy Officers' service records. Records for those officers of the RNAS who transferred to the Royal Air Force in 1918 can be found in series AIR 76.

The officers' records contain:

- Name.
- Date of birth.
- Marital status.
- Name and address of next of kin.
- Previous occupation.
- Service history both for Navy and Air.
- Royal Aero Club details.
- Appointments.
- Details of accidents.
- Honours and decorations.
- Character, promotion assessments, abilities, confidential reports.

RNAS officers can also be found in the Navy List.

Ratings service records

For Ratings within the RNAS you will need to consult the Registers of Seamen's Service which run up to 1923 in series ADM 188 and can be found online using Discovery. This applies to all ratings in the RNAS who served prior to the formation of the RAF and all their service numbers will have an 'F' prefix.

Many RNAS personnel transferred to the RAF in April 1918 and their records can be found in AIR 79 which is name indexed on Discovery although digitised images are not available for download. In some cases a new record is generated from transfer so you would need to look at both sets of documents. In other cases the RNAS record has been annexed to the AIR 79 record.

When a RNAS airman transferred to the RAF the 'F' prefix was replaced with a '2' and if the service number then contained less than six digits '0s' were added to the number. By way of clarification:

- RNAS number F5692.
- RAF number 205692.

If your ancestor's service number within the RAF is between 313001 and 316000 then there is likely to be a separate Royal Navy service record in ADM 188 as the numbering system shows that he served with the Royal Navy prior to the formation of the RNAS.

Royal Aero Club Aviators Certificates

These records can be searched by name using ancestry.co.uk. They cover the period 1910 to 1950. It is the records in the early years that are likely to be of greater interest bearing in mind the Royal Navy used this as a qualification for pilots when establishing their air services. The original records are held at the RAF Museum at Hendon, north London.

An Index card exists for every pilot. On the front it carries basic personal information including: name, date and place of birth, nationality, rank, profession and Navy division (if applicable), date, place and aircraft type certified to fly and certificate number. There is usually one card for each type of aircraft a pilot is certified to fly so there may be more than one card in the system. On the rear of the card is normally a photograph of the pilot.

There are also photograph albums including pictures of qualifying pilots which are organised by certificate number as opposed to name so it is necessary to find the card first. In some cases the ancestry database links the card and the photograph in the album.

Royal Naval Aviation (Fleet Air Arm)

The Fleet Air Arm had its origins within the RAF Coastal Command which was seconded into the Royal Navy in 1937 having been the RAF's premier maritime arm. Naval aviation was almost forgotten about between the two world wars; a consequence of which was that the service did not receive the resources it needed to develop properly or efficiently continuing until the outbreak of the Second World War, during which it rose to prominence.

Operational records of the Fleet Air Arm

The surviving Operations Record Books of Fleet Air Arm Squadrons can be located in both Admiralty series documents ADM 207 and RAF series documents AIR 27. The Coastal Command Operations Record Books can be found in series AIR 24 - AIR 27 depending upon which squadron your ancestor belonged to.

Unfortunately Aircraft Carrier Flying Log Books do not appear to have survived but both Fleet Air Arm and Coastal Command combat reports are in series AIR 50. In some cases the flying log books of RAF personnel serving in Fleet Air Arm are in held in series ADM 900.

The information in the ADM classes of documents of most use to the researcher is detailed below:

The series ADM 207 covering 1939 to c.1957 contains squadron diaries for some of Fleet Air Arm's squadrons mainly from the World War Two period but there are some post-war diaries relating to the training and RNVR squadrons. These records are supplemented by other diaries and squadron line books, photographs etc. held at the Fleet Air Arm Museum at Yeovilton, Somerset.

The series ADM 900 comprises a sample of documents of which the majority have been destroyed and covers the period 1870 to the early years of the Second World War. As such they may not exist for particular squadrons. They typically include examples of flying log books of Fleet Air Arm personnel alongside some Royal Naval Volunteer Reserve divisional air record books, 1904-1939.

Fleet Air Arm Museum Centre for Naval Aviation Records & Research

The collection covers a wide range of documents from official and private sources, related to the Royal Naval Air Service and the Fleet Air Arm. They cover areas such as aircraft, ships, equipment, air stations, operations and personnel. Amongst the most regularly consulted are the Squadron Line Books and Record Books, Air Publications and aircraft accident records.

The Centre also holds documents relating to service in the Royal Navy and Royal Marines before and during the First World War. Personal papers from important figures in aviation are held.

The very large photographic collection covers all areas within the Museum's remit and is widely used by researchers and authors. It comprises material from both official and private sources.

Items mentioned on these pages are only a sample of what is held. The collection is growing continuously.

Service records

Fleet Air Arm personnel service records are currently held by the Ministry of Defence and are subject to relationship disclosure and the payment of the statutory fee.

Women's Royal Naval Service (WRNS)

The WRNS was formed in November 1917 and by the end of the First World War had 500 officers and 5,000 ratings. In addition there were about 2,000 members of the Women's Royal Air Force who had previously served with the WRNS mainly connected with the Royal Naval Air Service. The WRNS was disbanded in 1919 but was revived at the start of World War Two.

The WRNS were formed so that women could take on the 'land jobs'. Many seamen based on land needed to be released to the fighting ships. The Admiralty felt that by employing women to do these jobs, the men would then be able to go to sea. The recruitment campaign for the Women's Royal Naval Service used the slogan 'Free a man for sea service'.

Initially, the Admiralty was only going to employ 3,000 women who would perform basic domestic duties, such as cooking, serving meals and general cleaning but the reality was that double that number were recruited to perform other naval duties as well. Some were based overseas and the first foreign naval station to use the WRNS was Gibraltar. A basic royal blue uniform was designed without any gold lace trimmings.

With the revival of the service in 1939 nearly 200 different jobs were being performed by women, many of which related to naval operations and maintenance of ships, aircraft etc. By 1944 the service personnel numbered 74,000. Again large numbers of WRNS served overseas. Unfortunately during the Second World War 303 women lost their lives on active service. The WRNS became a permanent part of the Royal Navy in February 1949.

The uniform of the Women's Royal Naval Service was blue with rating badges being of a lighter blue. For the duration of the First World War officers stripes were surmounted by a diamond as opposed to a curl but the non-substantive (rating) badges peculiar to the WRNS were:

• Shell (Scalloped) - household worker.
• Spoked steering wheel - motor driver.
• Quill pens crossed - clerical staff.
• Crossed keys - storekeepers and pursers.
• Crossed hammers - technical staff.
• Envelope - telegraphists and postwomen.

As with other branches of the Navy the inclusion of a crown or star (or both) within the ratings badges denoted seniority and were more meaningful during the Second World War than in the First.

Records of Service

Registers of Women's Royal Naval Service officers appointments between 1917 and 1919 can be found in series ADM 321. The service record cards for the same period are in ADM 340.

The officers' files hold official forms, dossiers and letters concerning appointments and promotions. In some cases a file can also include an identification certificate showing date and place of birth, marital status, occupation, religion, physical description and name of next-of-kin.

Officers who resigned for personal reasons in 1918 are not included in ADM 340 so you will need to look at ADM 321 which contains details of appointments, promotions and resignations.

Service records for both officers and ratings within the Women's Royal Naval Service are found in series ADM 318 for officers or series ADM 336 for ratings. These can be searched online via Discovery.

The ratings' records in this series cover service in the Women's Royal Naval Service during the First World War only and the record consists of a single form listing:

- Name.
- Date of enrolment.
- Age on joining.
- Character.
- Whether willing to work away from their home area or not (immobile - those working near their home were usually found in London or at strategic naval bases).
- Service appointments.
- Name and address of next of kin.
- Whether discharged from the service.

Engagement papers which duplicate the information in these service records are held by the Royal Naval Museum, Portsmouth.

Any member of the WRNS decorated in the First World War can be found in the naval medal rolls online on Ancestry or in series ADM 171/133 at The National Archives.

Queen Alexandra's Royal Naval Nursing Service

The Royal Navy did not officially employ female nurses until 1883. Regulations for Nursing Sisters in the Royal Naval Hospitals were published in 1884 and as a result a nursing service was established at Haslar. In 1897 the service was extended to Plymouth, Chatham and Malta and from the early 20th century in all Royal Naval Hospitals. There had of course been 'nurses' employed at the Royal Greenwich Hospital from as early as 1704 for which many records exist in series ADM 73 at The National Archives.

Before 1884 the Royal Navy generally employed only male nurses. Formal healthcare for sick and injured sailors became effective in the mid-18th Century when each ship had its own surgeon and sick-bay. The first hospital ships were established in 1801. Some of the women who had sailed with their husbands volunteered to attend the sick and injured on these vessels and as such gave the first opportunities for women, as nurses, to go to sea. Before then women had put to sea but had done so disguised as men.

By the mid-1800s and particularly at the time of the Crimean War middle class nurses started to be trained to serve on hospital ships. Florence Nightingale was one such nurse who sailed early to the Crimea. She became the Superintendent of female nurses in the Crimean War hospitals. She was accompanied by 38 other nurses. Eliza Mackenzie accompanied by her clergyman husband took six nurses at the start of the war to a naval hospital at Therpia close to Constantinople.

It was not until 1897 that female nurses actively went to sea. Two nursing sisters sailed on a hospital ship when British soldiers were sent to Africa to quash a rebellion. It was this action which brought naval nursing to the attention of Queen Alexandra. In 1899 the authorities had debated the establishment of a Naval Nursing Reserve. It was subsequently decided that a civilian female nursing reserve would be established to be activated only during times of conflict. So great was Queen Alexandra's intervention that in 1902 the Queen Alexandra's Royal Naval Nursing Service (QARNNS) was born.

In the First World War they undertook their first official active service and their places in hospitals were quickly filled by VADs (Voluntary Aid Detachments). VADs were non-military organisations created in 1909. Its members were trained by the St John Ambulance Brigade. By the end of the First World War it was very obvious that a nursing reserve proved invaluable. The QARNNS worked in civilian hospitals during peacetime and were called back to military service in times of war.

At the start of World War Two the QARNNS were engaged both in this country and near the front line overseas on hospital ships and in land hospitals. Some lost their lives and many became prisoners of war particularly in the Far East. During the Korean War, *HMHS Maine* was the only hospital ship conveying the sick and wounded from Pusan to Osaka. The heat, humidity and minimal staff made the nursing task most difficult for at least four months. (Remember the TV programme *Tenko*.)

The service recognised nursing sisters with officer ranking and as such they appeared in the Navy Lists. Nursing Sisters and Senior Nursing Sisters were the equivalent of Lieutenants, Superintending Sisters equivalent to Lieutenant Commander, Matron equivalent to Commander, Principal Matron equivalent to Captain and Matron in Chief equivalent to Commodore.

The badge of the nursing service is quite distinct and comprises of four insignia, the crown, the foul anchor crossed with the letters AA, the red cross and EiiR. The ranking system is denoted by gold borders.

- Matron in Chief - double gold border.
- Principal Matron - single gold border with a bar below the red cross.
- Matron - single gold border.
- Nursing sister - single red border (senior sisters have a red bar under the red cross).

Those who serve in the reserve have a silver border and the word Reserve in silver below the red cross. There are also various hat bands with similar borders denoting ranks.

Records of Queen Alexandra's Royal Naval Nursing Service

The records in series ADM 73 relate to Royal Hospital Nursing. There is an alphabetical List of Nurses for the period 1704-1864 together with registers of service with names, date of entry and date of leaving.

The formalisation of the nursing service took place in 1884 when a staff of nursing sisters in Royal Naval hospitals was put in place initially at Haslar and Plymouth. By 1887 this was extended to include Malta and Chatham. However it was not until 1901 that the service was extended to include all naval hospitals.

After 1884 the names of the senior nurses and matrons were included in the Navy lists and records of the members of the Royal Navy Nursing Service and later the QARNNS exist in different piece numbers.

The varied records in series ADM 104 relate to post 1884 naval nursing:

Nursing Sisters 1884-1910 (name indexed) providing name, rank, date of birth, date of entry into the service (can be retrospective) and discharge date.

Annual report of nursing sisters 1890-1908 - seniority, name, age, name of hospital where they are serving, dates of service, character and work involved. (The latter can be very brief.)

Nursing Sisters' appointments 1894-1929 (name indexed) - name, rank, date of birth, date of entry, next of kin, date of discharge, training and qualifications, character, ability and medals awarded.

Nursing establishment books 1911-1927 - relate to each Navy establishment or hospital. You need to know roughly when a nurse joined the service as the entries are listed as such (as opposed to being an alphabetical listing) - name, rank, date of appointment and date and reason for discharge.

Queen Alexandra's Royal Naval Nursing Service Reserve 1914-1919 - covers only those nurses who signed up for the duration of the war.

Many records are also found in various surgeons' volumes.

Case books relating to the Royal Naval Hospital Bermuda between 1832 and 1883 together with a history of the hospital, and wages and salary lists of persons employed in the care of prisoners of war. There are also registers of reports of deaths and of those killed and wounded.

The records in this series can be viewed in PDF format via Discovery.

The QARNNS has its own archives which were originally at Haslar. When the hospital closed they were transferred to the Institute of Naval Medicine in Alverstoke, Gosport, Hampshire. The records collection includes collections of photographs, articles, diaries and memorabilia of both the service and individuals and chronicles the history of the service from the outset. The archive is staffed purely on a volunteer basis but is an invaluable resource for those with ancestors who served with the QARNNS.

Royal Fleet Auxiliary

From the reign of Henry VIII and the subsequent expansion in size of Britain's Royal Navy there has been a requirement for a Merchant Fleet. From early Tudor times, the ships accompanied Admirals carrying livestock, canvas, wood and lesser fleet requirements. The ships, manned by merchant seamen, were referred to as 'Pinks'. Without these ships blockades could not have been carried out.

The Royal Fleet Auxiliary (often referred to as the 'Fourth Force') was a civilian manned fleet established in 1905 and became a permanent organisation in 1911 when it was necessary to provide coal and oil to ships as they changed means of power from sail to steam. Coal and oil fired engines were the main source of power and ships could not carry all that they needed for voyages away from home. Although there was a network of bases around the world the fleet still needed to be supplied with coal, hence the birth of the RFA although initially its role was fairly minor. This was particularly true in the First World War period. Its main role, besides the supply of fuel, was to replenish general supplies and ammunition at sea. It also had a role both in peacetime and war in transporting personnel around the world.

The Royal Navy relied on the RFA during the Second World War when the British fleet was frequently away from the various bases and the need for ships to remain at sea for much longer periods than in peace time. The RFA was largely a freighting service, with some officers and all ratings signing on for one voyage at a time.

Until 1921 officers of the RFA were RNR officers but since then have been ranked as Merchant Navy Officers.

Records of the Royal Fleet Auxiliary

The Fleet Air Arm Museum has the Crew Books of the RFA and the Mercantile Fleet Auxiliary (MFA) for the period of the First World War. The books contain alphabetical indexes of ships and the crew lists which include names, next of kin, date of entry onto the ship and date of discharge and rates of pay.

All service records are held by the RFA Human Resources but it is possible that some members of the RFA may well have Merchant Seamen tickets and a record could be included with the surviving seaman's pouches.

Crew of HMS Ramillies at Liverpool, c. 1940, by H W Tomlin, (Lt). Public domain image.

CHAPTER EIGHT

*Records of Royal Navy personnel
in service after 1923*

Many Royal Navy servicemen who served throughout the Second
World War or at the time of National Service took their service
records with them when they were dismissed from the service. It
is possible therefore that they are amongst individual family collections
rather than being available through the Royal Navy. The records follow a
similar style and format of ADM 188 documents.

The Ministry of Defence is the custodian of all records of service personnel
after 1923. Subject to the payment of a statutory fee of £30 for each record
and the provision of a death certificate (except where death was in service),
certain information can be provided from the records of service of Royal
Navy personnel. Also up until 1972 the records of their service were given
to Royal Navy personnel on their leaving the service.

If a copy of this Form is required,
Form S. 1243 is to be used.

CERTIFICATE of the Service of

SURNAME (in Block Letters)		CHRISTIAN NAME OR NAMES

in the Royal Navy.

NOTE.—The corner of this Certificate is to be cut off where indicated if the man is discharged with a "Bad" character or with disgrace, or if specially directed by the Admiralty. If the corner is cut off, the fact is to be noted in the Ledger.

Port Division	Portsmouth.
Official No.	MX 109488.

Man's Signature on discharge to Pension

Leeds HFC8994

Nearest known Relative or Friend (To be noted in pencil.)

Date of Birth **22 December 1923**

Where born { Town or Village — **Harrogate** | County — **Yorkshire**

Relationship: **WIFE**
Name:

Address: **BALDWIN STREET**
NEW PARK. HARROGATE

Trade brought up to **Yard Labourer.**

Religious Denomination **Church of England** 3N3

All Engagements, including Non-C.S., to be noted in these Columns.			Swimming Qualifications.		
Date of actually volunteering	Commencement of time	Period volunteered	Date.	Qualification.	Signature.
1. 7 Mch. 43	1 June '43	Until the end of the period of the present emergency (VOLUNTEER)	1.		
2.			2.		
3.			3.		
4.			4.		
5.			5.		
6.			6.		

Medals, Clasps, &c., L.S. and G.C. Gratuity (see also Page 4).

Date received or forfeited	Nature of Decoration	Date received or forfeited	Nature of Decoration
		Woollen Clothing Granted	18 June 46
	Harrogate 56 303	K2A7 9513	

Description of Person	Stature	Chest	Colour of			Marks, Wounds, and Scars
	Feet	In.		Hair	Eyes	Complexion	

	Feet	In.	Chest	Hair	Eyes	Complexion	
On Entry as a Boy.........							
On advancement to man's rating, or on entry under 25 years	5	8½	37	Brown	Grey	Fresh	Scar right knee.
On re-engagement or re-entry for C.S. or for Non-C.S. after attaining 25 years							
Further description if necessary							

CAUTION : This is an Official document. Any alteration made to it without proper authority, will render the offender liable to severe penalties.

N. P. 11 2892/1927.
N 7863/38.

NE175165

(8843) Wt. 34332/D239 200m. 8-41 P.L. Co. 544/3
S. 459.

Name of Ship (Tender to be named in brackets)	Substantive Rating	Non-Substantive Rating	From	To	Cause of Discharge and other notation authorised by Article 460, Cause 9, K.R. and A.I.
Glendower	S.B.A. Prob.		June 42	14 July 42	
Malay (R.N.B.)			15 July 42	14 Aug 42	
	P.S.B.A.		15 Aug 42		
	S.B.A.		10 Aug 42		
Victory (Rn. of Taylor)			1 Jan 43	31 Jan 43	
			Feb 43	29 Feb 44	
Victory (Rn. of Taylor)					
	L.SBA (qy)		24 Apr 46		released Class 'A'

Date	Wounds received in Action and Hurt Certificate; also any meritorious Service, Special recommendations, Prize or other Grants; temporary advancements to Acting (higher) ratings, with inclusive dates	Captain's Signature
1. 6. 45	LS.9 (3 year)	
1 June 46	WS1 (d)	
4 July 46	PAYMENT OF WAR GRATIS AND P.W.X. AUTHORISED	

51. World War Two service records handed to the seaman on discharge.

Under the Freedom of Information Act and in recognition of the duty of care owed to the family of the deceased they are subject, for a period of 25 years following the date of death and without the consent of the next of kin, to limited information disclosure by the MOD, namely:

- Full name.
- Rank.
- Service number.
- Date and Place of birth.
- Date of death if this occurred in service.
- The date of joining the service.
- The date of leaving.
- Good conduct medals, orders of chivalry and gallantry medals.

If the record requested relates to a person who died more than 25 years ago and no next of kin permission has been obtained then additional information will be given namely:

- The ships and land bases in which he/she served.
- The dates of service thereon and the locations if relevant.
- The ranks held whilst in the service.
- Details of any World War Two or subsequent campaign medals.

Where the consent of the immediate next of kin has been given the full record will be released and the 25 year threshold will not apply. The provision of the record is still subject to the payment of the statutory administration fee of £30 and the provision of a death certificate.

In all cases the Ministry of Defence will not disclose any information where this could prejudice the capability, effectiveness or security of its armed forces irrespective of division. In order to apply you will need to download the appropriate forms from the website: **www.gov.uk/requests-for-personal-data-and-service-records**.

For commissioned and non-commissioned officers the completed forms with the fee should then be forwarded to:

RN Disclosure Cell
Room 48
West Battery
Whale Island
Portsmouth, Hampshire, PO2 8DX

For records of Royal Navy ratings (all divisions) who enlisted between 1924 and the start of the Second World War, Royal Naval reserve officers 1920-1950, Royal Naval Volunteer Reserve officers up to 1950, WRNS ratings enlisting 1939-1955 and QARNNS personnel 1923-1955 applications and fee should be sent to:

Ministry of Defence
Directorate of Personnel Support (Navy)
Navy Search
TNT Archive Services
Tetron Point
William Nadin Way
Swadlincote
Derbyshire DE11 0BB

For records of Royal Navy ratings after 1939, Fleet Air Arm after 1939, Royal Naval Reserve and Volunteer Reserve after 1945 and QARNNS and WRNS ratings after 1956 applications and fee should be forwarded to:

NPP(Acs)AFPAA
Centurion Building
Grange Road
Gosport PO13 9XA

For records of all personnel who served with the Royal Fleet Auxiliary the application and fee should be forwarded to:

Royal Fleet Auxiliary
Human Resources Bureau
Fleet HQ
West Battery
Whale Island
Portsmouth PO2 8BY

It is vitally important that applications are addressed to the correct department as failure to do so will result in delays for you obtaining the service record.

HMS Birmingham 1917, by Oscar Parkes. Public domain image.

CHAPTER NINE
Royal Navy war casualties

M any of you will have ancestors or perhaps even close family who tragically lost their lives in either the First or Second World Wars. It is feasible that you will have a record of the death but if not then you should look for a death certificate and also try and locate a grave or memorial.

Civil Registration of Deaths

The General Register Office (GRO) has the following indexes for Naval deaths:

First World War
Royal Navy - All Ranks 1914-1921.

Second World War
Royal Navy Officers 1939-1948.
Royal Navy Ratings 1939-1948.

If Naval Personnel died in conflict abroad after 1948 deaths are recorded in GRO Deaths Abroad.

Like all civil registration indexes these are available on the main websites, Findmypast, Ancestry, Family Relatives and TheGenealogist. On some there are combined listings but on others the indexes can be searched as separate databases, for example on Family Relatives.

Searches can be undertaken using name of person, ship, naval number, rank and year.

Searchable online Databases

UK Royal Navy War Deaths Roll

Names of Royal Navy personnel who died in The First World War are listed in this database. This is currently an index but does contain significant information about each individual. The original collection is available at The National Archives. This is currently available to search using **Ancestry.co.uk**

Two lists of those who died during the Great War were published in 1921 by HMSO. Volume One gives the basic details of nearly 42,000 officer casualties. The other volumes relate to ratings. During WWI the Royal Navy lost more vessels and had more casualties than the Germans.

The index contains the following information:

• Name.
• Rating (occupation, rank or classification).
• Branch of the service.
• Date and cause of death.
• Ship or Unit.
• Theatre of war.
• Which relative was notified.

In some instances additional information is also included:

• Date and Place of Birth.
• Where the grave is located.
• Decorations and awards.

Commonwealth War Graves Commission

Since the foundation by Royal Charter in 1917 as the Imperial War Graves Commission the now Commonwealth War Graves Commission (CWGC) has constructed war cemeteries, plots, erecting headstones over graves and, where the remains are missing as is often the case with those serving in the Royal Navy, inscribed their names on permanent memorials (see below). For all services over 1.7 million burials are now commemorated at 23,000 different locations in 150 countries The aims, laid out in the Royal Charter of 1917 have not changed and are as relevant now as they were then.

The Commission is governed by certain principles namely: each of the dead should be commemorated by name on a permanent headstone or memorial and that there should be no distinction made in regard to rank or seniority.

It is possible to search the online database on cwgc.org by surname, date, war, rank, regiment, awards or any combination of these criteria.

The results will give: name, rank, service number, service or branch of the Navy or Royal Marines, date of death (or when lost), country of service, grave or memorial reference number, cemetery or memorial name - whether military or civil cemetery or one of the naval memorials. In some cases additional personal information is given such as name of parents or wife/husband, and address but this is not always the case.

Jack Clegg Memorial Database

The database searchable on Findmypast or Ancestry is a record of the deaths of Royal Naval Division servicemen who served in the First World War I as previously described.

The database includes:

All servicemen who were killed or died in service during the war, all who died after leaving the RND up to 1926 or in some special cases up to 1942, Army personnel who died while serving in a Naval Battalion or unit, ex-RND personnel who transferred from service in the Army or Air Force and army officers who were drafted to the RND. This mainly relates to senior officers who served with any of the Navy or Royal Marine battalions.

Royal Navy Memorials and Cemeteries

The Manning Port Memorials Portsmouth, Plymouth and Chatham

Your ancestor may well have been amongst the many thousands of Royal Navy personnel who were killed or subsequently died as a direct result of injury sustained whilst on active service. After the First World War the Navy commemorated those who died at sea without a known grave. This was achieved by the building of memorials at Plymouth, Portsmouth and Chatham which were the main naval ports of the time. These memorials are administered and maintained by the Commonwealth War Graves Commission.

An Admiralty committee recommended that the three memorials should be identical with an obelisk serving as a leading mark for shipping. The memorials were designed by Sir Robert Lorimer with sculptures by Henry Poole. The Portsmouth Naval Memorial was the first to be unveiled on 15 October 1924 by the then Duke of York who became George VI.

52. Portsmouth Naval Memorial (author's photograph).

After the Second World War the naval memorials were extended to commemorate those naval personnel without graves as a result of losses in the war, but this presented some challenges as the sites were not the same. The architect for the later extension at Portsmouth was Sir Edward Maufe. The Second World War extension was unveiled on 29 April 1953 by Queen Elizabeth, the Queen Mother.

Men from the Commonwealth who served in allied navies are also commemorated on the memorials and include those from Australia, South Africa, India, Pakistan, Hong Kong, Burma, Ceylon, Newfoundland, Fiji, Gold Coast, Kenya, Nigeria and Sierra Leone.

Portsmouth Naval Memorial includes the names of around 10,000 sailors of the First World War and around 15,000 of the Second World War.

Plymouth Naval Memorial commemorates 7,251 sailors of the First World War and 15,933 of the Second World War.

Chatham Naval Memorial commemorates 8,517 sailors of the First World War and 10,098 of the Second World War.

Haslar Royal Naval Cemetery

The Royal Hospital Haslar opened in 1753. Until 1858 all those who died in the hospital or aboard ships in Portsmouth Harbour or Spithead were buried in the hospital grounds. In April 1859 a new cemetery was opened for the naval burials. Over 1,500 British sailors, who died in the world wars, were lost at sea in other conflicts or in peacetime accidents are buried there.

Naval custom meant that the accompanying band was not permitted to play until it was away from the hospital and 'round the corner' in Clayhall Road in case the hospital patients were disturbed.

Various memorials were erected in the cemetery namely:

HMS Archer Memorial - In Memory of those who died of Yellow Fever on the West Coast of Africa between 1864 and 1866.

HMS Thunderer Memorial - On the 14th July 1876, a boiler explosion killed more than 40 crew on board *HMS Thunderer* at Stokes Bay.

Zulu War Memorial - In memory of Navy personnel killed in action and who died of diseases during the Zulu War of 1879.

HMS Eurydice Memorial - On 24 March 1878 on a return voyage from the West Indies *HMS Eurydice* sank in a blizzard, off the Isle of Wight. The ship sank in minutes with only two survivors from a crew of 364. *HMS Eurydice* is reputed to still sail as a ghost ship.

HM Submarine A1 Memorial - On 18 March 1904 the submarine sank off Isle of Wight after collision with *SS Berwick Castle* whilst on exercises. She was struck near the conning tower, by *Berwick Castle*, travelling from Southampton to Hamburg.

Burial registers at the Royal Naval Cemetery, Hampshire (1826-1911) are in series ADM 306 at The National Archives and can also be accessed using Deceased Online.

During both the First and Second World Wars Gosport was a significant naval depot as well being home to the Haslar Naval Hospital. It was also home to the Royal Navy Light Coastal Forces in World War Two.

The Haslar Royal Naval Cemetery was attached to the Hospital and houses 763 First World War graves, two of which are unidentified and many of which are scattered throughout the cemetery. The crew of HM Submarine 'L.55' whose bodies were brought back from the Baltic in 1928 are interred in a 'collective grave' with their names inscribed on a separate memorial.

611 Second World War graves of which 36 are unidentified, exist. The majority of them are together in groups, the largest containing around 350 burials, the smallest 25. There are, however some scattered around the cemetery. There are also Foreign National war burials.

The graves and the memorial are also maintained by the Commonwealth War Graves Commission.

Royal Navy Patrol Service Memorial

The Memorial dedicated in 1953 is situated in Lowestoft, Suffolk on a cliff top position aptly overlooking the sea and Sparrow's Nest Gardens. It was erected and is maintained by the Commonwealth War Graves Commission and commemorates only those members of the Patrol Service who died at sea during the Second World War and who have no known grave. Those of the service whose burial is recorded on graves elsewhere are not included on the memorial.

Around the base are 17 bronze panels listing 2,385 names including 49 from Newfoundland. The names can be searched online and the accompanying images of the panels enable anyone who could not visit the memorial to obtain the information it contains.

The data can be searched using either the name of the individual or the name of his ship at: **www.rnps.lowestoft.org.uk/memorial/memorial.htm**

There is also a small museum of the Royal Naval Patrol Service close by maintained and run by the RNPS Association.

Royal Naval Volunteer Reserve Memorial

Crystal Palace was used as a training establishment for the Royal Naval Volunteer Reserve during the First World War where volunteers trained to serve. *HMS Crystal Palace* trained 125,000 men.

The original RNVR Memorial was unveiled on 6 June 1931 by the then Prince of Wales, later to become Edward VIII, as a memorial to all who had served in the RNVR and trained at Crystal Palace, particularly for those who were killed or died of wounds. The memorial has a history as it originally stood in front of the bandstand and luckily was not damaged in the great fire of 1936. It was moved in the early 1980s by the Greater London Council and subsequently replaced by a replica because of continued vandalism. This was refurbished and subsequently re-dedicated on 6 June 1992 by the then Admiral of the Fleet, Sir Henry Leach, GCB. The memorial is maintained by the Borough of Bromley. Because of on-going damage the bronze plaques are held elsewhere for safe keeping.

Royal Naval Division Memorial

A fountain in memory of the men of the Royal Naval Division was erected in Horse Guards Parade in 1927 supposedly commemorating the Gallipoli landings in which the RND was heavily involved. It was designed by Sir Edwin Lutyens. It commemorates those of the Royal Naval Division who lost their lives in the First World War. It was relocated to the Royal Naval College at Greenwich in 1951 but returned to its original position in 2003.

Royal Naval Cemetery, Sandys, Bermuda

The cemetery is located close to the Royal Naval Dockyard, the land having been purchased by the British Royal Navy in 1809. The cemetery was first consecrated in 1812 at the time when the Dockyard was still being built and is known as The Glade.

Initially the cemetery was open to all for burial but the convicts who were involved in the dockyard construction could not be buried there. Many of those buried in the cemetery were the victims of the mid-19th century yellow fever outbreak

During the Second World War, many British Royal Navy personnel died while fighting the battle in the mid-Atlantic. Within the cemetery there are many graves of Royal Navy seamen who lost their lives in those battles. There are also other graves from both wars maintained by the Commonwealth War Graves Commission.

Royal Navy Cemetery, Portland, Dorset

Originally known as the Naval & Military Cemetery the burials exist from c. 1875 although the majority of burials relate to losses in both world wars. 65 burials exist for the First World War with 103 burials for the Second World War. In the post war period a Cross of Sacrifice was erected to commemorate these men. Most of the Second World War graves are near the Cross of Sacrifice.

The records are available on Ancestry and give name, rank, service number, ship, date, age and in some cases family relationships, particularly recording 'son of____'.

Royal Naval Cemetery, Shotley, Essex

During the Second World War *HMS Ganges*, the naval training establishment was based at Shotley. In the early days bodies of seamen not repatriated to their own parish were buried in Shotley churchyard. Many burials relate to the trainees and training staff of the establishment.

In 1940 an additional burial ground opposite the church owned and administered by the Admiralty was consecrated. There were many deaths during and immediately after the First World War some of which died from the effects of Spanish Flu.

Most of the records of burial are recorded in Shotley parish registers or the registers of St George which was *Ganges* own chapel. There is also an online burials database.

Royal Naval Cemetery, Lyness, Hoy

The cemetery was established in 1915 when Scapa Flow was the base of the Grand Fleet. Lyness was a Royal Naval base until July 1946 and the cemetery contains graves from both wars.

There are 439 burials of the First World War and of these, 112 relate to unidentified personnel. Most of the graves are from the crews of HMS *Hampshire, Vanguard, Narborough* and *Opal*. The 200 burials of the Second World War in the cemetery include those of the men from HMS *Royal Oak*, which was sunk off Longhope in Scapa Flow.

The cemetery also contains the graves of sailors from the German Navy as their High Seas Fleet was interned at Scapa Flow after the 1918 Armistice.

The cemetery is administered by the Commonwealth War Graves Commission through which burial records are available.

Royal Naval Cemeteries, Greenwich

The Royal Naval Cemetery was opened in 1857. The former burial ground of the Royal Hospital for Seamen is within the grounds of Devonport House although some memorials are outside the boundary. The Devonport Mausoleum was built in 1750 and has a plaque recording the first burial in 1749. By the time the Hospital closed in 1869, 24,000 men and some women had been buried there. Since then many of the remains have been cleared.

With the Royal Hospital Greenwich graveyard full by the 1840s, and due to construction of a railway tunnel as part of the London and Greenwich Railway, the Royal Navy needed a new burial site. In 1857, the Admiralty bought an orchard in East Greenwich for use as the new cemetery. The remains of around 3,000 men including some who fought in the Crimea War and at Trafalgar were removed from the Hospital site in 1875 and reinterred in the new cemetery. In 1926 the cemetery was sold to Greenwich Metropolitan Borough. The Admiralty reserved rights of further burials.

The burial registers can be seen at The National Archives as part of series ADM 73 (see basic genealogical sources).

Royal Naval Cemetery, East Stonehouse, Plymouth

Seamen were buried in the Hospital burial ground between 1824 and 1897. The incumbent of St Andrew's Church held the right to officiate but that role was often undertaken by the hospital chaplain. Today the gravestones are around the boundary wall as a local school now uses the ground as a playing field.

In 1756 an area of land known as No Place Field was purchased which remained unused for burials until brought into use in 1824. A further part of the land was opened for burials in 1833 and became known as the New Ground.

The burial register was maintained by the vicar of St Andrew's Church and is in the custody of the Plymouth and West Devon Record Office.

CHAPTER TEN
The life of a Navy Rating

Naval seamen experienced a very organised and disciplined way of life on board a ship. The way in which a ship was manned depended upon its rate and a specific compliment of men was attached to each rate although frequently ships were under-manned.

Most ships would have a large number of petty officers such as gunner's and carpenter's mates, quarter masters, clerks and stewards who were appointed from the able seamen on the crew. Able and ordinary seamen existed in about equal numbers on any ship. Your ancestor's capability determined what his rating was. An able seaman would have a better rate of pay and a greater prospect of promotion. Individual captains progressed ordinary to able seamen depending upon their rate skills. The base criteria enabling progression to able seaman was to be at least 18 years of age and have at least three years' sea experience. Boys were official rates from 1749 and this related to boys aged 12-17 years who were seeking to be trained as seamen or budding midshipmen. Hence many served in the capacity of officers' servants.

In the late 1800s a rank of 'leading seaman' was introduced which was a stepping stone between an able seaman and a petty officer. A landsman was a person who showed little aptitude for a particular skill and was frequently someone new to the Navy or perhaps a Merchant Seaman who landed a naval voyage.

Before a ship could put to sea every man had to be fitted into the job he was best suited to either as result of his sea experience or his civilian job prior to naval service. The ships company was divided into two groups, the 'watches' and the 'idlers' Idlers were those with specialist jobs but the basis of all ship organisation was the watch system. Watches were divided into two. These were the Larboard or Port watch and the Starboard watch. Each was for four hours.

The watch system was an advantage to the sleeping arrangements of the ship's company which were usually intolerable due to overcrowding. Each man was only allowed 14 inches in width for his hammock. With the watch system only half the hammocks were in use at any one time so each seaman had double the width in real terms, i.e. 28 inches of space.

Watches and all other activities on board ship were controlled by a series of bells sounded each half hour. This was eight bells per watch. The watch system was thus:

1st watch - 8pm to midnight
Middle watch - midnight to 4am
Morning watch - 4am to 8am
Forenoon watch - 8am to noon
Afternoon watch - noon to 4pm
Dog watch 4pm to 8pm (usually divided into 2 x 2 hour sessions)

The idlers were divided into divisions made up of the rest of the crew who were not allocated to watches. The divisions were a cross section of skilled ratings, landsmen and boys and were under the control of one of the Lieutenants. The surviving Lieutenants' logs give a valuable insight into this aspect of life on board a ship.

The peacetime role of all men was to be trained for war. Gunnery practice was an important element of daily duty for many men on board. The skills of each man were put to the test in warfare. The order 'prepare for battle' meant the whole ship mobilised for its function as a fighting machine. Bulkheads were removed, furniture stored, decks wetted and sanded, water buckets were placed throughout to deal with fires, vital equipment was taken out of use but cutlasses, powder etc. were ready. The main element of preparation was to ready the guns by loading them and putting the battle lanterns by each gun. All of the hammocks were strategically placed for the protection of men and vital equipment and nets were placed to save falling spars and wounded men from being drowned if they fell overboard. Because of the activity the men usually went bare breasted and tied a neckerchief around their heads to lessen the noise and to keep their hair out of their eyes.

The ordinary British seaman was known as 'Jack Tar' because tar was commonly used on sailing ships. The hands and clothes of ordinary seamen were commonly tarred by the ship tacking. British sailors once wore tarred pig tails. Wearing pig tails was fashionable in the 18th century. Why sailors added tar is anybody's guess as the fashion rapidly disappeared at the end of Napoleonic Wars. The last recorded instance of tarred pig tails was reported in 1827.

On the gun decks the gunner was in charge of the men and the guns on which the survival of the ship relied. The gunner had the responsibility of inspecting the guns and to prevent nitre from separating in the powder which would lessen its firing effectiveness.

Each gun crew consisted of six men namely a gun captain, assistant captain, loader, assistant loader, sponger and assistant sponger (who also acted as the powder man). The range of a broadside gun was less accurate at more than 400 yards from its target.

Over time different strategies were employed in naval gunnery and various examples exist of 'Fighting Instructions' which had to be strictly adhered to. If necessary the ship could 'strike their colours' in other words surrender.

Health and illness

The British Empire fully depended on the health of the seamen in the Navy to survive and grow and these were frequently exposed to dangerous new infections. Once a ship left the port it was not unusual for a number of crewmen to become very ill and die. In fact the chances of getting home without ailments, sickness or injury was fairly low.

Living conditions on board ship meant that inevitably seamen would have been ill at some time during a voyage or at least had to suffer from intemperate conditions. Ships were often infested with rats so much so that the Navy employed official rat-catchers. On HMS Duke 2,475 rats were caught in a single voyage! The rats were killed using an arsenic, wheatmeal and sugar paste. Some seamen who came into contact with the paste when laid often did so with fatal results.

Accidents on board ships were frequent. Falls from masts and rigging were the most common. Sometimes injured men fell directly into the sea. If they were not rescued, they drowned because they could not save themselves due to their injury. Crushed hands and feet, broken limbs, ruptures, muscular strains etc. were also very common. Injuries sustained from enemy actions also needed to be treated but were not as common as accidents. Nonetheless the naval hospital system and payments of pensions for wounds were introduced which will be addressed later.

Naval medical officers spent a great deal of time debating strategies and courses of action to help alleviate diseases because the Navy needed healthy crews to fulfil its operational requirements, They were also innovative in securing treatments for the diseases manifesting themselves on board ships.

Naval surgeons were exposed to, and had the opportunity to observe fevers in different parts of the world and to study their symptoms and causes, and experiment with new but often limited treatments. They were involved in both post-mortems and with observing living patients.

Poor food with little nutritional value and little fruit and vegetables resulted in scurvy which was perhaps the most common disease amongst seamen. Scurvy manifested itself as swollen gums, bleeding, spots and debility. By way of counteracting scurvy individual captains saw to it that their crew received fresh vegetables as often as possible. By the early 19th century citrus fruits became standard issue aboard the Navy ships.

As scurvy killed more men in the Royal Navy than sea battles fruit juice was available on every ship from 1799 which drastically reduced the effects of the disease. It was not too long after that it was more or less fully alleviated. In context however the Royal Naval Hospital at Haslar dealt with more than 1,500 cases of the disease in every year of the 1780s the period when scurvy was at its height.

Typhus fever which plagued many Navy ships' crews was directly attributable to overcrowding and unhygienic conditions on board. This sometimes rose to epidemic proportions particularly on early convict ships and hospital ships. Again it was alleviated by the early 1800s when Navy physicians and surgeons managed to improve standards of cleanliness and hygiene on board their ships. This also improved the efficiency of the ships as fighting units. Cholera was also a huge problem in Navy ships involved in the Crimean War.

The tropical and hot climate diseases, particularly yellow fever remained until the late 1890s / early 1900s. The cure for yellow fever which was discovered by accident also cured malaria as the common carrier was the mosquito. Royal Navy surgeons pioneered the use of quinine which proved to be a particularly effective treatment for malaria and yellow fever.

On home ground, the general public were not impressed with the Navy as it felt they were the cause of many diseases being introduced to the country. Cholera reached Britain from India in the early 1830s and there was an outbreak of yellow fever in Swansea in 1865. To try to counteract this ships arriving back in ports were often quarantined on arrival but the quarantine regulations were often inadequate.

Ships were often quarantined for only a day or two and those seamen who were ill and quarantined for a significant period may well have died as a result. Many ships were actually sent to Quarantine Stations away from their home port. For example ships docking at Portsmouth were frequently sent to the Quarantine Station at Stangate Creek in the Medway.

In the early to mid-1800s it was very common for Royal Navy vessels to return to their home port in Britain with a significantly depleted crew due to the effects of yellow fever or some other disease.

From the 1840s onwards the health of seamen and practice of ship quarantine came under close scrutiny and there was a complete reform of naval health. The transition from sail to steam power in that period also had an effect, somewhat fuelling the idea that heat in engine rooms etc. actually incubated diseases.

The new steam-powered ships changed occupational accidents as the equally hazardous jobs of engineer and boiler maker created different types of injury both on board ships and within the naval dockyards.

It is highly unlikely that an ancestor serving in the Royal Navy would have escaped some form of injury or disease as they travelled around the world. To find information necessitates research in the operational records as little mention will be noted on the service records.

Ships' Complements

The number of men serving on a ship was determined by the Admiralty Office and depended upon the rate of the ship. An example of ships' complements at the end of the Napoleonic wars is given below. Each complement included 'widows' men'. Usually allocations were for some reason deliberately left short.

'Widows' men' did not exist. The attachment of widows' men to a ship's crew depended upon the ship's rate. Widows' men were fictitious seamen whose wages were applied to funding of widows and had no resemblance to the number of widows left in that state because of deaths of a particular ship's crew.

1st rate - 110 gun ship - 829 men
Officers 17
Petty Officers 78
Able Seamen 175
Ordinary Seamen 175
Landsmen 174
Boys 1st class - 8, 2nd class 13, 3rd class 19
Marines 170
Widows' men 8

2nd rate - 90 gun ship - 731 men
Officers 17
Petty Officers 75
Able Seamen 152
Ordinary Seamen 150
Landsmen 150
Boys 1st class 8, 2nd class 13, 3rd class 16
Marines 150
Widows' men 7

3rd rate - 80 gun ship - 693 men
Officers 16
Petty Officers 56
Able Seamen 147
Ordinary Seamen 146
Landsmen 145
Boys 1st class 6, 2nd class 11, 3rd class 16
Marines 150
Widows' men 7

4th rate - 50 gun ship - 340 men
Officers 13
Petty Officers 40
Able Seamen 69
Ordinary Seamen 69
Landsmen 69
Boys 1st class 4, 2nd class 7, 3rd class 9
Marines 59
Widows' men 3

Sloop - 120 men
Officers 10
Petty Officers 22
Able Seamen 19
Ordinary Seamen 18
Landsmen 18
Boys 1st class 3, 2nd class 4, 3rd class 6
Marines 20
Widows' men 1

Discipline on board ships

Within the ship's community and because of the discipline regime on board it was not unusual for crimes to be committed or regulations to be broken. The severity of the misdemeanor depended upon the degree of discipline administered. Sea captains or commanders could use their summary jurisdiction to degrade non-commissioned officers to ratings such as ordinary or able seamen. Examples of this type of action can be seen in musters, log books etc. Some were transferred to a lower rate ship. Courts martial also administered punishments for certain actions but it was usually down to the Captain or master to do so. Major punishments could only be imposed by Courts Martial but ships discipline was in the hands of the captain (and sometimes other officers).

Some of the common punishments to which seamen would be exposed to included:

Running the Gauntlet - was often a punishment for theft. The ship's company each armed with a knotted rope formed a line round the deck and as the offender passed through the ranks usually prodded by a sword tip, his backside (often bare) was flayed.

Starter or colting - a colt was a short knotted cord carried by petty officers and used on the head, arms or back of the offender.

Gagging - inflicted for swearing or bad language or in the contradiction of an officer. The offender had his hands tied behind his back and had a marlin spike lashed in his mouth. The offended officer decided the length of time a seaman had to endure the punishment.

Ducking - used for blasphemous speech or uncleanliness. It was not a frequent type of punishment and fell into disuse around the time of the Napoleonic wars. The offender was lowered into the sea several times by rope from the yard-arm. He was usually weighted down so he really went under each time.

Flogging - perhaps the most common form of naval punishment inflicted with the 'cat-o-nine tails' Admiralty regulations stated that no one should have more than 12 lashes but it is believed this was frequently ignored and in Courts Martial the number of lashes to be administered was specified and could be as many as 500. It was administered for being drunk, fighting, being incapable of duty etc. The number of lashings could accumulate if more than one charge was brought at the same time. The offender was taken onto the deck stripped to the waist tied to one of the gratings and flogged. It was deemed to be a degrading punishment and sometimes had severe consequences which occasionally resulted in serious injury or even death. In some instances flogging was followed by a period of imprisonment.

Transcript PRIS11/16 - Marshalsea Prison Admiralty side - Florence McCarty 1800:

'Florence McCarty a seaman belonging to H M Ship Phoebe bt int Cust the 11th July 1800 by Warrant of their Lordships pursuant to the sentence of c Ct Martial held on board His Majestys Ship Cambridge on 7th of April 1800 for the trial of Florence McCarty for having uttered traitorous seditions and mutinous words and the charges having been fully proved the Court adjudged him to receive five hundred lashes and afterwards to be confined in Solitary Confinement in the Marshalsea prison for the space of Two years from the date of the Court Martial.'

Other punishments - Mast-heading was used to punish high spirited midshipmen for minor misdemeanors and was treated as a bit of a joke. The midshipman was sent up to the main top-gallant cross tree on the mast where he remained without food or water for 24 hours.

For mutiny or murder and some other capital offences seamen were hanged from the yard arm. Hanging as a capital punishment for mutiny took place on board a ship until it was banned in 1860. In order to do this a yellow flag had to be flown from the admiral's mast head. The resultant dead body was then buried at sea without ceremony. In the musters the 'discharge' of a seaman was frequently recorded as DD (discharged dead).

In the case of officers another frequent punishment was that of being dismissed from the service. Depending upon the severity, conditions regarding pay being forfeited was also imposed. This was normally imposed for warrant and petty officers who as an alternative could have been demoted to lower ratings.

Other punishments were often 'invented' to fit the crime. Punishment was usually recorded either in the log books or sometimes mention was made in the ship's muster.

CHAPTER ELEVEN
Royal Navy Ratings service records

Men serving in the Royal Navy were rated according to skills they had and the tasks they performed, hence the term 'rating'. There were many different ratings, such as Ordinary Seaman, Able Seaman and Leading Seaman.

The records kept by the Royal Navy in regard to ratings underwent changes throughout history. Tracing a seaman before 1853 can be challenging as there were no central records kept specifically to track a seaman's time in service and the researcher is principally reliant upon ships' musters, pension records and some other operational records. From 1853 the system of record keeping tended to be by name of the individual and contained more detail though there is never a guarantee that you will find who you are looking for particularly in the period between 1853 and the mid-1870s. Records of ratings that joined the Royal Navy after 1923 are still held by the Navy itself.

Continuous Service Records 1853-1923

Over 600,000 service records dating from 1853 are available to search and download online via The National Archives Discovery Online Documents section. Although most terminate in 1923 there are some which contain records of service to c.1928.

The original records which can now be collectively searched were in two series:

- ADM 139 - continuous service engagement books from 1853 to 1872.
- ADM 188 - registers of seamen's services from 1873 to 1923.

From 1853 new ratings signed up for ten years' service if they were 18 or older. Existing ratings could sign up for seven years' service. Both new and existing ratings were given a Continuous Service (CS) number. Service CS numbers remained unchanged throughout a serviceman's career. The CS form was summarised and recorded at discharge and were not recorded continuously through a seaman's career. However they form the basis of a service record.

Since 1894 the Navy had three managing ports: Chatham, Portsmouth and Devonport (Plymouth). All ratings belonged to their designated port during their service and the following designations were included in their service numbers C (Chatham), P (Portsmouth) and D (Devonport).

It is important as you research to understand the service number system as these changed over time. Originally the service numbers were known as CS numbers up to 1872 and from 1873 to 1894 as ON official numbers. Numbers issued up to this time were those before 178000 without further classification.

The allocation of service numbers changed in 1894 and up to 1970 different sets of numbers were allocated to different branches.

The numbering system changed again in 1908 running to 1923 and this time they were prefixed by a letter and within each letter class they commenced at number 1.

Seamen	*Artisans and misc.*
1894 to 1907 - 178001 - 240500	1894 to 1907 - 340001 - 348000
1908 to 1923 - J1 - J110000	1908 to 1923 - M1 - M38000

Engine room artificers	*Sick berth attendants and police*
1894 to 1907 - 268001 - 273000	1894 to 1907 - 350001 - 352000
1908 to 1923 - M1 - M38000	1908 to 1923 - M1 - M38000

Stokers	*Officers' stewards and cooks and boy servants*
1894 to 1907 - 276001 - 313000	1894 to 1907 - 353001 - 366450
1908 to 1923 - K1 - K63500	1908 to 1923 - L1 - L15000

Note that for the 'M' numbers the same sequence covers more than one branch.

In 1903 a short service scheme was introduced where men could serve for a period of 12 years. The first seven years was spent in Royal Navy service and the remaining five years in the Royal Fleet Reserve which consisted of pensioned ratings who were still of age. Continuous service records with the prefix SS relate to those engaged on short service.

It is also useful to note that if seamen joined before 1928 and continued service after that date then his career details up to 1928 are in ADM 188 but the remainder of the record is still held by the Ministry of Defence. It was not unusual for ratings who were serving in the early 1900s to join the Coastguard Service and in this case they frequently kept their Royal Navy service number. (See later.)

Information within Continuous Service Records

All documents reveal basic information: name, year of birth (or age) - you may also find the full date of birth in some records, place of birth, names of ships with dates of service in each, Period of time actually served, details of engagements which may have not been completed, usually supported by the reason.

From 1892 you will normally find additional details including: seaman's occupation on joining, badges issued, character and ability, details of physical description including hair, colour of eyes, complexion, height and details of tattoos, information relating to wounds, death date (but only if the seaman died in service).

There may also be a cross reference to the 'new register' for which the other record will be in one of the Continuation Books (ADM 188/83-90) so you may need to look for a second record.

If the record was contained in ADM 139 (Continuous Service Engagement Books) you may also find details of any service within the Merchant Navy, although this is not that common. The Official Number may also enable you to trace records of service in later registers. This is particularly important if your ancestor's service was both sides of 1872/73.

The registers of seamen's services, from series ADM 188, may also reveal continuous service numbers (which conversely can be used to locate records of service in the Continuous Service Engagement Books).

If you locate the service records of men whose number is prefixed by the letter 'F' then they served in the Royal Naval Air Service (RNAS) during the First World War and you will need to use the records for that branch (see below).

53. Post 1878 Service record (TNA document ADM 188/549/361422, William Edward Heasman).

If you find an Official Number with a 'Y' prefix then the rating may have volunteered for service without being called up in which case a further record should be found in the records of the Royal Naval Volunteer Reserve.

Because of the numbering system and Navy administration some ratings could have records in both ADM 139 and ADM 188, but others may have two records of service within ADM 188. If you are researching online and there is more than one related document then the two documents should have been linked together. However you may need to check for different surname spellings and how the seaman is addressed relating to forename, initials etc. as this is not always the case.

The record(s) may indicate that the rating became a Warrant Officer (gunner, boatswain, carpenter or artificer engineer). You will then need to undertake research for a Warrant Officer's service record using ADM 196.

Certificates of Service 1802-1919

This series of records forming series ADM 29 comprises service records compiled by the Navy Pay Office from the ships' musters and pay books and relates mainly to ratings and Warrant Officers although occasionally commissioned officers are included whose information is taken from full and half-pay registers. In the early 1800s pensions were generally only be paid to Warrant Officers but after 1834 pensions, and therefore records for seamen, become more common.

There were two sets and one was sent to the Admiralty for the granting and administration of pensions, superannuation, gratuities or medals (ADM 29) and another sent to Greenwich Hospital (ADM 73). The prime purpose of the records was to support applications made by naval servicemen for pensions, gratuities or medals. ADM 29 also included applications for the admittance of orphaned children to the Greenwich Hospital School and applications for discharge from foreigners or apprentices who were originally press ganged into the Royal Navy. Applications were made in some instances by those whose record included the term 'run' (desertion) where this had been entered inaccurately alongside an individual's entry in a ship's muster and needed to be removed. Service records were also compiled for the same reasons in regard to Coastguards, Naval Dockyard workers, Sea Fencibles and Convict Guards as many saw previously service in the Royal Navy.

The dates shown are the dates the certificates of service were given and as such a man's service details occurring prior to that date should be included but some records do not necessarily cover all the service to date. In some cases where a certificate was issued while a man was still in service further certificates could have been issued later and in many, but not all cases, annotations have been made in later entry books to that effect. The main index to the whole series is found in ADM 29/97-104 although records up to piece number ADM 29/73 are searchable by name using the Discovery Online documents. The indexing on Discovery is an on-going project so additional piece numbers are likely to be included later. Each entry includes the folio number within the piece for easy identification of the document. The documents are available on microfilm at The National Archives.

Before the introduction of continuous service registers for ratings, in the mid-19th century, these certificates formed the only official evidence of the careers of ratings. The original certificates were those sent to Greenwich. If a Continuous Service (CS) or Official Number (ON) is given in ADM 29 documents you should find a more composite service record in the Continuous Service Engagement Books or the Registers of Seamen's Services online .

Ships' Musters and Pay Lists 1667-1878

If a seaman served before 1853 one way to trace the service of a seaman is the use of ships' musters and it is possible to trace a seaman's service both backwards and forwards using ships' muster rolls provided you know the name of at least one ship on which he served. Men signed up to serve on a particular ship and were paid off when the ship was decommissioned. The available ships' musters also cover the period to 1878 when there may not be a comprehensive service record as described above.

Available musters can be accessed through Discovery by entering into the search field the name of the ship without using any prefix such as 'HMS' i.e. *Trident* as opposed to *HMS Trident*.

Ships' musters were maintained for every ship in commission. They were either monthly or quarterly purely for pay and accounting purposes. Muster rolls along with associated pay lists were the only record of everyday seamen's service kept by the Navy until 1853. Between 1715 and 1830 at least three sets of pay books were maintained for every ship. Each had a different function and destination. One was kept at the Navy Treasurer's Pay Office, one at the Ticket Office and one at the Navy Comptroller's Office. The Treasurer's Pay Office set has been preserved as the nucleus up to 1832 when it was discontinued. Where gaps exist in the series these have been filled by records from the Ticket Office set which continues to 1856. It is not unusual for different information to be included in the different sets so if more than one record exists for a ship, then all should be searched.

A ship's muster from around 1761-1764 should provide a seaman's age and place of birth although this was not always been entered. The age given is that of the seaman when entering the ship, not necessarily when he joined the Navy. Unfortunately the information can often be vague or inaccurate but it may give clues which can be followed up in other genealogical sources including parish baptism registers. From about 1800 description books which provide additional details relating to age, height, complexion, scars and tattoos may be included with musters and these can provide a wealth of other information besides the physical description such as details of previous ships on which the seaman served; a valuable resource when tracing a man's career before 1853.

If a muster is missing you can, as an alternative, use the ship's pay books to confirm that a man served on a particular ship. Most pre 1688 musters were destroyed by fire and the musters and some ledgers for 1878-1909 were destroyed by enemy bombing in 1941.

Some of the musters contain 'alphabets' which are surname indexes sewn into the actual books. They exist in pay lists from about 1760 and in musters from about 1797. Where these can be found the number alongside the name is the sequential number in the muster.

On joining a ship a crew member was provided with a pay book number which should have remained unique to him throughout that ships voyage/commission. It is also believed that surviving muster and pay books were copied from rough musters and therefore errors in interpretation may exist. In musters it may be that some of the columns which ought to have been filled out were not.

Voyages in general would not have lasted any more than five years and each seaman signed up for the duration of a voyage/commission and prior to or after a voyage the seaman may have been in the service of the Merchant Navy. Thus there could be difficulty in finding earlier or later ships. However many seamen remained loyal to a Captain so a tip to try and locate other ships is to look for which ships were captained by the same person.

Musters and pay books are contained in various, but different classes. The ships' musters can be found in ADM 36, ADM 37, ADM 38, ADM 39, ADM 41, ADM 115 and ADM 119 and the pay books in ADM 31, ADM 32, ADM 33, ADM 34, ADM 35 and ADM 117.

Pay Books

ADM 31 covering 1691-1710
Pay books recording the names of all officers and men on board each ship. Office of the Comptroller of the Navy: Ships' Pay Books.

ADM 32 covering 1692-1856
Pay books from the Ticket Office (the Accountant General's Department from 1832) recording the names of all officers and men on board each ship.

ADM 33 covering 1669-1778
Navy Pay Office: Ships' Pay Books (Series I).
Pay books recording the names of all officers and men on board each ship. The various books are arranged chronologically and alphabetically by vessel.

ADM 34 covering 1766-1785
Navy Pay Office: Ships' Pay Books (Series II).
Pay books recording the names of all officers and men on board each ship.

Muster Books

You will find that musters are filed by standardised spelling of ships names and these frequently relate to variations in a ship's name because the letters a and e are interchangeable as well as phonetic spelling where letters are sometimes missed out. This is peculiar to the Royal Navy records and can present problems if researchers are unaware.

ADM 36 covering 1668-1808
Royal Navy Ships' Musters (Series I).
Muster books of HMS ships of the Royal Navy, recording the presence of every person on board a ship. The series also contains (along with series ADM 37) musters for some shore establishments particularly garrisons and dockyards.

54. *Ship's Muster (TNA document ADM 36/8199, HMS Valiant ship's muster).*

Description books are also bound within the musters for certain ships which give a record of previous service, birthplace and a physical description of each crew member.

ADM 37 covering 1757-1842
Ships' Musters (Series II).
This series relates to Series II muster books again recording every person on board ship. There is a clear break between the years 1828 and 1836 but the exact date varies from ship to ship depending upon the termination of the particular voyage. After the 'break' the musters are slightly more elaborate.

ADM 38 covering 1793-1878
Ships' Musters (Series III).
Within this series of musters the following abbreviations are used:

C: Muster, or Complete, Book.   O: Muster Open List.
D: Description Book.   V: Victualling List.
M: Quarterly Muster Book.

ADM 39 covering 1667-1798
Ships' Musters (Series IV).

ADM 41 covering 1794-1815
Hired Armed Vessels, Ships' Musters (relates only to the Napoleonic War period).
This series includes all the musters of hired armed vessels where they are not included in any of the above series of muster books.

Establishment and Ledger Books

ADM 115 covering 1853-1879 (supplements information in service engagement books)
Ship Record and Establishment Books.
For each vessel these volumes show full details of the complement of officers and ratings. The records include ship's pay book number, whether in continuous service, ratings birth information, badges issued, date of entry, information on the last ship served on and all draftings and desertions.

ADM 117 covering 1872-1884
Ships' Ledgers.
An Admiralty regulation in 1872 instituted the ships ledgers which were a record of the full pay and allowance of every officer, man and boy on board, and all particulars relating to victualling. The introduction of this system superseded all former muster

and pay list formats. Most ships' ledgers do not include birth information but officers' dates of appointment are included. There is full information in regard to discharge showing date, place, and name of the ship and cause of discharge. Details of character are sometimes provided as are lists of wills made with a brief synopsis of who made the will, the date and the beneficiary.

Most of the ledger books for the period 1878-1909 were amongst records destroyed in 1941.

Terminology of Musters, Pay Lists and Description Books

Because most of these records were used for accounting purposes an explanation of the terminology and abbreviations used will help in understanding what the document is actually telling you about your ancestor.

VICTUALS - bedding, blankets, clothing, tobacco.
UNSERVICEABLE or DUS - unfit on medical grounds.
SUPERSEDED - where an officer is replaced.
STRAGGLE or R (run) - deserter.
SLOPS - clothing/uniform.
QUALITY - rank (officer) - rating.
MEN IN LIEU - men 'persuaded' to join the Navy to maintain a ship's compliment, (sometimes referred to as substitutes).
D - discharged.
DD - discharged dead (cause of death may be given).
DSS - discharged to shore as sick.
SLVO - supernumerary list for victuals only (supernumerary means men over and above the ship's compliment).
LV - leave.
Lt - lent to another ship.
HS - Hospital ship.
HH - Haslar hospital.
E - entered.
DS - discharged to sick quarters.
A - H - codes used relating to methods of recording when wages were paid.
NB - Scotland (used to replace the place born).
ORDINARY - from the reserve.

Within the musters and pay lists various abbreviations are used to indicate the type of ship. This system particularly applies to records found in classes ADM 36 and 37 but can apply to all classes.

Abbreviations relating to the type of ship as found in the musters are given below:

Type of Ship	Abbreviation	Type of Ship	Abbreviation
Armed	A	Galley tender	GYT
Armed brig	AB	Hired armed cutter	HACU
Armed cutter	ACU	Hired armed tender	HAT
Armed cutter tender	ACUT	Hired armed vessel	HAV
Advice boat	AD	Hog boat	HG
Armed galley	AGY	Hired gun boat	HGN
Ambi navigator	AN	Hires hospital	HHP
Armed prize tender	APZT	Hired hospital ship	HHPS
Armed ship	AS	Hulk	HK
Armed schooner	ASC	Hulk ship	HKS
Armed sloop	ASL	Hospital	HP
Armed tender	AT	Hospital ship	HPS
Armed transport	ATR	Hired schooner	HSC
Armed treasury ship	ATRES	Hired sloop tender	HSLT
Armed transport ship	ATRS	Hired tender	HT
Armed tender vessel	ATV	Ketch	K
Armed vessel	AV	Lighter	L
Brig	B	Prison hospital ship	PHPS
Bomb	BB	Packet tender	PKT
Bomb ship	BBS	Privateer	PR
Brig tender	BT	Receiving ship	RS
Convalescent ship	CO	Schooner	SC
Cutter	CU	Sloop	SL
Cutter tender	CUT	Sloop bomb	SLBB
Floating battery	FBY	Sloop tender	SLT
Fireship	FI	Smack	SM
Frigate	FR	Supernumerary ship	SNS
French ship of war	FSW	Store ship	ST
Galleott	GA	Tender	T
Gun brig	GB	Troop ship	TPS
Gun barge	GBG	Transport	TR
Gun boat	GN	Tender vessel	TV
Guard ship	GS	Wherry	W
Gun vessel	GV	Yacht	YT
Galley	GY	Yacht tender	YTT

Navy ships have carried Royal Marine regiments since the mid-1600s. Their sole purpose was two-fold, to transfer from sea to land as a fighting force and also to fight on board ship to repel the enemy attacks. The ships' musters contain details of all the marines on board (see *My Ancestor was a Royal Marine*).

CHAPTER TWELVE
Royal Navy Officer service records

The methods of collecting and preserving Royal Navy service and operation records varied depending upon the period. Within the records terms and abbreviations have been used which again changed from time to time. Many records of use in tracing an officer ancestor date from around the time of the Napoleonic Wars but some are much earlier. Tracing an officer's career depends upon your ability to logically use the available records to the fullest advantage which in places can be fairly complex.

Warrant Officers

Warrant Officers on board a ship had specialist knowledge and a high level of experience which meant that they were primarily responsible for making sure that the ship was always in a high state of readiness. A ship had to be well maintained and its guns always ready for use, with ample charges and projectiles. More importantly it had to be in the right place at the right time. Most Warrant Officers were attached to the ship throughout its life, whether it was in commission, or laid up. They held a Warrant signed by members of the Board of Admiralty.

Warrant Officers' responsibilities were outlined previously.

In 1843 the Master and in 1859 the Chaplain became Commissioned ranks and in 1861 a Commission was also granted to a Schoolmaster if he was involved in the instruction of naval officers in shore training establishments. They ultimately became Naval Instructors.

In 1808 the status of some of the Warrant Officers altered significantly. Masters, Pursers, Chaplains and Surgeons were made 'Warrant Officers of Commissioned Rank'. As such other Warrant Officers primarily carpenters, gunners, cooks and boatswains, had their roles diminished. Cooks were subsequently rated as petty officer in 1838.

In 1837 with the advent of steam powered warships the warranted engineer was established. Some warranted engineers were commissioned in 1847. Some boatswains were promoted to chief boatswains as of 1865 and in 1920, became Commissioned Boatswain. In 1903 the rank of Carpenter Lieutenant was introduced. Warrant Officers were required to have achieved a higher educational standard although some promotions particularly in the earlier periods when education was not compulsory were made on the basis of service. Those seeking promotion to a Warrant Officer were usually required to have qualified for Petty Officer rating and in some cases they would have to have served in that rate for a period of time. As such few promotions were made under the age of 30 years and most occurring in the early to mid-30s. In some cases promotions were made without regard to suitability.

Advancement to Commissioned Officer from Warrant Officer normally required 10 years of service as a Warrant Officer. There was an increase in the number of Warrant Officers promoted to Lieutenant during the Second World War and after.

Commissioned Officers

For almost the full duration of the Royal Navy's existence the rank of Lieutenant was the basic commissioned rank. All commissioned officers had to pass an examination in seamanship in order to qualify for a commission. They also had to prove that they had served a minimum period of time at sea. From 1677 this was three years, of which one year had to have been spent as a midshipman. In 1703 this was increased to four years with two years as a midshipman or master's mate. In 1729 the time at sea was increased to six years, which remains in force today. Because of an ambiguity as to whether or not time in the Merchant Navy would count towards sea service the Admiralty stated the following in 1745 'that service in merchant ships was acceptable for the four years of 'non-rated' time'. The qualifying age for a Lieutenant's commission was normally 20 but evidence suggests that in some cases (particularly where men had an ancestral history of Navy officers) some received their commissions at a younger age. Conversely some were much older. The Admiralty was inconsistent in its record keeping so, as you will see later, a very important piece of evidence for assessing their careers is missing.

There is need for explanation over two other ranks which appear to be commissioned officers when in fact this is not necessarily the case. 'Lieutenant-commander' up to 1914 simply meant a 'lieutenant in command' who was the captain of a ship which was too small to be under the control of a Commander. They were sometimes referred to as 'Captain' in the same way as other commanding officers were but they were still only commissioned Lieutenants. The official rank of Lieutenant-Commander was created at the start of the First World War for Lieutenants of eight years or more seniority.

You may also come across the term 'Sub-lieutenant' which was only used for a short period around the Napoleonic wars between 1804 and 1814 for a midshipman or a master's mate who had passed the Lieutenant's examination but had not yet been promoted as such. They normally served as watch-keeping officers on small vessels which only had a 'Lieutenant in command'. A Sub-lieutenant was in this context not the same as the commissioned rank which was not instituted until 1860.

Seniority

The key to understanding the careers of a commissioned officer concerns the application of the seniority rules and also the half-pay set up within the Navy.

The Navy has for a long time relied upon the authority of officers. It was all to do with successive appointments and the permanent status. Up until recently it was possible for an officer to serve in various capacities and guises perhaps as a Lieutenant, then a Captain, then Second Lieutenant, First Lieutenant, Master, Commander etc. In such a situation it was difficult to establish who had the authority and seniority thus Admiralty opinion was divided.

Samuel Pepys wearing his Admiralty hat wrote in 1675:

'I find there hath been wanting to this day a clear determination how commanders are to behave themselves in reference to precedence, and giving command one to the other when they chance to fall in company without any warrant from the lord admiral giving the command to some one of them, the want whereof hath three or four times within my knowledge begot very much ill-blood and some disorder to the king's service.'

Pepys assembled the first seniority list, but even after his efforts it was still unclear regarding who had seniority. Thus in 1691 the Admiralty made a further attempt to compile an official seniority list, but disputes between Captains continued to occur hindering the process.

Eventually seniority was clear cut and dependent upon when an officer was promoted to that rank. Separate records of seniority exist.

Half-Pay

Half-pay came into existence in 1668 and was fully instituted in 1674 as a reward to Admirals, Commodores and Captains who had served in the preceding wars. In 1694 half-pay was given to all Post-Captains, First Lieutenants and Masters of the first three rates (ships), who had served during the duration of the wars then occurring. By 1700 it was clear that the Navy wanted to keep an establishment of experienced Sea-Officers, who did not have a command at the time but who would be available to return to service should the need arise. Officers in receipt of half-pay were not allowed to go abroad or accept any other public employment.

Half-pay was at this time only granted to the first 50 Captains and the first 100 Lieutenants listed on the first printed seniority list; this therefore became a retainer for future services and the Navy List showed those on half-pay as a separate listing.

Half-pay was a sliding scale descending with seniority which in practice meant the elements of retainer and reward were totally mixed throughout the whole of the 18th century. For example half-pay could be granted to officers who had served in the previous war and withheld from those who had not.

It is known that officers were retained on the half-pay list even if they were known to be incapable simply because there was no other support for them in old age.

Though pensions for wounds and good service might be granted by the Admiralty to some more senior officers no regular superannuation scheme for any commissioned officers existed until 1738 and even then this was severely restricted.

Records of Officers

For both commissioned and Warrant Officers the officially produced Navy List enables the basics of tracing an individual officer's career.

The Navy Lists

The amount of information contained in the Navy Lists from 1814 to date varies with time and circumstances but besides recording officers details they include pay scales, uniform regulations etc. The Lists were published between one and 12 times a year depending upon the periods.

The Navy List includes officers in the Royal Navy, Queen Alexandra's Royal Nursing Service, Women's Royal Naval Service, the Coastguard and all the other naval branches including the Reserve Forces and the civil departments. The list enables researchers to determine names, rank, seniority, decorations and other significant career details.

It is also possible to see different groupings by rank for both commissioned and Warrant Officers by ship with their officers and current locations and stations, and separate lists of pensioners and retired officers.

Before the publication of the Navy List there were earlier reference publications which are useful in determining basic information about your officer ancestor.

Steel's Navy List: was the first such list with publications running from 1787 to 1816. Publication was sometimes erratic but they were printed as frequently as monthly. Steel's lists officers, ships and establishments and includes officers of Sea Fencibles before 1810, miscellaneous intelligence reports and vessels captured. Prize money awards are also noted in the publication.

Lean's Navy List: spans the period 1878 to 1916 sometimes duplicating information in the Navy List. Lean's records information on officers arranged both alphabetically and by seniority. This is particularly useful in providing dates of birth of officers and short biographies of their service and decorations. Like the main Navy List it also gives lists of ships and establishments with serving officers.

The Official Navy Lists: commenced in 1814 giving information on seniority and disposition of officers each year including commissioned officers, some Warrant Officers and officers associated with the Coastguard services. Certain officer categories were not included until much later. The following table is the earliest date at which certain officers appear:

- 1838 Naval Instructors and Schoolmasters.
- 1842 Mates.
- 1852 Chief Engineers.
- 1862 RNR Officers.
- 1870 Midshipmen, boatswains, gunners and carpenters.
- 1884 Naval nursing sisters.
- 1890 All other officers of the establishment.

The Official Navy List has other useful information that can help identify your ancestor or put 'flesh on their bones'.

Where serving.	Name.	Rank.	Seniority.	Where serving.	Name.	Rank.	Seniority.
349	FAGAN Christopher S. F. . . . . . RM	Maj	1 Sept 83		Field Arthur M. . . .	Cr	30 June 89
Ex	Fair George M K.(act)	S L	14 May 89		Field Cyril . . . RM	C	24 Nov 88
	Fairfax Henry . . CB	R A	1 July 85	376	Field Frederick L. . .	RM	15 Nov 86
	(A Lord Commissioner of the Admiralty.)			262	Field John G. M. . . .	Cr	30 June 88
79	Fairfoot William . . .	B	12 July 76	58a	Fielder John	Ch E	2 July 89
96	Fancey Henry . . .	Gr	3 Aug 80	76	Fildes John H. . . .	S L	24 Sept 86
14	Fane Augustus . . .	S Cr	5 Aug 85	490	Finch James J. . . .	E Ins	2 Nov 89
AdC} 540	Fane Charles G. . . .	C	9 Aug 75	474	Fincham William C. .	Ch E	1 Apr 88
52	Fanshawe Arthur D. .	C	31 Dec 81	405	Finlay George. . . .	P	19 June 86
118	Fanshawe Arthur H.	S L	1 Sept 86	475	Finnis Frank	Cr	1 Jan 86
362	Fanshawe Basil H. . .	S L	13 Nov 87	223	Firks William J. . . .	Ch E	31 Aug 88
CG	Fanshawe Lionel . .	Cr	29 June 83	53	Fish Francis J. . . .	B	12 Sept 88
312	Farewell Frank A. S..	L	11 Jan 81	485	Fisher Frederick W. .	Cr	21 June 87
53	Farie James U. . . .	Mid	15 Mar 89	RM	Fisher James W. MD	F S	2 Sept 82
14	Farquhar Arthur M.	Cr	30 June 89	NH	Fisher John	I H	1 Apr 87
168	Farquhar Richard B..	L	16 Sept 81	AdC	Fisher John A. . CB	C	30 Oct 74
93	Farquhar Stuart St. J.	L	24 Apr 86		(Director of Naval Ordnance.)		
	Farouharson Harry D. RM	L	27 Sept 89	192	Fisher Octavius S.. .	S	20 Aug 85
CG	Farr William . . .	L	29 Dec 71	277	Fisher Thomas H. . .	L	7 Feb 80
477	Farrant Charles D. M.	A P	14 Jan 83	NID	Fisher William B. . .	Cr	1 Jan 90
285	Farrell James	B	7 Feb 77		Fishley Robert D. (act)	Car	19 Nov 89
Ex	Farrington Alexander (act)	S L	14 May 89	111	Fitch Richard A. . .	S	20 Aug 85
231	Farrow Frederic G. .	S P	17 Feb 86		FitzGeorge Adolphus A. F.	C	14 Oct 81
96	Farwell Charles . . .	S P	19 Apr 88	115	FitzGerald CharlesC.P.	C	19 Mar 80
285	Fasham John	Gr	11 July 68	354	Fitz Gerald Richard P.	L	31 Dec 84
115	Fasken Edward R. D..	S	21 Aug 84		Fitzgerald Michael . .	S S	1 Apr 85
53	Faulds Arthur G. J. .	E	1 Sept 88		Fitzherbert Edward S.	L	24 Sept 86
526	Faulkner Percy F. . .	E	1 Sept 89		Fitzmaurice Henry . .	Gr	27 Apr 85
293	Fawckner William B..	L	15 Feb 82	443	Fitzmaurice MauriceS. (act)		
396	Fawkes Wilmot H. . .	C	30 June 86		FitzRoy RobertO'BCB	R A	14 May 88
366	Feak William M.. . .	S E	11 July 86	240	Fitzsimons Nicholas	B	21 June 87
517	Featherstone Walter J.	E	1 Sept 84	71	Fleet Ernest J. . . .	Cr	1 Jan 90
24	Fedarb William (b)..	E	1 Sept 83	347	Fleet Henry L. . . .	Cr	21 June 87
498	Feesey John H. . . .	AsCk	15 July 89	10	Fleetwood John L. . .	E	1 Feb 89
238	Fegen Frederick F. .	Cr	9 Aug 87	306	Fleming Frederick . .	Gr	1 Oct 88
172	Fell Herbert L. H. . .	Mid	15 Oct 88	370	Fleming Richard . . .	B	14 Sept 85
349	Fellowes John . . CB	C	29 Jan 80	533	Fleming Thomas (act)	Gr	31 Dec 89
417	Fencock William T. .	S P	23 Apr 87	48	Fletcher Edward B. .	L	24 July 71
14	Fennell Samuel M. . .	A P	14 Jan 87	115	Fletcher William B. .	F S	1 Aug 83
	Fenton Thomas C. . .	L	15 Oct 75	50	Flevill Benjamin . . .	B	21 June 87
287	Fenwick Charles E.	L	1 Jan 90	301	Flood Frederick J. . .	E	1 Sept 86
474	Fenwick Maurice G.F. B.	A P	7 July 80	373	Floyd Henry R. P. . .	L	23 June 80
180	Ferbracke William .	A P	1 May 82	485	Flux George J. . . .	Gr	11 July 82
	Ferguson Charles J. .	A P	17 June 84	354	Flynn David W. . . .	Gr	3 Aug 80
201	Ferguson Edward . .	S	30 Sept 78	553	Flynn Francis . . BA	Ch	25 Sept 84
366	Ferguson James H. .{	Ch / E Ins}	2 Mar / 83	501	Flynn Michael . . .	B	19 July 81
249	Ferguson John C. BA, MB	S	22 Feb 88	216	Foden Harry	Clk	14 July 88
499	Ferguson James A. .	Mid	15 Feb 87	316	Fogerty George J. . .	S S	30 Sept 88
65	Ferraro John S. . . .	Gr	19 July 81	409	Fogerty John S. . MD	S	20 Aug 85
35	Ferris John	Cr	31 Dec 84	CG	Foley Cecil F. . . .	L	1 Sept 74
512	Ferris Pierce . . .	Gr	8 Feb 86		Foley Francis J. . . .	Cr	1 Jan 89
517	Festing Henry M. C. .	Cr	31 Dec 87	90	Foll tt Samuel G. . .	Ch E	19 June 87
					Fookes Albert W. . .	Car	29 Dec 88
				338	Foord Henry D. G	Mid	15 Dec 86
				122	Foot Charles M. . .	Mid	15 June 89
				180	Foot Cunningham R. de C	L	31 Dec 86

55. Example of details within the Navy Lists.

Ships of the Navy

The most useful section apart from that relating to officers is the Alphabetical Listing of Ships. This gives the name, type of vessel, tonnage, horse power, the name of the station or port to which the ship is assigned, the date and place that the ship was commissioned and the names of commissioned and Warrant Officers serving on the ships at the time the publication was compiled. Of particular importance is an indication that a ship is assigned to the Coastguard or other naval division. The Lists are also very useful in furthering the information about the naval dockyards and foreign stations.

Tables and Regulations

Within each edition of the Navy List all of the tables and regulations currently in use (at the date of publication) are included. These relate to such aspects as details of the full and half-pay rates granted to each rank, the uniform regulations for both commissioned and Warrant Officers and for petty officers, men and boys, pension entitlement of widows of officers, the examination regulations relating to officers and naval cadets, information on prize money and the conveyance of treasure and salvage, the entry regulations for seamen and the regulations for the wearing of medals.

All of these vary from time to time and if you are aware of when a seaman or officer began or ended their service you should be able to find information about those aspects of the Navy career.

The UK Navy Lists from 1888-1970 can be searched on ancestry.co.uk although not every edition is available. Other online data providers also have a search facility for various editions including 'TheGenealogist' and 'Family Relatives' the latter being particularly useful for the Navy Lists editions published in both world wars though they do not appear to be the Confidential Navy Lists.

The confidential editions of the Navy List contained the complete information on officers and ships which was omitted from the generally available and published edition in wartime. The confidential Navy List was for official use only which indicated where individual officers were serving, with the names of ships and establishments. A complete list of all ships in the Royal Navy was included, together with details of tonnage and armament. This edition can only be seen under supervision at The National Archives and is contained within series ADM 177. It was published in January, April, July, October during the First World War but bi-monthly during the Second World War; namely, February, April, June, August, October, December.

There is a very useful online research facility for around 120 Navy Lists covering various periods from 1766 to the present (current lists of available editions are shown on the website home page) at **www.navylistresearch.co.uk**. This is a subscription site but offers generous discounts for continuous subscriptions. The database is progressively being updated to include both the current lists and lists from earlier years.

There are several advantages in using online research as these publications are expensive to buy, older editions can sometimes be difficult to find and in other cases the cost of travel to either The National Archives, Society of Genealogists or National Maritime Museum (which all have good runs) can be expensive.

Seniority Lists

The whole system of officer promotion was based on seniority to their rank and lists were published for sea officers and those on half-pay between 1717 and 1846. For Warrant Officers the lists started slightly later running between 1780 and 1844. Although there is not much information contained in the lists they are worth searching because as a minimum they provide name and date of seniority to a particular rank. They can be found in series ADM 118.

Succession Books

These provide an alternative way of researching the career of both commissioned and Warrant Officers. Succession books allow you to follow an officer's career from ship to ship. The books are arranged by the ship's name and name successive officers appointed to each ship listed as well as promotions and transfers between ships. Many of the books have an index by both ship and name. They cover the period from c.1673 to the end of the First World War although there are some gaps particularly in the early period and up to around 1764. The books also generally list dates of appointment and discharge.

The succession books which are found mainly in series ADM 11 cover Flag and Commissioned officers with some separate lists for Captains, Commanders and Lieutenants. For Midshipmen, cadets and boys the books run from 1815 in series ADM 11. For Warrant and Standing Officers the books are split between classes ADM 11 and ADM 29 with separate series for Masters and Mates and for Standing Warrant Officers (gunners, boatswains, pursers, carpenters). Succession books for Medical Officers can be located in series ADM 104.

There are other series of succession books for personnel such as cooks, chaplains, naval schoolmasters from as early as 1673 and these along with many of the early series of records can be found in series ADM 6. Using Discovery and searching on Succession Books ADM will locate all available resources.

Commissioned Sea Officers of the Royal Navy

For those with ancestors who served as commissioned officers for the period 1660 to 1815 there is a searchable database available through **ancestry.co.uk** taken from the three published volumes. This is a listing of each officer and alongside the name of each officer are his rank and the first year in which he served at that rank. The original list was compiled from a number of sources. The list was compiled by Royal Naval College, Greenwich and the National Maritime Museum. Before using this database or searching the published book the introduction should be consulted as this contains information relating to the scope and nature of the list as well as providing the source information and an explanation of abbreviations used.

LEEKE, Sir Henry John				LEGGATT, William	d	1817 (PRO)
L		24 Nov	1810			
CR		15 June	1814	L	23 Jan	1779
CA		27 May	1825 (MB)	d		1783 (PRO)
Kt		1 Apr	1835 (OB)	LEGGE, Hon. Sir Arthur Kaye		
KH		25 Jan	1836 (OB)	L	3 Aug	1789
Ret RA		15 Apr	1854 (PRO)	CR	19 Nov	1790
KCB			1858 (DNB)	CA	6 Feb	1793
RAR		14 Aug	1858 (PRO)	RAB	31 July	1810
COM AD	23 Apr–28 June		1859 (AO)	RAW	12 Aug	1812
VAB		2 May	1860 (PRO)	RAR	4 Dec	1813
VAW		15 Jan	1862 (PRO)	VAB	4 June	1814
VAR		27 Apr	1863 (PRO)	KCB	2 Jan	1815 (MB)
AB		11 Jan	1864 (PRO)	VAW	12 Aug	1819 (CH)
				VAR	27 May	1825 (CH)
d		26 Feb	1870 (PRO)	AB	22 July	1830 (CH)
LEEKE, Thomas Samuel						
L		7 Nov	1806	d	12 May	1835 (CH)
				LEGGE, Hon. Edward		
KIA		2 Nov	1810 (PJP)	L	2 Mar	1734

56. Commissioned Sea officers of the Royal Navy (from the publication of the Navy Records Society).

Other published information

Officer biographies can be located through printed sources. *Biographia Navalis* by John Charnock, the details of service of 2,200 naval officers covering 1660 to 1794 can be searched using Google Books. The 'Original and Correct List of the Royal Navy' is useful from the end of the 1700s when it started to list many officers together with their ships. Between 1780 when it was first published and 1799 it normally listed only ships. If researching at The National Archives you can of course use ADM 118 which are the indexed official seniority lists. If you find a name crossed out in the ADM 118 series this usually means that the officer concerned was not in receipt of peacetime wages. It does not indicate death.

Admiralty List Books in series ADM 8 cover the period 1673 to 1909 are monthly returns showing the disposition of ships together with the names of officers. None are indexed but they were used to compile the three volumes of 'Commissioned Sea Officers, 1660-1815' (see above) which can be used as a guide index to officers' names in ADM 8, but only up to 1813. From 1815 it is easier to refer to the Navy Lists.

For the mid-Victorian period O'Byrnes 'A Naval Biographical Dictionary' published in 1849 is searchable on ancestry.co.uk and is available in hardback at the Society of Genealogists. This is useful for identifying the careers and fairly detailed biography of all naval officers still living in 1845.

Officers' Service Records

You may be lucky enough to locate within a family archive the actual certificate issued to an officer on admission to a particular commission but you will still need to search the official records for further details of an officers' career.

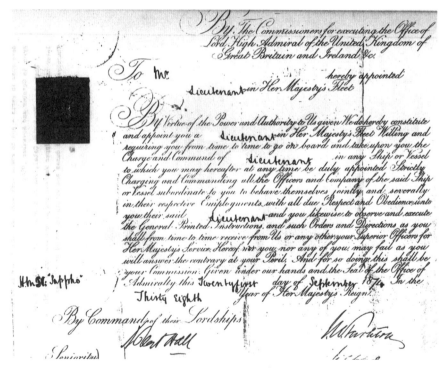

57. Officers commission appointment (personal papers of W G Lawrence).

Once a career pattern has been established it is then straightforward to search the official records for more information. Some of these records are available digitally. The records of officers both commissioned and warranted are both comprehensive and sometimes complicated to use. Records for the 18th and early 19th century are sparse but for the later periods are considered to be reasonably complete.

The basic records for Warrant Officers can be located in two classes of service record: Royal Naval Officers' Service records (1830-c. 1930) in series ADM 196 and the service records 1802-1894) found in series ADM 29. The latter series only covers Warrant Officers whereas ADM 196 is for both commissioned and Warrant Officers. Both of these classes can be searched by name using Discovery.

The records contained in ADM 196 relate to the service records of officers who joined the Royal Navy between 1756 and 1931 and include service records for commissioned officers joining the Navy up to 1917 and Warrant Officers joining up to 1931. Records for Warrant Officers in the Royal Navy before 1830 are incomplete and patchy as there were no central service registers for personnel. After 1931 the records are still held by the Royal Navy.

By way of clarification Commissioned Officers are Admirals (also known as flag officers), Commodores, Captains, Commanders and Lieutenants. Warrant Officers are gunners, boatswains, carpenters, surgeon's mates, armourers, sail makers, masters at arms, rope makers, caulkers and coopers, masters (before 1808), surgeons (before 1843), pursers (before 1843), chaplains (before 1843) and engineers (before 1847).

In the case of some Warrant Officers their record may be held in a different record series. Most of the records relating to carpenters or boatswains who joined between 1848 and 1912 and engineers who served between 1839 and 1862 can be found in ADM 29. If you are looking for records of surgeons or assistant surgeons it may also be worth looking at ADM 104.

Before the late 1800s the records of service tended to be very basic in content. Most contain:

• Name.
• Rank Quality.
• The ships on which they served together with date of entry and discharge.
• Some may include a date of death, particularly if this was in service.

From the late 19th century additional information is included by way of birthdate and place and the details of immediate next of kin.

Because of the way the Navy was organised and administered it is possible for an officer to have more than one service record but fortunately in undertaking a name search on 'Discovery' if more than one record is in existence then it will show in the catalogue entry.

You may encounter challenges in finding service records which may be attributable to the fact that an officer died or left service before records were systematically kept or an officer served with the Reserve.

The other obvious search should be in the records of ratings as he may not have been an officer at all. You will be surprised how often someone who served in the Navy enhanced their status or family stories handed down have been enhanced or corrupted - keep an open mind. One other anomaly which you should be aware of is if you are searching for an Admiral rank he may be described as a flag officer.

Officers' Service Record Cards

These records in series ADM 340 covering the period from about 1840 to the end of the First World War can be accessed by an online search through Discovery and consists of around 5,000 officers' service records for men and women serving in the Royal Navy, Royal Naval Reserve, Royal Naval Volunteer Reserve and Women's Royal Naval Service. The series is not complete for all officers.

Some of the cards may contain information about service dating back to the 1840s (although most tend to commence in the 1880s) while others may detail service through the Second World War.

The information in these records supplements the details in the actual service record and can include:

• Name.
• Rank.
• Date and place of birth.
• Seniority and promotions.
• Any training undertaken.
• Ships' names and dates of service.
• Home address.

There may also be more than one card for an officer. Information is included on both sides of the card. Although most of the genealogically important data is on the front the rear of the card lists the ships, details of pay and any voluntary training undertaken.

Officers' Passing Certificates

It was usual for some officers to sit an examination to assess their suitability for a particular rank for which they were awarded a certificate when they passed. These certificates are important for ascertaining a man's service, frequently as a rating or Midshipman, prior to the examination. In some cases supporting documentation of genealogical value exists such as a birth or baptism certificate.

Lieutenants' Passing Certificates

Examinations for Lieutenants were introduced in 1677 and were originally held at the Navy Board Offices in London. All prospective Lieutenants were interviewed by three senior Captains and the interview related to seamanship and the theory of navigation. The questions asked were made up by the captains and there were no set examination questions. The candidates who passed were not guaranteed a commission with many having to wait a number of years for such. In times of war it was easier and quicker to obtain a commission. By 1813 the Navy employed around 2,000 commissioned Lieutenants.

The records are a valuable source of genealogical information as they frequently give age (some will state 'above twenty one years') the names of the ships on which they served as ratings prior to passing their examination, together with the name of the Captain they served under, their rating on each ship, the names of the examining officers and the date of examination. Between 1744 and 1819 there may be two certificates each containing slightly different data. There is a gap in the availability of records of passing certificates between 1677 and 1690 and also between 1833 and 1853.

The List and Index Society has published an alphabetical listing of 'Royal Navy Lieutenants' Passing Certificates 1691-1902' in two split volumes each giving the name of the candidate, year of passing and the ADM reference together with the page/folio number in that piece. There is also a short synopsis at the front of volume one which outlines the procedures employed in obtaining the certificate.

58. Lieutenant Passing Certificate (TNA document ADM 6/96 - Edward Nathaniel Greenwood).

The certificates are contained in three record classes ADM 6 and ADM 106 as well as ADM 13 specifically for engineers.

Apart from lieutenants as above you can only search by rank and date for other officers by using Discovery. As part of the search you would need to use keywords such as 'passing certificate' and the rank of the officer. If you are searching for Masters and Surgeons you will need to restrict your search to ADM 106.

Commission and Warrant Books

Up to 1860 the commission and warrant documentation was the only official method of appointing an officer to a specific ship. The books form part of series ADM 6 and cover the period 1695 to 1849. The commissions or warrants were always issued for each different appointment. They are not the easiest documents to search as they are organised primarily by date but give basic information i.e. officer's name, the name of the ship to which the appointment relates, the officer's rank and sometimes why the appointment was made.

Returns of Officers' Surveys

In the period between 1817 and 1861 various surveys were conducted by the Admiralty with a view to making their records more comprehensive. This did not work too well because some officers never received the survey forms and others did not bother to return them. Those that have survived are however extremely useful in supplementing career information.

Surveys which survive for commissioned officers can be found in series ADM 9. There is a printed index to the surveys carried out in 1817 and 1846. There is a name index in the TNA search room but the index to ADM 9/1-9 can be searched using Discovery.

Using the index is straightforward. You will need to locate the name of the officer in whichever index you are looking at and then note the folio number alongside the name. In some instances, particularly for the 1817 survey you may find his rank also listed. The actual surveys are organised by folio numbers.

The system to find Warrant Officer surveys is slightly different as there appears to be a more frequent sequence of surveys in some instances, some of which are indexed and some which are not. Most of these surveys and associated indexes can be found in ADM 11.

Surveys of masters were taken in 1822, (ADM 106) 1833-35, 1851, 1855 and 1861. The 1822, 1855 and 1861 surveys are not indexed. The 1833-1835 surveys have indexes covering each volume and the 1851 survey has a separate index.

There was only one survey for gunners, boatswains and carpenters undertaken in 1816-1818 which is not indexed. For pursers and paymasters the survey was undertaken in 1852 and again each document volume has its own index. Royal Naval chaplains were subject to a survey in 1833-1834 but again there is no index.

Full Pay Registers

These registers are useful as a supplement to the other records of officers. They record the wages paid to both commissioned and Warrant Officers when on active service. Alongside the half-pay registers it is possible to piece together any gaps in an officer's career within the Navy. They can be found in series ADM 24 covering the period 1795 to 1905.

Up to 1829 the registers are compiled by each rank all with separate name indexes. After 1830 all ranks are combined into one general register, again indexed by volume. For certain Warrant Officers (engineers, gunners, carpenters and boatswains) details of pay can be found in series ADM 22 covering the period between 1847 and 1892.

The registers provide the officer's name, his wage and the name of the ship on which he served. Later from c.1830 you may also find recorded the reason that officer left the ship. In some cases the address of the officer where pay was sent and sometimes a death date are also included.

Officer Obituary Book

This record is not exactly what the title suggests because it records details of officers who were dismissed from the service or resigned as opposed to deaths (although deaths in service are recorded). The entries relate to those who are no longer in active full time service. Many entries also relate to alterations in seniority as a result of disciplinary actions. The books are arranged chronologically as the following example transcript illustrates:

Transcript ADM 6/445 - Commissioned Officer Obituary Book.

Name	Date	Whence	Authority
Lieut. Albert F Hurt	1 Feb 1860	Cossack	Resigned service
Lieut. M H M Mundy	14 Feb 1860	H Pay	Resigned service
1st Lieut. John R Mascall	14 Mar 60	Trafalgar	Dism'd ship & release 2 yrs time
Lieut. Geo P Heath	3 May 60	H P to	Reserved list
Lieut. Thomas W Simeon	4 May 60	Perseverance	Dismissed ship and placed at bottom of the list of Lieutenants
Lieut. Philip J Patrickson	10 May 60	Asia	Dismissed ship and placed at the bottom of the list of Lieutenants

CHAPTER THIRTEEN

Personal papers, diaries etc.

One of the most prolific series of documents outside the official collections relates to the records deposited by individuals or their families in many of the major museums or archives dealing with the Royal Navy. Although they obviously relate and in most cases are personal records of the individual concerned they frequently provide excellent information about conditions, happenings and conflict which happened on the ship on which that person served. You should always seek information from colleagues or crew members of the vessel on which your ancestor served. Many contain photographs, scrapbook entries etc. which may just show your ancestor. Some will mention others by name in diaries, log books etc.

It is also worth checking with 'non-naval' repositories as they too may hold personal papers as the example below.

The London Metropolitan Archives hold personal papers of Charles Todd who was a naval chaplain between 1881 and 1899. His personal papers include his certificates of ordination as a deacon and priest, his commission as a Navy chaplain, letters, diaries and notebooks some of which also describe expeditions in Ceylon and East Africa, various newspaper cuttings, photographs and most significantly a description of his Navy service.

One repository which is worth considering for extended research is the Liddell Hart Centre for Military Archives which, although mainly relating to the army does contain information and private papers for some Royal Navy officers. Most of the records relate to the 20th century. The centre is located at Kings College in the Strand, London. By way of example you can find the records of Captain Eric Bush, RN.

Liddell Hart hold photographs relating to his naval career and press cuttings relating to the publication of books that he authored or was involved in, including 'Bless our ship'. From his biographical history you can find details of his life and service which can be expanded by looking at ships' logs, operational records etc:

'Capt. Eric Bush RN

Birth 1899; education Stoke House, Stoke Poges, Royal Naval Colleges at Osborne and Dartmouth; Midshipman, HMS Bacchante, 1914; HMS Revenge, 1916; Sub-Lt, 1917; Lt, 1920; HMS Thunderer, HMS Erebus; Lt Cdr, 1927; graduated from RN Staff College, Greenwich, 1931; Cdr, 1933; Capt, 1939; Chief of Staff and afterwards Capt, Auxiliary Patrol, 1939-1940; commanded HMS Euryalus, 1941-1943; commanded HMS Malaya; Chief of Staff, Naval Force 'W', South East Asia Command, 1945; commanded HMS Ganges at Shotley, 1946-1948; retired 1948; died 1985.'

The Wellcome Library also holds various records associated mainly with the medical arm of the Royal Navy for example: an early case book (mid-1800s) of the surgeons on *HMS St George* which was a guard ship stationed at Devonport. Patients from around 30 ships stationed at Devonport appear in the case book. It names the surgical team on St. George as surgeon James Browne, MD, assistant surgeon William Webber, MD, assistant surgeon Hart Gimlette, MD. It indicates that a number of patients were treated in the sick bay with others being sent to the Plymouth Royal Naval Hospital.

Many of the family histories held by the library at the Society of Genealogists contain personal accounts of men who saw service in the Royal Navy. Searching the catalogue under 'Royal Navy - Family History' will enable access.

CHAPTER FOURTEEN
Royal Navy pensions

The use of records relating to pensions for both officers and ratings is essential for your research. However finding records of pensions can be complex and perhaps slightly confusing. Nevertheless it is an essential to identify the most appropriate record. A number of bodies have had responsibility for administering pensions throughout naval history, namely: The Chatham or Greenwich Chest, The Greenwich Hospital, The Admiralty and the Navy Pay Office. The Compassionate Fund was also a charity responsible for the payment of pensions to widows.

Background

The Chatham Chest was set up in the late 1500s specifically to grant pensions to disabled seamen after many who had been disabled in the war against Spain petitioned the monarch for relief and maintenance. Deductions were made from the pay to enable contributions to be paid out as and when required. The name relates to the chest in which the assets of the fund were held, hence the name 'Chatham Chest'. The chest itself is now on display at Chatham Dockyard.

For many years seamen who were completely or partially disabled through accident or wounds were issued with a 'smart' ticket which gave details of the accident or wound suffered and the amount of pension awarded. The ticket acted as a pass to either Greenwich or pay out from the Chatham Chest and ensured that all such seamen basically did not starve.

The fund was initially financed by members' contributions amounting to sixpence per month. Pensions were granted on a fixed scale depending upon disability and each pensioner was given smart money, a lump sum, equal to one year's pension.

The chest could not always balance its books but in the early days when in credit the money was invested in property. Whether all of the contributions deducted from seamen at the end of voyages actually reached the Chest is unknown. By 1660 the Chest was encountering financial problems because of an increase in the number of pensioners and a decrease in income due to a reduction is personnel after the end of the wars against Spain. From the early 1670s the Government subsidised any deficit in the fund so it could continue its obligations to the pensioners. However despite this many pensioners did not receive their pensions on time. In 1803 under Act of Parliament the chest was merged with the Royal Hospital Greenwich but this took about 10 years to be fully integrated. It was not until 1814 that Greenwich took over the full responsibility for the fund when it became known as 'the Chest at Greenwich'.

The Royal Hospital Greenwich was founded in 1694 as a home for superannuated seamen and marines. The Royal Charter which established the hospital had the objective of providing support for seamen's widows, education for their children and to improve navigation. The first in-pensioners were admitted in 1705. By 1716 the hospital also maintained payments to out-pensioners and provided pensions and allowances for widows and orphans of seamen and marines. At this time it also provided relief for a limited number of officers. By the end of the 1700s there were more than 2,000 pensioners living there.

A school for the sons of seamen was attached to the hospital and in 1829 was amalgamated with the Royal Naval Asylum.

After 1832 the hospital was administered by the Board of Admiralty. It stopped housing in-pensioners in 1869 and from 1873 onwards became the Royal Naval College. The Royal Hospital School was established by Royal Charter in 1712 and was originally located at Greenwich Hospital. The Hospital however continued to administer out-pensions and other allowances as well as continuing with the school administration until the school moved to Holbrook in the 1930s.

Greenwich Pensioner

Frequently civil registration certificates and other genealogically valuable documents will refer to the occupation of someone as a 'Greenwich Pensioner' who, for want of a better description was the Navy equivalent of a 'Chelsea Pensioner'.

Those living in the Royal Hospital Greenwich were known as an 'in-pensioner' and those who lived elsewhere but received a naval pension were known as 'out-pensioners'. Some out-pensioners became in-pensioners if their situation and condition so warranted. In such circumstances the families of these men were not allowed to reside with them. In-pensioners were free to leave the hospital whenever they wanted but re-admission was not possible for at least a year.

In-pensioners lived to fairly strict naval regulations and dressed in a unique uniform consisting of a tri-corn hat and blue coat a uniform which existed long before the Navy as a whole adopted a standard uniform. Any in-pensioners who did not abide by the regulations became known as a 'canary' and his blue coat was swapped for a yellow one and he would have to perform menial tasks as a punishment.

Pension Administration

Besides the Chests and the Greenwich Hospital the other bodies that organised pension payments were the Naval Pay Office operating under the direction of the Admiralty and the Charity for the Payment of Pensions to the Widows of Sea Officers. The Admiralty eventually assumed overall responsibility for pension arrangements with the exception of Greenwich Hospital. After 1853 with the introduction of continuous service for ratings they were rewarded with a pension after 20 years of service. Although the Continuous Service Records exist there are not that many records thereafter relating to actual pensions.

Dependents of officers or ratings killed in action were eligible for payments of a year's wages which was paid to them by the Naval Pay Office. For most of the 19th century there was no formal pension provision for officers as they relied on half-pay or retirement pay which eventually evolved into a pension system. Some officers however received out-pensions from Greenwich Hospital or the Chatham Chest depending upon time period. Pensions were also paid to widows and orphans of officers, which in some cases were administered by the Paymaster General as opposed to the Admiralty. Although the Greenwich Hospital closed in 1869 it continued with the distributing pensions.

The system was entirely different for those suffering from mental illness. Royal Navy servicemen who were suffering from any form of mental illness were treated at Hoxton House assylum, London until 1818 and from then up to 1854 by the Royal Hospital, Haslar.

Pensions to Naval Officers

Because there was no specific pension entitlement for officers up to the mid-19th century the Admiralty had the task of deciding what to do with officers who because of age were unsuitable for employment. To some extent this was taken care of by half-pay. After the mid-19th century the Admiralty established a proper method of retiring officers which was based on seniority and having accrued a number of years' service. By 1837 good service pensions were introduced for both flag officers and captains. Up until then, however, the pension system was primarily for those killed or wounded when pensions were paid to widows.

Retirement pensions as such (superannuation) were paid to different ranks at different times, but it did not happen across the board until 1836. Some had existed since the mid-1600s as shown below:

1666 yard officers and some captains.
1672 the most senior Warrant Officers.
1737 senior lieutenants.
1747 yellow admirals (superannuated rear admirals - retired captains).
1786 captains.
1836 all commissioned and Warrant Officers.

There are various classes of records which need to be researched when tracing superannuation payments.

Registers of Pensions and Allowances

These cover the period 1830 -1934 and can be located in ADM 23 which contains the registers of pensions to commissioned and other civil officers, half-pay officers, coastguard, artificers, widows of naval officers, allowances for the Victoria Cross and meritorious services and compassionate allowances.

It is also necessary to search in related records of the Paymaster General for the period. (Some information in these also applies to those of rating rank.) If these records are not searched then some vital information will be missed. Classes of importance are:

• PMG 15 covering 1836-1920 Naval Officers' half and retired pay
• PMG 16 covering 1836-1920 Pensions and allowances to commissioned and Warrant Officers, pensions and allowances to relatives of naval officers killed or dying in service, pensions for meritorious services, retired flag officers' pensions

awarded between 12 July 1837 and 25 June 1851 and compassionate allowances to late officers granted under an Order in Council of 23 October 1876.

- PMG 18 covering 1837-1921 Compassionate allowances to children and relatives of both commissioned and Warrant Officers. These must also be cross referenced to registers of pensions in series ADM 22 particularly for the earlier period as these records commence in 1734.
- PMG 19 covering 1836-1929 Pensions to widows of commissioned and Warrant Officers.
- PMG 24 covering 1836-1918 Pensions and civil superannuation to salaried staff of Dockyards and shore establishment at both home and abroad, Civil superannuation to staff of Greenwich Hospital and School from 1867 to 1875.

Registers of Salaries and Pensions

The series ADM 22 covers the period 1734-1934 and in addition to the registers of salaries and pensions includes pay books of widows' pensions and of naval out-pensions. The series also includes records of payments under the Compassionate Fund/List and an index to full pay ledgers of certain Warrant Officers such as boatswains, carpenters and gunners

Bill Books and Navy Estimates

Researching this class of document in ADM 18 covering the earlier period of 1642-1831 becomes a little more complex and it is necessary in these to search by date. The series includes other documents besides the pensions and half-pay which is payable on Navy Estimates.

The Navy Estimates are basically the annual budget of the Royal Navy covering the period from 1708 to 1970 and are in series ADM 181. They are annual estimates of the cost of the Navy both at home and abroad and include wages, pensions and victuals of all serving men and dockyard personnel and also cover the upkeep and supplies of naval establishments, etc.

Under the section concerning pensions the details that can be obtained include a description of the pension payment often explaining why the grant was made, the date of the order allowing the pension and the annual amount paid.

Admiralty miscellaneous files

This series is a series of miscellaneous administrative matters in class ADM 7 covering the period 1563-1956. The section under the heading 'Establishment Records - Pensions' for the period 1694-1916 is that which may contain some useful information.

Half-Pay Registers

Half-pay has been described above but the registers are in series ADM 25 and cover the period 1693-1924. They are searchable by date. They list date of allowance, name, rank, ships served on, with dates of entry and discharge, total time served, to whom the pay was made which is sometimes next of kin and whether they were ever re-employed. Some of the later registers include death dates.

Half-pay was granted to officers in stages:

1668 to Admirals and Flag Captains	1729 to Surgeons
1674 to Masters	1814 to Pursers
1675 to Commodores	1817 to Navy Chaplains
1697 to Captains and Lieutenants	1840 to Mates
1715 to Commanders	1856 to Engineers

Earlier half-pay registers to c. 1689 and within series ADM 18 are much less informative providing only basic information of name, rank and pay.

There is also a register for 1837 (the start of the superannuation) in series PMG 73/2 which lists all officers on half-pay and gives their addresses at the time:

Transcript PMG 73/2 - Addresses of Naval Officers on Retired or Half-Pay 1837 Pg 125.

700 Lieutenants at 6s 0d per Diem

John M'Galdery	Innis Bofin, Donegal
John Hancock	Swanage, Dorset
John Robert Woodruff	Union Rd, St Helier, jersey
George Tardrew	Beam, Torrington, Devon
Harry Wilson	Wigwam, Carisbrooke, I of Wight
Alexander Makenzie (B)	Porlock, Somerset
John Weir	Strachin, by Edinsdown, Argyle
Herbert Mackworth	2 Place Belle vue, Boulogne

William Hollamby Hull	Maze, Hill St, St Leonards on the Sea, Sussex
Francis Roberts	Burton, Bridport Kingston, Littlehampton
Edward Simmons	New Rd, Rochester
Benjamin Alpin	Charles St., Bath

Royal Bounty

The Royal Bounty paid from 1675 to 1822 was one year's wages paid to widows, dependent children or in some circumstances to mothers of officers killed in action. When dependents applied for a payment it was usual to submit marriage and death certificates as well as documents which proved age, relationship and sometimes their financial situation particularly if they were poor.

Pay lists of the royal bounty exist for the period 1739-1787 and can be located in series ADM 106. They give the name, address and relation of the payee, the name, rank and ship of the dead man, and the sum paid.

As an additional resource and covering a wider period 1675-1822 the Bounty papers, also in series ADM 106 will provide the background information for any claim and this is where you may find certificates, accounts etc.

Compassionate Fund/List

The compassionate fund, later known as the compassionate list was administered by the Admiralty and was established in 1810. The fund paid grants and pensions to the orphans or other dependents of commissioned officers killed in action. Warrant Officers' dependents later became eligible for the compassionate list from 1885.

Records in previously mentioned classes i.e. PMG 18 and ADM 22 need to be searched for relevant information. ADM 2 also contains letters to the compassionate fund and this series will enable the researcher to see if any background information, appeals, disputes etc. were lodged. The letter coverage runs from 1809 to 1845.

Widows Pensions

The 'Charity for the Payment of Pensions to the Widows of Sea Officers' was established in 1732 and paid pensions to the poor widows of all officers regardless of how or when they died.

The charity received money from a compulsory deduction of three pence in the pound from officers' wages as well a parliamentary grant. It was considered to be an official pension fund but registered as a charity and hence controlled by trustees.

Between 1830 and 1864 widows of Warrant Officers appointed after 1830 were precluded from obtaining a widow's pension but in 1836 the Admiralty took over responsibility for widows' pensions and made them payable regardless of the widow's income. From 1848, widows of engineers became eligible for pensions.

Searching for widows' pensions can be a little complex but records should be searched in the following sequence. Many of these records have already been described but additional comments if relevant are made alongside each entry:

- Widows of Naval Officers Pensions PMG 19 - 1836-1929 arranged alphabetically by date.
- Registers of pensions or allowances ADM 23 - 1830-1934.
- Pay Books of Widows pensions ADM 22 - 1734-1934.
- Commission of the charity for relief of officers' widows ADM 6 - 1673-1960 searchable by name.
- Chatham Chest Pay Books ADM 82 - 1617-1807. Some of these records are held by the National Maritime Museum, Greenwich and not The National Archives.
- Officers Marriage Certificates ADM 13 covering 1806-1866. These are searchable on Discovery by the name of the officer and relate to the proof of marriage needed where a potential claim for a widow's pension was lodged. The series of marriage certificates runs to c.1902 but not all pieces are indexed by name.

Other records, as detailed above, under 'Registers of Pensions and Allowances' should also be systematically searched.

Pensions to Naval Ratings

Until the late 19th century, the Navy Pay Office, The Chatham Chest and The Royal Hospital Greenwich were the three principal bodies responsible for the payment of various naval pensions to ratings.

Their records are held at The National Archives. In the very early period of naval history and before pensions were granted as of right there may be some information contained in the records of the Privy Council or the State papers. From the 1870s pensions were also administered by the Paymaster General and later still the Ministry of Pensions.

Greenwich Hospital paid a large number of Navy ratings as out-pensions as well as admitting in-pensioners to the hospital. Out-pensions were usually in the form of superannuation with claimants having to prove former service in the Navy. These claimants were able to hold other employment as in reality the superannuation was barely enough to live on. In many cases the recipients of a pension were still fairly young men. A somewhat unique feature of a Greenwich pension was that recipients were able to re-enter the Navy at any time but of course their pension then ceased to be paid until their subsequent discharge.

To qualify for pensions, ratings had to prove their service, which they did by certificates issued by the Navy Pay Office that can be found in series ADM 29. The certificate showed details of all their postings which were taken from information held in the ships' musters and pay lists. Before the introduction of continuous service records these certificates were the only official record of the careers of ratings. Collections of these certificates survive as the original certificates received by Greenwich, and in the Pay Office's entry books. These certificates of service have minimal content as they are not a service record as such giving only the name, rating, the ships served on and the duration of service on each. It is assumed that they are accurate but it is known in some cases that omissions exist or do not record information back to the start of a person's career.

After continuous service was introduced the aim was to grant a pension to all who completed 20 years' service. Many ratings entered as boys or young men, commencing their engagement as teenagers and therefore being able to retire in their late thirties or early forties. The Navy continued to employ their younger pensioners in the dockyards and other naval establishments. In reality there are not that many records surviving covering pensions but it is possible to piece together a pension history from the certificates of service, hospital registers and later the Continuous Service records.

Pensions and grants for disability or wounds were paid to ratings through the Chatham Chest, on production of their smart ticket (see earlier). Such records can be found in ADM 82 for 1653-1799, or ADM 22 for 1831-1837.

Greenwich In-Pension Records

In comparison to out-pensioners there were only a small number of in-pensioners but the records which exist are far more detailed when admission was sought or granted. The records held by the Greenwich Hospital cover 1790-1865 and can be searched by name index in series ADM 73. This series comprises of in-pensioners' admission papers for the period 1790 to 1865 which give a description of the person with the services in the Navy and the nature of any disablement. The entry books for both officers and pensioners cover the period 1704 to 1869 and these give full particulars of the individual and are mostly indexed. The out-pension pay books cover a fairly short period from 1781 to 1809. There are also a series of registers of allowances paid to wives or guardians of children for men who are in receipt of a Navy pension but who have been admitted to public lunatic asylums during the period 1899 to 1948.

The entry books list date of entry, name, age, marital status, number of children, where they were born, last place of residence albeit sometimes just the town rather than actual address, time served in the service, Navy trade (if any), the name of the last ship on which they served and cause of wounds or disablement. Some registers will also give a physical description and there is also a register for those ratings whose applications as in-pensioners were rejected. This only covers a fairly narrow period of 1742-1764.

Series ADM 6 also contains a large collection of volumes concerning applicants for admission to Greenwich Hospital and should be searched also. It relates to registers of candidates for Greenwich Hospital pensions or other relief and covers ratings for the period 1737-1834.

Of interest and to enable additional, sometimes revealing, background information to be obtained is piece number ADM 65/83. This piece contains primarily in-letters relative to the admission of pensioners to the Greenwich hospital but only covers the period 1782-1801.

Throughout this series or record you may well come across unfamiliar abbreviations used where a decision is recorded in the registers. P = hospital pension, CP = Chatham Chest pension, A = admitted, R = rejected, Pr No. = pension number allocated.

For some reason there is also a register of Greenwich Hospital pensions covering 1868-1870 found amongst the records of the Royal Hospital Chelsea records in piece WO 23/24. If you are searching during this period then this should not be ignored.

Greenwich Out-Pension Records

The first place to search is the Admiralty out letters within series ADM 2. These run between 1763 and 1815 and concern the nominations of people to become out-pensioners. Some have surname indexes. The most comprehensive set of records can be found in ADM 73 and these relate to payments given to ratings that were accepted as out-pensioners. These cover the period 1781 to 1809 and include the death dates.

Records of payments to ratings for the period 1814 to 1846 are in series ADM 22 and these are arranged by date and then by the initial of the surname of the seaman. Generally these also provide a death date.

In conjunction with the Royal Hospital Chelsea (the Army pension administrators) the records relating to ratings' pensions for the period 1842-1883 are within series WO 22. These records provide the date of commencement of the pension and whether it was a permanent or temporary pension. If the pension was terminated owing to death then the age and the date of death are recorded. A peculiarity exists in the organisation of the WO 22 documents as they are arranged by various areas in United Kingdom and also by foreign places. For a short period, namely 1863-1869 ratings' pensions are also recorded in the Greenwich papers contained within series ADM 73. Some records relating to rating pensioners who reside abroad can be found with returns in PMG 71, alongside those for naval officers.

Pensions to widows of Ratings

Widows of ratings who applied for pensions through the Chatham Chest and Royal Bounty underwent the same process as those for widows of officers. The pay books for pensions given to widows of ratings who died in service can be found in series ADM 82 for the early period of 1695-1779. The Royal Bounty records for widows and dependent children are in series ADM 106 which are principally pay lists giving name, address and relationship of the claimant alongside the name, rating and name of the ship on which the dead man served. Registers covering the Greenwich Hospital pensions granted between 1882 and 1917 are located in ADM 166. These contain a surname index (for which it is essential to know the name of the widow or child claiming) and the registers themselves provide details of the applicant as well as information relating to the deceased seaman. In many cases however they do not cover persons who died as a result of 'warlike' operations during the First World War only deaths in service for those who died in non-combatant roles.

First World War pension records have not been preserved in any great quantity. It is thought that only about 10% have been retained. PIN 71 contains selected files in regard to widows' pensions of ratings killed before the advent of the war. These can be quite interesting as they contain medical records and often the men's own accounts of the circumstances. The official records within the files contain information including physical description, place and date of birth, names of parents, wives and children and religious affiliation. Some records in this series work beyond the 1920s and may be subject to research restrictions.

The actual widows' pension records relating to ratings killed in action and administered between 1922 and 1926 are located in series ADM 23 with similar details found in the records of the Paymaster General records in series PMG 72. A sample (roughly 8%) of widows' pension forms relating to all branches of the armed forces but including some ratings' widows have been included in series PIN 82. These were records which were necessary for the Ministry of Pensions to administer the pension in the aftermath of the war. The forms can be quite informative if those for your ancestral naval family have survived. They record widow's name and address, details of the deceased seaman including the date place and circumstances of the death, details of the award including date, how much and for how long the awards was made. In some cases a copy of the death certificate was lodged as part of the claim and can be found within the records.

'Kings Freemen' - Ex-Royal Navy Sailors

Kings Freedom was not a pension facility but it was aimed at securing employment for discharged seamen. The term 'King's Freemen' could be construed as a misleading term as the King's Freemen were not freemen of the city or town but were given the right to trade without having to be time served (apprenticed) and being granted freemen. After having served, particularly in the various wars and for pressed men there was a continuing financial problem for the large number of returning sailors which frequently gave rise to social and economic problems.

Men often joined the Navy at a young age or ran away in the middle of an apprenticeship so they were never fully trained to make a living. Thus when they were discharged they found it difficult to find gainful employment in civilian life. At the time it was usual for towns and cities to forbid anyone, unless they were freemen, to trade within the bounds and consequently seamen returning from service often found it difficult, if not impossible, to find work.

In the late 1700s and early 1800s steps were taken by the government to make the transition back to employment easier for returning seamen without the restrictions of local customs, controls or byelaws. The Government actually passed three Acts of Parliament which permitted servicemen of all military divisions, not just the Royal Navy, who served any time after 1763, except those who deserted, to work in their chosen trades upon discharge. The Acts allowed those who were not freemen to act as if they were freemen in the course of their work. This facility was offered in many of the towns and cities throughout the country.

It was normal procedure for someone wanting to become a 'King's Freeman' to produce his discharge certificate, and sometimes other documents, in order to obtain what was deemed to be a certificate of entitlement enabling the ex-seaman to be free to trade and more importantly free from any subsequent prohibition action. In the City of London this certificate had to be issued by the City Chamberlain.

In many cases there are records held in local record offices. The London Metropolitan Archives holds over 4,000 sets of records for the City of London, mainly in the form of discharge papers (Ref COL/CHD/FR/11/04/001-011). Some papers are indexed and in the case of London the original documents are infrequently produced because of conservation issues so the index includes most of the genealogical information which could be found had access to the original papers been possible.

Certificates of entitlement were generally issued between 1784 and 1873 but dates on discharge papers may be as early as the late 1760s. It should be emphasised that in most cases the certificates of entitlement are not available as these were given to the person and became personal documents. Deposited discharge papers vary in content but it may be possible to find summaries of a man's service, baptism information etc. It is incumbent on you as a researcher to search locally if your ancestor was discharged in the above time period as the documents may provide essential clues for further research in ships' pay lists and musters etc.

Casualty and Wound Records

This aspect of research is considered important where a serving officer or rating fell ill, was injured as a result of an accident or was wounded as a result of warfare. If your ancestor fell victim to any of the above then it is worthwhile looking at both the medical journals/records and also the casualty and wound records. This information can be found in a variety of documents including ships' logs, musters and the like but in any case they run alongside the service record. We have already detailed the pension records etc. where a serving officer or rating was killed but there are many other records which record deaths.

Official Records of Deaths

The registers of deceased ratings' wage claims in series ADM 80 for the period 1787-1831 are arranged alphabetically up to 1809 and then by date that the wages reached the Pay Office up to 1831. They list the name of the rating and the ship's names. Some include death dates and others don't. Some also list the person to whom the wages were subsequently paid which was usually the next of kin.

For a ten year period between 1755 and 1765 there is a list of seamen who died whilst at the Royal Hospital Haslar in Gosport. These are found in ADM 102 and their usefulness is the fact that they list the ships on which the deceased served. Death certificates of those men who died at Plymouth Hospital between 1809 and 1815 can also be found in ADM 102. A post mortem book for the period 1829-1838 for deaths in the Malta Royal Naval Hospital can be found in ADM 104 as can case books relative to the Royal Naval Hospital Bermuda for the period 1832-1883.

Various other classes of document cover different periods:

- Deaths of POWs - 1793-1816 (mainly in France). ADM 103. These show the name, rank/rating, place of imprisonment and date of death.
- Deaths on board ships and in hospitals between 1823 and 1833 - ADM 105
- Officers (commissioned and warranted) obituary books 1833-1846. ADM 11. These show name and rank, half-pay details and dates of death.

Those killed or wounded at Kagoshima in August 1863, at Tel-El-Kebir in 1882, and at Vitu in November 1891 are listed in various editions of the *London Gazette* for the time period in question. These can be searched online or using series ZJ1 when at The National Archives.

The main set of records for the mid-19th and early 20th centuries relating to casualty and wound records are in series ADM 104. There are two series: one covering non war deaths and the other covering deaths by enemy actions. There are indexes covering most pieces some by surname and some by ship's name which detail name, rank, ship and then give a report page and a year of death. It is from the page number and year of death that you can locate the entry in the relevant register.

A successful search will return all or some of the following details of a seaman: rank, ship serving on, service number, date of death, date of notification of death, relative informed and address of the next of kin.

For the First World War the records of those killed in action or died of wounds can be located in ADM 242. These are the official records which were used on the Commonwealth War Graves 'Debt of Honour' database although less information is included online than on the official record. They are arranged in strict alphabetical order so if the name was misspelt by the Admiralty the person will be out of order and this is perpetuated through to the Commonwealth War Graves listing.

The casualty rolls give valuable information including: name of the individual, gallantry awards if any, official number and port division, branch of the service (the listing includes the reserves etc.), ship or unit, date and place of birth, date of death, cause of death (indicated by a code number), name of cemetery (or left blank if at sea), grave location and next of kin including address and relationship.

The July 1915 Navy List also lists both officers and ratings killed in action and subsequent volumes also contain an obituary listing for the duration of the war.

Births, Marriages and Deaths at Sea

Any of the log books kept by the Captain, Master or Lieutenant may well be the source of the details of an event relating to a crew member either whilst at sea or if the event took place on shore away from the ship. Log books of the hospital ships may also be a prime source for information relating to deaths of seamen away from home. This is equally true for members of the crews of merchant ships seconded to the Admiralty whether or not the crew member was Royal Navy Reservist or a merchant seaman.

For a short period from 1842 to 1879 returns extracted from the ships' logs were forwarded to the Bishop of London's Registry via the Admiralty for all marriages performed on HM Ships by either the Captain or the Navy Chaplain. Between 1880 and 1889 like returns were forwarded direct to the General Register Office. The records returned to the Bishop of London's registry are available through the City of London Joint Archive Service on microfilm and all the records form part of series RG 33 (indexed in RG 43) at The National Archives.

The returns made of births and deaths at sea are also part of the Bishop of London's Registry with an extended period of coverage from 1816 to 1924. Alongside this series are the Bishop of Gibraltar's baptisms for the early 20th century. Again these are in the custody of the City of London Joint Archive service and are on microfilm at the London Metropolitan Archives.

The Marine Births and Deaths registers held by the GRO also include events taking place on board Royal Navy ships from 1837.

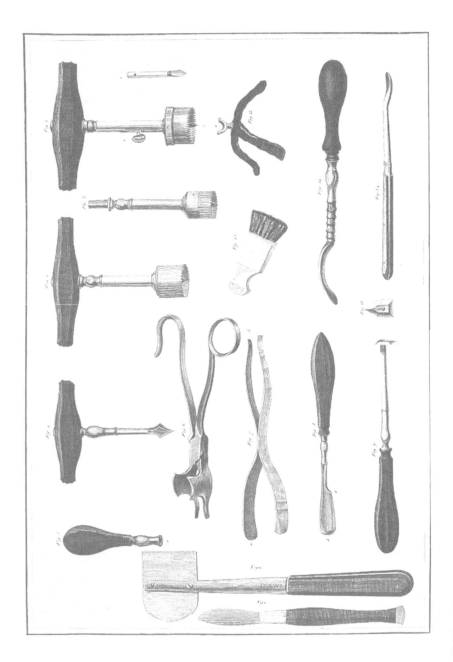

Royal Naval Surgeon's supplies from 'The Naval Surgeon Comprising the Entire Duties of Professional Men at Sea', by William Turnbull 1806. Public domain image.

CHAPTER FIFTEEN
Royal Naval Medical Service and its records

The Royal Navy Medical Service, as the name suggests, has been responsible for medical care where the medical officers were either surgeons or physicians. Throughout history every commissioned ship carried either a surgeon or assistant surgeon who treated patients, performed surgery and administered medication. Surgeons were certainly on board ships which sailed against the Armada of 1588.

The Barber-Surgeons Company undertook the training and examination of ships' surgeons for the Navy from the early 1600s and they also administered the supply of medicines and surgical instruments. Surgeons were occasionally subject to impressment.

The first milestone in naval medicine began with James Lind whose clinical trials aboard *HMS Salisbury* in 1747 developed a cure for scurvy, one of the most prevalent diseases amongst ships' crews at the time which was thought to have killed far more men than injury in battle.

Even in the early 1800s around the time of the Battle of Trafalgar there were massive losses amongst the seamen as a result of various diseases particularly relevant to the Africa stations. In the 1840s Alexander Bryson, a naval physician researched preventive measures against yellow fever and malaria. Mosquitoes were not identified as the cause of these diseases until the 1890s.

Medical officers and naval surgeons were allocated naval officer status in 1857 and at the same time became uniformed for the first time. In 1863 surgeons had to wear red distinction cloth between their gold ranking rings.

Officers and men of the service served in commissioned and convict ships, naval hospitals around the world and with the Naval brigades during the Crimean War. That war also signalled the founding of the Naval Nursing Service. During the First World War personnel saw service both ashore and at sea. With the development of other naval divisions such as the Submarine Service and the Royal Naval Air Service new and different medical challenges existed.

Medical Records

For those who were wounded or injured and did not die as a result you may be able to find details within the medical records which are essentially the journals compiled by the Navy surgeons who served on ships, in hospitals with the Naval Brigades or at foreign stations. Unfortunately only a selection of these journals survives but where they can be located they contain a wealth of information which can enhance any genealogical information.

The journals cover dates from around 1785 and many of the earlier journals relate to surgeons who served on convict transportation ships. Up to 1915 they are organised by ship's name and after then by year. They can be located in series ADM 101. Some of these journals can be accessed through PDF files online as part of the Wellcome Trusts' project 'Surgeons at Sea'.

Although the content of journals varies slightly most will provide information relating to the medical treatments given, the date of admission and discharge (often either back to the ship or on to a hospital), if the injury/illness was fatal, patients name, rank and number. If the patient was transferred to a naval hospital it is often possible to locate the person being admitted by reference to the hospital musters.

Hospital musters are available in series ADM 102 for hospitals at both home and abroad or on stationary hospital ships. Some hospital ships were attached to naval hospitals and as such the musters form part of that hospital's muster.

Up to the early 1790s the musters include:

• Name.
• Number.
• Pay number associated with the muster for the patient's ship.

- Name of ship.
- Date of admission.
- Type of disease or wound/injury.
- Discharge details. (The discharge details use the same coding as the ships' musters use).

After 1792 the musters include date and amount of allotments and information on stoppages from wages which was around 4d. per day.

It is also possible to find information in a series of other health and sickness returns maintained by the Admiralty. These can be located in the following classes:

- ADM 1 - Medical certificates of officers examined for pensions for wounds covering the period 1718-1816. A list of men discharged from Haslar as unfit in 1792.
- ADM 30 - Payments made to sick men at Plymouth and Gosport 1739-1742 and at Rochester, Woolwich, Plymouth and Deal in 1757-1758.
- ADM 97 - Correspondence specifically from medical staff relating to patients 1817-1832.
- ADM 105 - Reports on wounded officers 1779-1848. Case papers for men deemed to be lunatics 1812-1832. There are also lists of lunatics admitted to Haslar up to 1817 in series ADM 305. Various returns of patients at both Haslar and Plymouth hospitals during the 1820s and information on officers who were invalided whilst abroad between 1847 and 1863 can also be located as can a register of cases treated at Sheerness by the staff surgeon at the time 1867-1896.
- ADM 304 - relates to an entry book of patients to Malta RN Hospital 1804-1840. Muster books later admission and discharge registers for Malta Naval Hospital 1836-1895 and medical records of in-patients at Malta 1857-1859.
- ADM 305 - various records relating to Haslar including prescription books 1787-1792, surgeons' admission books 1897-1898, lunatic musters 1863 and the same for the outpost asylum at Haywards Heath for 1861.

There may be other records relating to health and sickness and as such you should filter your search using Discovery.

Unfortunately few records survive for patients during the First World War. However it may be possible to locate information about casualties using the war diaries of the various field ambulances, casualty clearing stations and H M Hospital ships. These diaries can be located in series WO 95 although clearly you will need to have some idea of the location of the medical units which can be found listed in series MH 106.

The MH 106 series of documents which is not complete mainly consists of admission and discharge registers and medical board reports. Researching the documents can however be fairly revealing as they include name, service number, rank, nature of illness and/or wounds, religion, surgical operations undertaken and fatality information, if that was the result.

The series which exists because of a collection of records for a statistical study of medical treatments at the time also includes operation records, x-ray registers and some WRNS medical sheets relating to certain hospitals.

Sick Berth Ratings

After several petitions and because of the inadequacy of the Greenwich Hospital capacity the Admiralty eventually heeded the recommendations of the Sick and Hurt Board and opened Haslar in 1753 followed closely by a second hospital at Stonehouse in 1762. This resulted in a significant improvement as up until this time many sick and wounded seamen from Portsmouth Naval base were billeted ashore in local taverns. Prior to 1762 it is known that in any one year approximately 800 were accommodated in this manner with many dying or absconding. By 1805 as well as the establishment of the base hospitals each ship was also fitted out with a sick berth using the space in the in the ship's bows.

By 1833 there were also around 40 Navy 'sick quarters' in the British Isles and at the same time the rating of sick berth attendant was also established. By 1884 the Navy had an establishment of trained sick berth rating staff. Their training consisted of professional training for a period up to one year at Haslar or Plymouth hospital - initially for three months, extended to six months, then to 12 months at Haslar or Plymouth Hospital. Further specialist training was also undertaken covering many medical specialities such as physiotherapy, dispensing, X-ray and operating theatre duties. During 1902 the Royal Navy Auxiliary Sick Berth Reserve was also created to work alongside trained sick-berth and nursing staff together with VADs and they did so in both world wars. The service records of medical reserve personnel are amongst those of the Royal Navy Volunteer Reserve as detailed previously.

Royal Naval Hospital at Haslar

The Royal Naval Hospital Haslar was opened in Gosport, Hampshire in 1753 and was not closed until 2007 thus making it the longest established military hospital in the UK. During its long and distinguished history it was the prime establishment for the medical care of naval personnel and included an asylum for sailors with psychiatric disorders.

In the early days of Haslar patients had to be transferred from their ships to the hospital by rowing boat and then be taken to the hospital wards and departments in basic wheeled cradles. By the late 1790s a bridge was built over Haslar Creek (after which the hospital was named) and a rail track was built to make the transfer of patients much easier.

Royal Naval Hospitals, Malta

The Royal Naval Hospitals at Bighi and Mtarfa were the major naval hospitals on the island of Malta. They served the eastern Mediterranean area throughout the 19th and into the 20th centuries.

The Bighi hospital took casualties in the first instance from the Crimean War and during the First World War took a large number of wounded from the Dardanelles campaigns.

The Royal Navy Hospital at Mtarfa was commissioned in 1912 and became the hospital for all British Forces, not just the Navy, in the eastern Mediterranean until the end of the 1970s. During the First World War it also took the wounded from the failed Gallipoli landings of 1915. Its main strategic importance was during the Second World War after it had expanded significantly.

British Military (later the Royal Naval) Hospital Gibraltar

Although technically this was an 'all service' hospital it again was heavily used by the Navy in both world wars. The British Military Hospital Gibraltar opened in about 1903 to provide medical care for local seamen based in or visiting Gibraltar which had a strategic Naval Dockyard.

During 1915 and throughout the First World War there was a continuous stream of wounded arriving from hospital ships coming from Gallipoli. Because the hospital's capacity was soon reached a series of satellite hospitals were created so that wounded sailors did not have to endure a long sea voyage back to the UK. Immediately prior to the Second World War the hospital was the main treatment base for wounded men from the Spanish Civil War.

In the Second World War casualties from the eastern Mediterranean, particularly Malta were treated at Gibraltar while their ships were serviced at the large Royal Navy Dockyard but again because of growing demand and the vulnerability to air attack a second subterranean hospital was built into the rock using a system of tunnels. The hospital was officially transferred to the administration of the Royal Navy in 1963 when it became known as the Royal Naval Hospital Gibraltar.

Royal Naval Hospitals

Royal Naval Hospital Great Yarmouth

The Royal Naval Hospital at Great Yarmouth had a capacity of 200 patients and was completed in 1811 and was principally used to treat the sick and wounded of the North Sea Fleet engaged in war with France.

The Hospital site covered an area of about 15 acres and was designed as four ward blocks around a courtyard. One block contained staff accommodation and utility offices and the remaining three blocks had two storey wards, chapel, operating theatres and mortuary.

For a period of time after the end of the wars with France the army used it as barracks and this continued until 1844 when it returned to medical use as a naval lunatic asylum. From 1846 when the Chatham hospital was no longer used the Chatham patients were transferred there. In 1849 patients from the Royal Hospital Kilmainham (Ireland) were also transferred there.

Following the outbreak of the Crimean War in 1854 the Hospital reverted to naval use only to take in naval wounded from the Baltic Fleet. There were none so it reverted to a soldiers' convalescent home.

By 1863, the Admiralty had reclaimed the hospital for use as a naval lunatic asylum and expanded the accommodation to provide new wards. When it re-opened patients were again transferred from the overcrowded Royal Naval Hospital Haslar. The Yarmouth Naval Hospital Act 1931 restricted admissions to naval (and Royal Marine) patients or to those civilians who had previous service within either branch.

Some medical registers are held by Norfolk County record office for the late 19th and early 20th centuries and it is thought that the James Paget NHS Hospital Trust at Gorleston may have further records within its archives. Victorian census returns will provide a 'snapshot' of patients and staff within the establishment.

The New Cemetery, attached to St Nicholas Church was the official burial ground for the Royal Naval Hospital patients until the latter part of the 19th century, covering the period 1883 to c.1906. There are 233 stone crosses with engraved metal plates giving name, rank, date of death and age but these are being systematically relocated so information is included below.

The listing below is of known Royal Navy personnel who are buried in the cemetery and for whom the memorials have been moved.

Name	Rank	Burial Date	Age
F W Adams	Gunner	11 Mar 1895	72
James Akhurst	Pensioner	29 Sept 1888	52
Thomas Anderson	Chief Engineer	14 Sept 1886	65
James Avery	Leading Shipwright	13 Oct 1899	37
William Bailey	Boy	20 Oct 1885	40
William Baker	Boatswain	19 Nov 1897	54
Frederick Barrett	Able Seaman	17 Aug 1896	60
Charles Barrington	Pensioner	19 Jan 1900	70
Patrick Barry	Petty Officer	4 Dec 1903	38
John Bartlett	Pensioner	18 Oct 1887	47
George Beasant	Stoker	10 Oct 1883	35
William Beer	Petty Officer 2nd Class	26 Jun 1898	32
Charles Bloomfield	Landsman	28 May 1894	73
William Board	Petty Officer 2nd Class	4 Jan 1895	33
William Hy Bolitho	Chief Stoker	27 Sept 1904	38
William Boniface	Pensioner	15 Jun 1906	47
John Booth	Boatman Coast Guard	24 May 1890	No age given
Edward Briggs	Pensioner Shipwright	3 Dec 1890	53
Charles E Briggs	Pensioner	8 May 1886	38
William Callaghan	Leading Seaman	19 Nov 1892	32
Walter Carr	S Actg Paymaster	11 Aug 1886	36
Henry Chadwick	Boatman Coast Guard	5 Dec 1897	32
Richard Chandler	Fleet Paymaster	30 May 1896	55
Alfred Chittenden	Able Seaman	21 Apr 1886	31
George Churchill	Boatman Coast Guard	1 Feb 1896	46
Job Clark	Commander	17 Dec 1885	89
George Cochlan	Able Seaman	27 Mar 1903	69
Michael Connolly	Petty Officer 1st Class	13 Jan 1898	38
William Cooper	Pensioner	6 Dec 1887	54
Edward Couch	Chief EBA	21 Dec 1902	48
Joshua Courtenay	Fleet Surgeon	8 Apr 1900	65
Samuel Crann	Leading Stoker	31 Oct 1896	36
Charles Crawley	Ordinary Seaman	1 Oct 1895	60
William Curling	Able Seaman	27 Nov 1894	34
John Curtis	Able Seaman	23 Jan 1900	83
Charles Davey	Pensioner	14 Oct 1886	56
David Day	Stoker	23 Jan 1901	44
Henry De Ridder	Paymaster In Chief	21 July 1900	62
George Deal	Pensioner Coast Guard	29 Mar 1902	69
Edward Dee	Able Seaman	23 Oct 1894	54

Name	Rank	Burial Date	Age
George Dimmick	Chief ERA	22 Dec 1900	39
Henry Downing	Sail maker	11 May 1895	30
Dennis Driscoll	Quarter Master	11 May 1886	38
Harry Duke	Armourer	27 Jan 1893	34
Samuel Edmiston	Pensioner	2 Mar 1888	47
Thomas Edney	Pensioner	3 Jun 1892	35
John Evans	Stoker	27 Dec 1893	33
Andrew Fardy	Leading Seaman	11 Aug 1884	32
William Farley	Boatman Coast Guard	5 Oct 1892	39
Mark Ford	Pensioner	13 Nov 1885	69
John Forse	Boatman Coast Guard	14 Jan 1894	39
William Fowler	Ordinary Seaman	14 Dec 1884	45
Edward Fryer	Seaman	4 Feb 1901	69
John Furneaux	Midshipman	24 Nov 1887	75
Joseph Gank	Petty Officer	9 Sept 1893	43
Edward Gibbs	Stoker	28 Dec 1884	54
George Gibson	Boatman Coast Guard	18 Aug 1902	38
Robert Gilchrist	Asst. Engineer	1 Nov 1902	67
Joseph Gillias	Captain Quarterdeck	17 May 1889	45
John Grady	Able Seaman	16 Dec 1898	56
William Greenslade	Ship's Corporal	26 Feb 1884	32
Edward Gregory	Pensioner	24 Dec 1887	73
William Groom	Pensioner	24 Feb 1893	45
Harry Harris	ERA	22 May 1895	33
William Harwell	Able Seaman	10 Feb 1900	78
Richard Hayes	Stoker	12 Aug 1896	69
Charles Heal	Able Seaman	3 Feb 1890	44
James Hegarty	Asst. Engineer	12 May 1888	32
Samuel Hemer	Master At Arms	8 Jun 1899	43
Joseph Hemmings	Pensioner	5 Aug 1896	75
John Henessey	Boatman Coast Guard	4 Aug 1884	53
William Henty	Able Seaman	13 Mar 1890	42
Alex Heseltine	Vice Admiral	16 Feb 1885	76
Byron Hext	Ordinary Seaman	30 Mar 1890	31
John Holmes	Pensioner	29 Sept 1887	51
John Jackson	Able Seaman	16 Nov 1891	56
William Jennings	Leading Stoker	4 Jun 1900	42
David Kirk	Gunner	25 Nov 1888	45
Thomas Lakerman	Boatswain	30 Mar 1898	70
William Lamb	Gunner	25 Nov 1886	65

Name	Rank	Burial Date	Age
Charles Lamerton	Chief Stoker	21 Dec 1904	35
John Lane	Able Seaman	18 May 1884	34
Henry Light	Leading Stoker	27 Aug 1886	41
Richard Lloyd	Boatman Coast Guard	8 July 1901	39
John Locock	Boatman Coast Guard	17 Apr 1895	37
William Lugg	Boatman Coast Guard	22 Nov 1901	31
John Lundy	Schoolmaster	14 Oct 1886	32
James Lydon	Cdr Bman. Coast Guard	25 Jan 1905	35
Bryan MacDermott	Fleet Surgeon	28 Nov 1892	49
Arthur Madden	Chief ERA	29 Mar 1904	50
John Maher	Boatman Coast Guard	3 Nov 1888	57
Richard Marchall	Stoker	5 Feb 1892	35
James Martin	Pensioner	17 Mar 1896	35
Thomas Matthias	Cdr Bman Coast Guard	23 Dec 1898	43
William May	Pensioner	3 Dec 1885	63
Henry May	1st Class Petty Officer	6 Aug 1902	37
John McCarthy	Able Seaman	2 May 1903	86
James McCarthy	Seaman	7 Mar 1900	88
William McLaughlan	Pensioner	26 Sept 1899	74
Donald McLeod	Leading Seaman	21 Feb 1895	27
William Metcalf	Petty Officer Pensioner	19 Jun 1901	46
John Miller	Lieutenant	3 Dec 1889	66
John Miller	Pensioner	24 Apr 1895	49
Joseph Minhinnick	Fleet Surgeon	29 Jan 1892	51
Thomas Miseroy	Seaman	8 May 1894	74
Frederick Mitchell	Petty Officer 1st Class	31 May 1898	33
Mortimer Montague	Able Seaman	24 Apr 1891	40
Archibald Moorhead	Boatman Coast Guard	18 Oct 1895	35
Charles Morley	Caulker	20 Mar 1884	73
John Morris	Petty Officer 1st Class	17 Dec 1893	49
Henry Morrish	Petty Officer 1st Class	10 Jan 1898	45
John Mosedale	Pensioner	6 Jan 1885	43
Samuel Moseley	Pensioner	3 Aug 1892	38
William Motton	ERA	29 Aug 1890	42
Edward Murch	Painter	29 July 1895	37
Edward Murphey	Boatman Coast Guard	26 Mar 1887	29
Arthur Napper	Boatman Coast Guard	12 Feb 1893	37
Edwin North	Pensioner	27 Aug 1890	68
James Outen	Chief Armourer	16 Mar 1899	35
William Parkin	Gunner	14 July 1888	34

Name	Rank	Burial Date	Age
Frederick Peate	Pensioner	22 Jul 1887	84
Albert Petworth	Petty Officer 1st Class	22 Jun 1898	29
John Porter	Armourer	19 Dec 1884	57
Edwin Pritchard	Pensioner	7 Jul 1884	39
William Rabbage	Staff Engineer	9 Mar 1896	41
Frank Rawlings	Petty Officer 1st Class	25 Feb 1898	32
William Rees	Ordinary Seaman	24 Jun 1894	62
Arthur Renfry	Engineer	6 Feb 1894	45
Thomas Rice	Boatswain	7 Feb 1902	50
Frederick Rich	Chief Stoker	22 Oct 1902	34
John Roper	Seaman	11 Dec 1893	82
George Sackville	Petty Officer	2 Jul 1904	45
Frederick Saill	Petty Officer	20 May 1896	35
John Scott	Lieutenant	23 Feb 1888	42
William Searle	Bandsman	22 Feb 1894	54
George Skates	Boatman Coast Guard	29 Nov 1883	40
John Smith	Cmd Bman Coast Guard	23 Dec 1899	55
H. Smith	Petty Officer 2nd Class	6 Sept 1901	32
Henry A. Smith	Pensioner	14 Feb 1890	49
Arthur Snell	Boatman Coast Guard	2 Oct 1897	33
William Spain	Acting 2nd Master	15 Jan 1898	57
Francis Staddon	Painter	20 Feb 1902	31
William Staddon	Boatman Coast Guard	23 Oct 1900	33
Arthur Stewart	2nd Class Petty Officer	21 Feb 1886	33
Edward Stone	Ship's Cook	14 Oct 1886	37
James Stuart	Boatswain	29 Apr 1887	53
Charles Suitors	Cmd Bman Coast Guard	9 Feb 1884	48
Charles Tamlin	Boatman Coast Guard	2 Jan 1892	35
John Taylor	Leading Stoker	20 Jun 1898	32
John Thomas	Able Seaman	4 Jan 1898	69
Thomas Thompson	Boatman Coast Guard	15 Jun 1901	37
Edwin Thorn	2nd Class Petty Officer	15 Apr 1902	37
Francis Tighe	Bandsman	21 Jun 1894	41
James Tool	Able Seaman Pensioner	10 Oct 1894	49
William Trew	Boatman Coast Guard	1 Dec 1900	43
Richard Truskett	Domestic 1st Class	16 Apr 1899	44
Joseph Turner	Yeoman of Stores	12 Jun 1891	57
Michael Ward	Cmd Bman Coast Guard	6 Apr 1898	43
William Waterman	1st Class Petty Officer	23 Nov 1902	36
William Weller	Pensioner	10 May 1887	65

Name	Rank	Burial Date	Age
Arthur West	ERA	22 Jan 1894	39
John West	Ordinary Seaman	3 Jan 1892	73
George Westlake	Boatman Coast Guard	9 Dec 1897	34
James White	Petty Officer 1st Class	26 May 1901	47
Thomas Williams	Ordinary Seaman	5 Sept 1894	69
Samuel Wilson	Stoker	13 Nov 1883	48
James Wilson	Engineer	28 May 1889	53
John Wood	Staff Surgeon	26 Jul 1887	38
Henry Wood	Pensioner	1 Nov 1889	42

There were also memorials to members of the Royal Marines and the various East India Marine services.

Medway Maritime Hospital

The hospital was a Royal Naval Hospital opened in 1905 to replace the Melville Naval Hospital which was too small to accommodate an increasing number of naval personnel moving into Chatham. When it opened it had a staff of nine medical officers, seven nursing sisters and around 70 attendants. The Melville subsequently became a Royal Marines barracks.

From 1810 to 1828 sick and wounded sailors who were suffering mainly from diseases such as cholera, smallpox and typhoid were looked after on hospital hulks moored on the River Medway. In 1828 Melville Naval Hospital was opened in a location opposite the Chatham Dockyard main gates catering for 252 patients.

Burials from the hospital took place in the Woodlands cemetery where there is a large naval section which was reserved by the Admiralty and served the Royal Naval Hospital in Windmill Road.

Hoxton Naval Asylum

In 1695 Hoxton House, then privately owned, became the asylum used by the Royal Navy up to 1818 housing those servicemen and ex-servicemen (both officers and seamen) who became mentally ill. They were financed by Chatham Chest funds. Records exist at The National Archives in the form of Hoxton House hospital muster books in ADM 102 for the period 1755 to 1818. Generally the naval lunatics were maintained at public expense and an allowance was made each year in the naval estimates for their upkeep. After 1818 they were transferred to Haslar. The number of Royal Navy lunatics housed in the hospital varied. In 1793 there were only 19 Navy patients but this gradually increased reaching its peak in by 1814 at around 140/150 men.

CHAPTER SIXTEEN
Royal Navy and the Coastguard

It is possible that you will find someone who has served in the Royal Navy transferring to the Coastguard service. The Navy controlled both officers and boatmen who transferred. The organisation was particularly popular amongst Petty Officers and senior ratings and any Coastguard service is usually noted on their Royal Navy Continuous Service record. However many served much earlier and this section deals with the records that will enable you to confirm whether or not your ancestor served in the Coastguard. Not all coastguard officers were previously employed by the Royal Navy.

Members of the Coastguard were frequently transferred to different stations ultimately with men settling in the last place of appointment on retirement which was often miles from their established family or places of birth. With this in mind it is sometimes difficult to keep abreast of the movement around the country and there is a useful database **www.genuki.org.uk/big/coastguard** compiled mainly from the Victorian census returns of coastguard officers that includes: name of the officer, date and place of birth, the location of employment and details of the family (wife, children etc.). Men of the Coastguard also spent time on board HM ships undertaking 'drill service', normally for a period of about 10/14 days.

The establishment and history of the Coastguard Service

The Coastguard Service as we know it today, commenced in 1822 following the amalgamation of three services which had been in operation prior to that time namely the Revenue Cruisers, the Riding Officers and the Preventive Water Guard. In 1832 they were joined by the Coastal Blockade. Its purpose was to prevent smuggling. From 1856 it also provided a reserve for the Royal Navy and from 1925 it undertook its modern role of saving lives and salvaging wrecks.

Throughout its modern history the Coastguard has fallen under the control of various government departments. The Admiralty had control of the Coastguard from 1856-1923 and during the Second World War.

It was on the revenue cruisers that Royal Navy crews existed. The cruisers were used initially to patrol the coastal waters of south east England as well as the Thames estuary but from 1800 the cruiser fleet was enlarged to cover all of the United Kingdom and Ireland.

The Boards of the Customs and of Excise were responsible for the prevention of the avoidance of duty due on imported goods and by the end of the 17th century they had a relatively small fleet of boats and some men who were shore based around the coast. The service continued to expand throughout the 18th century by the use of Navy vessels and Navy manned revenue cruisers. Because the organisation struggled to prevent smuggling the Preventive Water Guard was established in 1809 and Britain's coast was divided into three divisions with a Royal Navy officer known as an Inspecting Captain appointed for each division and given command of a fleet of cruisers and boats.

At the end of the Napoleonic wars the preventive cruisers came under the control of the Admiralty having previously been responsible to the Treasury. The preventive Water Guard operated in coastal waters to try and tackle the smugglers who evaded the Revenue Cruisers. All recruitment at this time was from discharged Royal Navy sailors. (Continuous service had not commenced at this time so sailors were discharged at the termination of voyages.)

In 1816 the Preventive Water Guard was withdrawn from the Kent coast and replaced by a shore based Naval Brigade whose job it was to intercept smugglers as they came ashore. This was the start of the coast blockade which patrolled from the Isle of Sheppey to Seaford in Sussex. The blockade proved to be the most effective force to counteract smuggling although some of its methods were unorthodox. It functioned as a separate unit until it became part of the Coastguard. A similar force was established in Ireland in 1819.

In 1820 the organisation comprised of 2,375 men employed on Navy ships and vessels, 1,533 men in Admiralty controlled Revenue Cruisers, and 1,276 in the Coast Blockade. From 15 January 1822 the component organisations joined forces to become the Coastguard.

On inception certain Navy ships were assigned to the coastguard service. The ships from Plymouth were *Spartan, Lee, Helicon, Wolf, Alban, Pigmy, Dwarf* and *Scorpion*; from Portsmouth were *Redpole, Hind, Cameleon, Grecian, Starling, Linnet, Viper* and *Quail*; from Sheerness were *Wye, Alert, Brisk, Surly, Swan, Pioneer, Severn, Asp* and *Seagull*; and from Leith were *Nimrod, Driver, Cherokee, Swinger, Martial* and *Nimble*. They formed part of the Permanent Cruiser Force and the Guard ships.

In 1831 the Admiralty obtained the right to appoint Coastguard officers and to select boatmen from paid off naval crews thus enabling the organisation to become a Royal Navy reserve force as well as a recruiting facility for the Navy. The Coastguard was popular because the salary was usually better than they were getting as seamen in the Navy.

During the Crimean War over 3,000 coastguards served as members of the Royal Navy. At the end of the Crimea War in 1856 the Coastguard was transferred to the Admiralty. By this time smuggling was declining and Naval Reserve aspects were of much more importance.

Royal Navy battleships became the headquarters of the coastguard and these were stationed at various ports around the country. In 1858 the coast was divided up into districts, four for England, Wales and Scotland and two for Ireland. As things progressed towards the 20th century the Coastguard had become an outmoded naval reserve. The Admiralty wanted to reduce the establishment within the Coastguard which was opposed by the public and also by the Board of Trade and the Board of Customs as they felt this would reduce its effectiveness in both life-saving and revenue protection.

The Coastguard was staffed by Royal Navy personnel, naval pensioners, Merchant Seamen (who may have also seen Royal Navy service), former Customs and Excise men and civilians. They were frequently awarded prize money for the capture of smugglers and the seizure of contraband.

59. Coast Guard crew of a Sussex station.

During the First World War many from the Coastguard establishment crewed Royal Navy ships. In 1914 the German submarines sank five Cruisers resulting in the deaths of nearly 1,400 coastguard officers. At this time the shore based Coastguard stations also performed an essential role for the Admiralty sending messages between the Admiralty and ships at sea, using their wireless telegraphy facilities. The shore based members of the Coastguard service also served to render beached mines safe.

Conditions of Service

Throughout its history regulations have determined who can serve and under what conditions. In June 1831 the following Admiralty regulations applied:

'All Seamen who may enter the Coast Guard Service from His Majesty's Navy are to be subject in every respect to the control, the discipline, and the regulations by which the Coast Guard Service is governed'.

'The vacant situations of Boatmen will be filled up from time to time, by Seamen, as Ships o! War are paid off; of which the Captain or Commanding Officer shall select a given number according to the vacancies, of which he will be informed, from the Ships' Company, of the men whom he shall judge to be entitled to fill these situations, and who may be desirous of entering this Service'.

'The Captain or Commanding Officer shall make this selection with the strictest impartiality, and shall transmit to the Admiralty, to duplicate, a list of the names so selected, stating them to be the men best entitled of the Ship's Company: together with a duplicate Certificate of each, according to the following form, one copy to be kept as a Record at the Admiralty, the other to be transmitted with the appointment to the Board of Customs'.

Typical certificate for a candidate for the situation of Boatman:

'This is to certify that _____ has served under my orders ____ years. (Former service was also usually included - if known)

That he has been sober, attentive, and obedient to command, and is a healthy, active, and good Seaman, not more than 30 years of age, nor under 5ft. 5in. high, and is in all respects fit for the situation of Boatman in the Coast Guard Service; and I consider him as one of those best entitled to that reward, for good services, of any Seamen under my command who are fit for the Coast Guard and desirous to enter it.'

Under the Coastguard Act in 1856 the following Admiralty Regulations applied:

'Seamen who have served seven years* with 'man's ratings' in any ship of Her Majesty's navy, and not exceeding 37 years* of age, are eligible, on their ship being paid off, for service in the Coastguard, upon their receiving the necessary certificate of good conduct from the commanding officer of such ship.

When a ship is ordered to be paid off, the commanding officer will send to the Admiralty a list of the men whom he recommends for admission to the Coastguard.

Continuous service men are eligible for the Coastguard, although they may not have completed the term of service for which they entered

Seamen gunners on board the gunnery training ships may be recommended for the Coastguard by the captains of those ships when they have completed the five years' service as seamen gunners, provided they are otherwise qualified.

Men who have served seven years, with 'man's ratings,' in a revenue cruiser, and not exceeding 37 years of age, may be appointed to the Coastguard on the recommendation of the Controller-General.

The men so selected will be directed to join any district where there maybe vacancies, and will be placed on the books of the Coastguard ship of that district, and victualled on board until lodgings are provided for them and they can be transferred to the shore.

They will be rated in the first instance as boatmen, and may be promoted, if deserving, to be commissioned boatmen, and from commissioned boatmen to be chief boatmen.

Boatmen will receive the pay of A. B. continuous service.

Commissioned boatmen that of leading seamen continuous service.

Chief boatmen that of first-class petty officers continuous service.

Coastguard-men doing duty on shore will be allowed 1s. 4d. per day in lieu of their provisions, and lodgings will be provided for themselves and families free of rent'.

Yet again in 1875 the regulations changed as follows:

'Seamen of good character who have served in Her Majesty's Navy 8 years with Man's rating (continuous service), provided their age does not emceed 37 years will be eligible for entry in the Coast Guard upon the recommendation of their Commanding Officer.

There will be no restriction as to the number of Candidates to be recommended from any particular Ship: but the admissions will depend upon the number of vacancies.

None but Trained Men and Seamen Gunners will be appointed, and all Candidates must be Badge Men.

Seamen Gunners will not be allowed to retain their Gunnery Pay, except when actually doing as Instructors, but all Trained Men, including Seamen Gunners will be allowed their Gunnery Pay of One Penny a-day.

All Coast Guard Men will be liable to be embarked in turn for such cruise as the Lords Commissioners of the Admiralty may appoint, and if found unfit for active service at sea, they will be discharged with such pension or gratuity as they may be entitled to from their services.

The age for absolute discharge from the Coast Guard whether fit for service or not, will be for:-

Boatmen - 50

Commissioned Boatmen - 50

Chief Boatmen - 50

Chief Boatmen in charge - 55

A limited number of Stokers will be admitted, provided they have qualified as Trained Men.

Divisional Carpenters of the Coast Guard will be appointed, as vacancies occur, from Artificers of the Carpenter Class serving in the Fleet.

Men who enter the Coast Guard must renew their continuous service engagements while serving in that force, and they will only be appointed on that condition.'

Uniforms

There was no set uniform for early Coastguard personnel although uniforms of sorts had existed from 1821. If you have a photograph of a coastguard officer in a uniform then the following may be a useful but not conclusive guide. Details of the uniforms in the early days are sketchy. The first attempt at an official uniform took place in the 1820s.

The items which were used to identify a coastguard officer were the belts and braces which were made of leather and included a portfire case, pistol holster and cartouche.

60. Examples of Coastguard Uniforms.

In 1821 it was deemed that every person was to wear the uniform according to his rank. Those who were Navy officers continued to wear their uniform of rank if they were appointed to Inspecting Commanders, Commanders on cruisers or Chief Officers of stations. Cruiser commanders who were not naval officers wore a different uniform.

For many other officer ranks the Navy uniform was the norm. Mates on Cruisers wore the same uniforms as Navy Commanders except the notched button holes at neck and cuff were black and not gold.

Chief Boatmen and Commander Boatmen wore blue round double breasted jackets with 10 uniform buttons on each side, a stand up collar, three notched button holes and cuff buttons. They also wore blue single breasted waistcoats with nine buttons and blue or white trousers. The wearing of trousers depended upon what task was being performed and also at the discretion of the station commander. The hat was a plain round hat. Boatmen wore the same uniform except there were no notched button holes or buttons to collar and cuff.

In 1841 the uniforms changed slightly. Naval officers wore a great coat with epaulettes, cap and side arms respective to their rank. Chief boatmen continued to wear the same uniform as earlier but with a cloth cap incorporating the 'CG' cypher and a badge on their right sleeve at upper arm level of an embroidered crown and anchor. Commander Boatmen wore an anchor badge only and boatmen had no insignia on their arm.

In 1866 Inspecting Chief Officers and Chief Officers of stations wore the naval uniform of a second mate with Coastguard buttons. Chief Boatmen wore the uniform of a Warrant Officer but again with CG buttons. Commander Boatmen wore the uniform of a 1st Class Petty Officer in the RN with either a hat or cap incorporating a band with the words 'Coast Guard' on the band.

61. Hat badge worn by Coast Guard Officers.

As we get closer to the 20th Century the uniforms were increasingly those as worn by equivalent ranks in the Royal Navy. Chief Officers on Cruisers and Inspecting Chief Officers wore the uniform of a 2nd Lieutenant with CG buttons. Mates on Cruisers wore the uniform of a Sub Lieutenant and boatmen wore either the uniform of a Warrant or Petty Officer depending on their rank. The only difference was the CG button. Coast Guard buttons were abolished on uniforms in 1902.

In the late 1800s and early 1900s officers of the Navy who held appointments in the coastguards were required to wear as their uniform 'the official undress uniform associated with their rank'. Their caps included a crown and the word 'Coastguard' surrounding the crown. Boatmen essentially wore the same uniform as a naval rating but the hatband would include the words 'Coast Guard' or reference to whichever group they belonged.

Just before the First World War the uniform included a double breasted frock coat with nine buttons on either side.

In 1921 the Coastguard uniform altered and the cap badge was the same as a senior petty officer in the Royal Navy. Other coastguard badges varied depending upon grade or rank.

Coastguard Service Records

As the Coastguard has been administered by many departments at different times during its existence documents relating to the service are widely scattered among those department records. This element relates mainly to those administered by the Admiralty as we are concentrating on the overlap between the Royal Navy and the Coastguard. Many Merchant Seamen were also in the Coastguard. After 1856 when the East India Company relinquished its Navy, many members of the Bengal Marine entered the Coastguard service having returned to the United Kingdom. There is an unexplained gap in the records of the Coastguard between 1866 and 1886 but it may be possible to build up a picture from published sources and administrative records. Available finding aids and indexes are not always complete so a search of the original records is always necessary.

Published Material

Various published material exists which enable identification of ancestors within the coastguard service. Most of these are available at The National Archives and in various copyright libraries:

• Coastguard officers and civilians appear in the Navy Lists from 1822 onwards.
• Returns of Officers and Men of the Preventive Boat Service 1816-1891 - this will provide name, age, place of birth, trade, time at sea, salary and list of appointments.
• Men of the Coast Blockade killed on the Kent and Sussex Coasts 1821-1825.
• Return of Captains and Commanders in the Coastguard Service and on Revenue Cruisers 1 July 1833.
• Return of Chief Officers of the Coastguard 1857.

The Coastguard service also had its official newspapers/magazines which are available at the British Library. Besides articles of interest to those serving as Coast Guards (both Naval and civilian) there were records of changes at stations and on cruisers, promotions, obituaries etc. Some of the newspapers were also the official organs of the Coastguard Benevolent Fund:

- *Hope* published February 1891 - December 1899.
- *The Blue Jacket & Coastguard Gazette* published from January 1900 - March 1909.
- *The Blue Jacket* published from August 1909 - June 1920.
- Various other magazines have been published since.

First steps in finding a record

In the first instance the service for any rating within the coastguard after 1873 should be recorded on the continuous engagement service record found in ADM 188.

The Coastguard Index

For many years the late Eileen Stage worked on indexing references to coastguards from various sources. Unfortunately she died while the index was still in progress so it is impossible to establish how complete it is but it is an essential starting point for information. The index is deposited with the Society of Genealogists and is currently being scanned and indexed for inclusion within the online records. Until then the original index is housed in the Lower Library and comprises of paper/card slips and document files.

The index consists of a series of individual cards originally thought to be an index in its own right to the many who served in the Coastguard service and also in part to the personal service sheets and a ring bound database. Some of the cards give basic information such as name, birth information, service together with a reference to the original documents and information about physical description etc. Others are just name and reference cards.

The *Personal Service Sheets* are extracted mainly from Admiralty records and census returns. These contain a wealth of information which summarises a coastguard's service including name, birth information, marriage details, children born whilst in the service, seamen's history, reference to any musters checked etc., information on the stations served at including dates, rank, promotions and the document reference, pensions or superannuation and death date. Where a coastguard also held a Merchant Seaman ticket that information is also included together with the reference to find the ticket in the original records. The content of the sheets does vary.

Samuel WAKERELL born Bermondsey, Surrey 11 October 1802

1818 First went to sea as an apprentice) see seaman's ticket
) 222,219   BT 113/112
Served 7 years in Royal Navy   )

COASTGUARD ESTABLISHMENT BOOKS
MARTELLO TOWER No.42 station: RYE port: HASTINGS district ADM 175/5 p278
Nomination No. 3395
Nominated 19 July 1832 from London
Samuel WAKERELL, boatman
Removed 15 September 1832 to COCKLESHELL HARD 17163/32

COCKLESHELL HARD station: ROCHESTER port: GRAVESEND district ADM 175/6 p10
15 September 1832 from No.42 TOWER
Samuel WAKERELL, boatman
Removed 14 June 1834 to PORTREATH R2962

PORTREATH station: ST.IVES port: PADSTOW district   ADM 175/6 p249
R2962 14 June 1834 from COCKLESHELL HARD
Samuel WAKERELL, boatman
Removed and promoted 2 November 1837 to LEPE R3544

LEPE station: SOUTHAMPTON port: LYMINGTON district   ADM 175/6 p164
R3544 2 November 1837 from PORTREATH
Samuuel WAKERELL, commissioned boatman
Removed and reduced 11 May 1839 to KINGSGATE R354

KINGSGATE station: RAMSGATE port: DEAL district   ADM 175/7 p47
R354 11 May 1839 from LEPE
Samuel WAKERELL, boatman

#1841 census KINGSGATE Coastguard station
WAKERELL, Samuel

Seaman's ticket No. 222,219   BT 113/112
Samuel WAKERELL born Bermondsey, Surrey 11 October 1802
Capacity: boatman coastguard
Height 5'5" Complexion dark Hair nearly black Eyes hazel
Marks: MERMAID & CRUCIFIX on right arm
First went to sea as apprentice 1818
Has served in Royal Navy: Yes 7 years
Been in foreign service [ie American, French merchant service] NO
When unemployed resides NO [sic]
Ticket issued RAMSGATE 4 June 1845
Age when ticketed 42:   Can write:: YES
CG boatman KINGSGATE station: DEAL district

62a. Example of information contained in the Coastguard Index (Society of Genealogists).

John WEEKS Born 1774 – Died 14 October 1842

*checked H M Revenue Cutter DILIGENCE muster & description books
ADM/36 13454 [sic] & ADM 37/1590
1st April 1809 – 31 December 1809 but John WEEKS not mentioned.

*Living Llanstadwell, nr Milford Haven where he was mate of the Revenue lugger
DILIGENCE from at lease 1795 – 1809.

*married twice at Llanstadwell, the 2nd time 12 Oct.1809. [per parish records]

*7 February 1811 birth of child in Muncaster, Cumberland
   father: Captain of a King's boat stationed at Ravenglass [per parish records0

PREVENTIVE WATER GUARD Establishment Books
*Ravenglass station; Whitehaven port   ADM 175/2
15 November 1816
John WEEKS, chief officer
Removed 19 April 1822 to Maryport
[notation in pencil bracketing John WEEKS with 7 other staff stated
transferred from Customs 15 November 1816

*Maryport station; Whitehaven port   ADM 175/1
R1157 19 April 1822 from Ravenglass
John WEEKS, chief officer
Station withdrawn 21 November 1822 when he was removed to
Port Eyron

*Port Eyron station; Swansea port   ADM 175/1
R1315 21 November 1822 from Maryport
John WEEKS, chief officer
Removed 21 August 1823 to Black Halls

*Black Halls station, Stockton port   ADM 175/3
R162 21 August 1823 from Port Eyron
John WEEKS, chief officer
Removed 25 September 1827 to Blyth Haven

*Blyth Haven station; Newcastle port   ADM 175/ 3 & 5
R1008 25 September 1827 from Black Halls
John WEEKS, chief officer
Discharged 13 January 1837 susperannuated

Permanent Superannuation – not listed   CUST 39/145

+Died 15 October 1842

62b. Another example from a Coastguard Index (Society of Genealogists).

The *Database of Merchant Seamen*, within the Coastguard Index has information contained in the bound volumes which is essentially a printout of a computer generated database relating mainly to the Merchant Seamen who joined the Coastguard Service. Some of these men also had Royal Navy service and are cross referenced to the personal service sheets. The database takes the form of name, year of birth, town, county/country, ticket number, the BT 113 piece number for the ticket, coastguard station and district, rank and whether served in the Royal Navy. As the database only mentions one station it is not possible to locate a date of service at that station so reference needs to be made either to the personal service sheet or individual record card.

In some cases there is a record in only one section of the index but a search of all three sections is needed.

Establishment Books

The main series of official records at TNA relate to the Establishment Books which run between 1816 and 1947 in series ADM 175. From 1921 onwards these records relate to what has become known as the 'New Coastguard Force'.

ADM 175 is part of the Digital Microfilm project and as such can be downloaded free of charge using Discovery. It is important to remember that they are not always comprehensive but the series does include records of service for Coastguards between 1816-1918; ships' record books, 1858-1879; registers of nominations for appointments between 1819-1866; service records of Royal Naval ratings between 1900-1923; registers of discharges from 1858-1868 and 1919 and; indexed service registers for coastguard officers 1896-1829.

More specifically if you know where your Coastguard officer served then there are registers of appointments for England (1819-1862); for Ireland (1819-1849); and for Scotland (1851-1856).

Within the establishment books certain abbreviations are used to denote ranks as follows:

* Chf officer - chief officer.
* Boatn - boatman (if preceded by chf then this relates to chief boatman).
* Permt extn - permanent extraman.
* Comd bn - Commissioned boatman.
* Tempoy exn - Temporary extraman.

Within ADM 175 there are various records which provide useful information for family historians.

Establishment books contain:

- Name.
- Rank (within the Coastguard organisation) - some give former RN rank.
- Name of Station or Cruiser.
- Cause of discharge.
- Date of discharge.
- Registered ticket number (if any).

Discharge records provide similar information but frequently include remarks regarding conduct, character and achievements.

The Coastguard record cards contain more useful information namely:

- Name.
- Official number (will be the same as the RN for continuous service).
- Date of birth.
- Religion.
- Place of Nativity (birth) for self and wife.
- Marital status.
- Last rating afloat (in the Royal or Merchant Navy).
- Passing date for proficiency examinations etc.
- Seniority (separated for the old and new force).
- Children (statistics giving sex and age).
- Awards.
- Remarks.

In order to locate a coastguard within the establishment books you will need to know where the officer served or was posted. In order to do this it is useful to access the Coastguard database through GENUKI (see above) as this covers the names of all coastguard officers as shown in the census returns from 1841-1891 which shows information including the name, date and place of birth, location at the time of the census and some family details usually including the name of the wife and names of children. All the entries have been transcribed from the census returns so the information may not always be accurate but it is an excellent tool to discover locations of Coastguards over a 50 year period. Not all Coastguard personnel are necessarily included as those whose careers started and ended between census returns will not appear.

Appointment Books

Between 1816 and 1831 selected Royal Navy officers were appointed to Revenue Cruisers. These were mainly Lieutenants, boatswains and master and as such the records of appointment can be found specifically in ADM 6/56. The appointment of boatmen to the coastguard for the period 1831 to 1850 can also be found in ADM 6/199. Even earlier before the actual coastguard came into existence, Navy officers were also appointed as preventive officers, mainly on Revenue Cruisers. The records for the 17th and 18th centuries can be found amongst the records of naval correspondence in ADM 1. You will need to refer to the indexes in ADM 12 to locate the information. As these are complex they are described later.

Cruiser Musters

There are separate musters for coastguard and revenue cruisers found in series ADM 119. These cover the period from 1824-1858. They basically follow the same format and contain the same information as any other Royal Navy muster book as previously described.

Pension Records

The records of pensions for Coastguard officers can be found amongst the records of Admiralty administered pensions as well as those for civilians administered by the Paymaster General. Specifically you will need to search for coastguards in:

- ADM 23 -1866-1923 for naval and coastguard pensions but they also include civil pensions.
- PMG 70 -1866-1928 for chief officers entitled to Greenwich in or out pensions.
- PMG 23 -1855-1935 mainly civil pensions.

Medals

Those who served in campaigns can expect to be awarded the appropriate campaign medals but the Coastguard had its own Long Service and Good Conduct medal. The medal rolls can be searched on Ancestry and form part of series ADM 171.

Coastguard Long Service and Good Conduct Medal were awarded for 20 years of full or part-time service with the Coastguard. The Board of Trade established the medal in 1911 and it was originally known as the Board of Trade Rocket Apparatus Long Service Medal. The medal was originally awarded for service with a rocket life-saving apparatus company or brigade, upon the recommendation of the Board of Trade, or

Ministers of Shipping or Transport. In 1954 it became the Coast Life Saving Corps Long Service Medal and in 1997 the Coastguard Auxiliary Long Service Medal It was not until 2012 that it became the Coastguard Long Service and Good Conduct Medal.

The medal has used two different ribbons with the same colors. The current ribbon (post 2012) is red with centre stripe of sky blue. The red edges are also divided by a thin sky blue stripe. The previous versions of the medal had a ribbon which was red at the edges with a broad centre stripe of sky blue.

Local Records and Resources

Some local records relating to the Coastguard can be found in county record offices and theses should also be considered when researching. As an example Pembrokeshire Record Office holds records between 1876 and 1970 to include the station books and log books for various Coastguard stations within the county. Whilst perhaps not covering actual staff information they would be useful in relation to the type of work, the time on watches etc. which an ancestor would have been involved in. It is likely that other record offices covering coastal Britain will have similar material including photographs.

It was not unusual for local districts to publish a newsletter or even a magazine and some of these are dated from the inception of the service in 1822. Where they exist they will be found mainly in local record offices or even at the local Coastguard stations. Many local newspapers carried reports and obituaries of the local Coastguard officers and events.

In many coastal towns there is often a memorial to the Coastguards and individual gravestones can be found in churchyards and cemeteries.

Administration of the Coastguard

Although most of these records relate to the way in which the coastguard organisation was administered by the various departments under whose responsibility it fell, some of the following records may provide useful information in regard to individuals, their salaries and some of the incidents they may have been involved in.

- CUST 147 - 1814-1907 Board of Customs correspondence to Coastguard establishments including divisional statistics and maps of divisions.
- CUST 29 - 1833-1849 Minute Books relating to the Coastguard.
- ADM 114 - 1822-1856 Entry books of orders, instructions and memoranda.
- CUST 38 and 39 - 1782-1832 Salaries and incidents in respect of Coastguard establishments. (CUST 39 relates specifically to the Thames Coastguard Division).

CHAPTER SEVENTEEN
The Royal Navy and the Royal Indian Navy

Throughout its history British men have served in various capacities (normally as officers) within the Royal Indian Navy and its earlier counterparts. There was also considerable co-operation between the Royal Navy and the Indian Navy with Royal Navy officers being loaned to the Indian Navy, so it is possible that your ancestor served in India in such capacities. Most of the officer ranks in India were the same as those for the Royal Navy, so it is possible that you may not be aware of an 'Indian connection'. If you have no success in finding details of your ancestor in the Royal Navy service records then it is worth searching the records of the Indian Navy for details. These are briefly outlined below. However, this is best illustrated by the following late 19th and early 20th century example which is one of many.

'JOHN TALBOT HALL
Born 30 November 1896 at Ticeshurst, Kent
Educated at Elstow School, Bedford and then underwent Navy training at Training Ship 'Mersey'
Married Agnes Maud Sherran in 1933 at Iver Heath, Buckinghamshire
Died 21 January 1964 in London.
Served in the Royal Indian Navy 1921-1944
Lt - 16 March 1921
Lt Cdr - 2 August 1908
Cdr - 20 April 1937
Capt - 25 January 1944 - retired at this rank on 1 September 1950
Rear Adm - 1 September 1950
During his service he served as:
Executive Officer on HMIS Lawrence and Clive (both minesweeper sloops)

Commanding Officer on HMIS Baluchi a patrol boat
Officer in charge of the Navy branch of the Defence Dept of the Government of India
Staff officer at HMIS Dalhousie the RIN Naval HQ
Commanding officer of HMS Achiles
Flag officer of HMIS Delhi
He then, in retirement became a Civil defence officer for N E Essex between 1951 and 1959.
He was also awarded the CIE (Companion of the Order of the Indian Empire) on 1 Jan 1944
- this order was founded by the British Government in 1878 rewarding British officials who
served in India.'

One of the problems the Royal Indian Navy faced after Independence was the inadequacy of personnel, especially officers, much of which stemmed from British policies relating to service in the Royal Indian Navy during the decades of the 20th century preceding Independence. Until 1947 Indian naval forces were led virtually by British, and to some extent, Anglo-Indian officers, because it was the Royal Navy that had no need for any other navy of any consequence and as such the Indian Navy was the last of the Services to which native officers were admitted.

After the Declaration of Independence all British officers of the Royal Indian Navy and its reserve forces were compulsorily retired, were paid compensation and granted pensions determined by their length of service. At the time these British officers were invited to volunteer for service and were transferred to a Special List of the Royal Navy. They were then assigned to either the Royal Indian Navy or the Royal Pakistan Navy. Some officers opting to serve with the Royal Indian Navy were granted commissions in the Service and in addition, further commissioned officers and Warrant Officers were loaned by the Royal Navy to meet a shortfall in the manning requirements.

In order to cater for the expansion of the Indian Navy the recruitment of native cadets was increased, as was recruitment of commissioned officers in all branches of the Navy. Some of these were Anglo-Indians or British people who chose to remain in India after independence. By the end of 1950, the number of Royal Navy and Royal Navy Special List officers in the Royal Indian Navy actually increased temporarily and all the India Navy officers underwent training under the auspices of the Royal Navy. It is therefore possible that records of service for these individuals will be included within both the Royal Indian Navy and the Royal Navy records.

Some examples of all ranks affected by the crossover are shown below:

Henry Ellis Passmore-Edwards
Royal Naval Reserve: Royal Navy:
Royal Indian Naval Reserve.

Commodore Robin Avelin Melhuish
Royal Indian Marine: 1906-1917; 1919-1934.
Royal Indian Navy: 1934; 1939-1945.
Royal Navy: 1917-1919.
Royal Naval Reserve: 1902-1906.

Commissioned Gunner Frank Charles William Meade,
Royal Navy: 1908-1916; 1940-1945.
Royal Indian Marine: 1916-1933.
born as Frank Charles William Glewitz, but changed his name, circa 1919, to Meade.

Commander John Clifford Mansell
Royal Navy Reserve:
Royal Indian Navy:
Royal Navy (Special List - Royal Pakistan Navy Liaison Officer).

Lieutenant Commander Jack Harrison
Royal Naval Volunteer Reserve: 1940-1944; 1946-1958.
Royal Indian Naval Volunteer Reserve: 1944-1946.
Royal Navy Reserve: 1958-1963.

Engineer Commander Carl Rousey Leopold Bergner
Mercantile Marine: 1907-1909.
Royal Indian Marine: 1910-1914; 1919-1940.
Royal Navy: 1914-1918.

Commissioned Gunner Albert Walter Baigent
Royal Navy:
Straits Settlement RNVR:
Malaya RNVR:

Record sources

The records relating to Royal Navy officers 'on loan' will be found amongst the records originating with the Admiralty and as described above. The records relating to British men serving with the Indian Navy will be found at the British Library amongst the India collection held in the Asia & Africa Studies department.

The Bombay Marine was the original fighting navy of the East India Company in Asian waters with records dating from around 1738. In 1830 it was renamed the Indian Navy, subsequently abolished in 1863 and replaced by a revived, non-combatant,

Bombay Marine. In 1877 both the Bombay and Bengal Marine were combined to form HM Indian Marine which became the Royal Indian Marine in 1892 and the Royal Indian Navy in 1935. For all of these there are records of both appointment and records of service available for research. 'Baxter's Guide for Biographical Sources in the India Office records' should be used as a reference for full details.

It is unlikely that you will locate personnel-type records for the Indian Marine. However, there are many relevant documents for both the Bombay Marine and Indian Navy while under the control of the East India Company although, like the Royal Navy, they may appear slightly confusing. Most of the records relating to appointments and service can be located in series L/MAR for the Bombay Marine and the Indian Navy up to 1863 whereas many of the post 1863 records for the Indian Navy can also be established in the series L/MIL. Administrative and pension information can be found generally within series L/AG. All of these records are held at the British Library. Those most useful for genealogical research are described below.

Officers' careers can be established from various published listings including the East India Register between 1803 and 1863 which shows individuals' appointments. The Indian Navy List has listings in a similar format to the Official Navy List. There are disposition lists covering 1854 to 1863 which also include brief details on naval vessels. The establishment lists cover the period 1767-1837 and from 1844 onwards. Surgeons were included from 1776 and pursers and captains' clerks from 1829. A separate listing survives for engineers and their apprentices as of 1847.

The records for Petty Officers and ratings are slightly more restrictive. The most useful sets of records take the form of musters mainly for the 18th century. A good number of these were taken at frequent intervals and tend to cover the 1760s to 1780s. The later musters for the 19th century take the form of Returns of Seamen organised both alphabetically and chronologically. It would appear that for the period 1816 to around 1865 a form of continuous service engagements was maintained albeit that there are some gaps.

There are European personnel casualty lists covering all ranks and ratings and recording both deaths and desertions and discharges for the period 1777 to 1834.

The records of service for commissioned and Warrant Officers covering c. 1840 to 1947 are a valuable source of information. There are a couple of exceptions relating to some commissioned and Warrant Officers in the First World War who appear in the Navy lists but for whom records seem to not exist. Additionally, there is a very useful volume of service records relating to Royal Navy officers loaned to the Royal Indian Navy in the Second World War (ref L/MIL/16-7) which is alphabetically arranged.

CHAPTER EIGHTEEN
Education and the Royal Navy

The genealogical information contained in school records is generally well appreciated and as you research your ancestors there is a strong possibility that you may find records of pupils or cadets with Royal Navy connections. At the beginning of the 19th century there was little general education available to children unless the family were fortunate. The Royal Navy arranged for the schooling of sons and later daughters of both officers and ratings, keeping them out of orphanages, workhouses etc. and also away from the charity schools.

By the 1830s there were four well established Navy schools in the London area, namely the Royal Naval School which was a public school for the sons of officers, the Royal Naval School for daughters of officers, the Royal Naval Asylum (rather inappropriately named!) which was essentially a lower school and the Greenwich Hospital School which essentially offered secondary education.

The records of the respective schools are both valuable and varied but it is not unusual to be able to find admission registers, claims for school places and sponsor nomination papers. These papers between them will be able to provide names and locations of fathers of pupils, information about the families of pupils and possibly career details after the pupils left school.

Alongside these schools were the various training ships which offered boys both a basic education and also training in seamanship.

Royal Naval Asylum

The Royal Naval Asylum was established as 'British Endeavour' in 1798. This establishment was a boarding school for needy children of seamen. It was located at Clarence House, Paddington Green, London. The number of children admitted to the school was always under 70. King George III made the asylum a Royal Foundation in 1807 and the school took over Queen's House, Greenwich (home of the National Maritime Museum today) where additional wings were built enabling education to be made available to over 700 boys and girls. In 1821 the asylum merged with the Greenwich Hospital School. In 1825 the asylum was renamed Greenwich Hospital Lower School.

Pupils were eligible for admission if their fathers served or were serving in the Royal Navy and were either orphaned or in dire need either because their father had been wounded or their mother had died. The boys had to be between nine and 12 years of age, free of any speech impediment or body infirmity. Formal written application was made to the commissioners for admission and in some cases a bondsman was required. In all cases no child over the age of 14 years could remain at the school and some were removed to the Greenwich Hospital School and some apprenticed to master mariners.

Many of the records of the Royal Naval Asylum form part of the Greenwich Hospital School archives (see later). There are some relevant documents at The National Archives in series ADM 73 detailing early admissions including those from Clarence House. Series ADM 6 includes the minutes of the trustees between 1800 and 1805 and the baptism registers between 1822 and 1856 are in series RG 4/1678 as previously noted.

Greenwich Hospital Schools

The founding charter of the Royal Hospital Greenwich included an objective relating to the education of residents' sons. As early as 1715 at least 10 boys living at the hospital were educated at a nearby academy. This was the start and schooling was later extended to the sons of out-pensioners of the hospital. The benefit of education at the school was later offered to boys whose fathers were or had been serving Royal Navy seamen. It is also known that the sons of some officers were also educated at the schools. By 1800 the school catered for 200 pupils aged 11 years and over. When the School incorporated the asylum the number of pupils was increased to 1,000 which included 200 girls although by 1841 the girls' school had closed on the grounds of 'evil communication'.

As early as 1756 the pupils wore a uniform not dissimilar to the 'sailor's dress' although they wore a rather unique leather cap. Later uniforms began to resemble those of boy sailors in the Navy.

Throughout the 19th century education was granted at three levels. The lower school (formerly the Royal Naval Asylum) taught those from the age of nine. The Upper School taught at secondary level with emphasis on seamanship and the Nautical School taught navigation to boys who were intent on entering the Navy at the age of 15.

It is thought that around 10,000 boys joined the Navy between the 1870s and 1930s as a direct result of being pupils at the school.

The Green Coat School was merged with the schools in 1886 as did the Boreman Foundation. The Foundation started in Greenwich in the 17th century specifically for the sons of local seamen, fishermen and watermen.

This school had around 100 boy pupils who attended as day pupils rather than boarders. Green Coat had local connections to Greenwich as it was the school attended specifically by sons of Greenwich watermen and seamen. In 1933 the school moved from Greenwich to its present home at Holbrook in Suffolk. Up to 1978 it still only took in pupils who could claim naval parentage. This proviso no longer applies.

Records of the Green Coat School are held by the Drapers' Company in London as it became the trustees. The company has lists of pupils and their parents for the 18th to late 19th centuries. The Drapers' Company also holds the admission registers and applications for pupils of the Boreman Foundation dating from 1886 to around 1930. Boreman boys were not obliged to join the Navy, although many did. The Drapers' Company archive is located at Drapers Hall, Throgmorton Avenue, London EC2N 2DQ. An appointment is needed for research.

The pupils of the Greenwich Hospital Schools led a regimented life in an environment which was deemed to be self-sufficient. All pupils undertook 'trades training' in such things as tailoring and bakery as well as having to undertake domestic duties.

From 1862 to 1876 the school expansion was completed and the buildings comprised those buildings which the National Maritime Museum now occupies. The first 'Fame' drill ship at Greenwich was built in front of the Queen's House in 1843 and this is where the senior boys practised their seafaring skills. Fame existed up to the time of the move to Holbrook.

Records relating to the Royal Hospital Schools, apart from admission registers dating from 1870, are held by The National Archives. The admission registers themselves are retained by the school at Holbrook.

Most of the extensive school records at The National Archives are held in series ADM 73 which contain a wealth of genealogical information. The application papers are the most prolific in such detail as a pupil's date of birth and baptism, father's information including details of his naval service, marriage and residence and in some instances details of siblings. Most applications are accompanied by a letter or form from the incumbent or parish officer of the home parish indicating that the family are in need. There is a very useful alphabetical list of boys from 1728 to 1870 in ADM 73/434-438.

Burial registers for pupils between 1807 and 1856 also exist in series RG 4/1679. It may also be worth extending your search for vital events into the series of Royal Hospital registers for baptisms, marriages and deaths.

The Royal Naval Schools

It is from the boys' school that former pupils frequently became high-ranking officers in the Royal Navy. The boys' school originated in Camberwell in 1833 but later moved to New Cross in 1844 and again in 1889 to Mottingham, Eltham. The school officially closed in 1910 but by that time around 4,000 pupils were educated there, the majority of whom joined either the Royal Navy or Royal Marines.

The records, which were found in a cupboard when the Royal Naval College closed, are now in the custody of the Lewisham Local History Library and include indexed admission registers for the period 1833 to 1910. There is a slight overlap for the periods around 1870-1888 so it is worth looking at all the registers covering this period. In general the records contain name, birth date (from around 1860), parents' names, father's rank, address and dates of entry and leaving the school. In some cases there is a potted biography of careers but this tends to relate to those who went on to hold senior ranks within the Royal Navy. A listing also exists of former pupils who received honours and decorations. Administrative records include information on scholarships, finances and news cuttings about the school and pupils.

The girls' school was founded in 1840 specifically for the education of daughters of Royal Naval officers originally housing 59 pupils in a boarding environment. At first the girls were admitted after a vote by registered members (those who made financial donations to the school). Many of the fathers were on half-pay or in some cases had died in service. The school was originally based at Richmond but in 1856 transferred to Isleworth. It was forced to move to Stoatley Hall, Haslemere, because of enemy bombing in the Second World War and where it remained until 1995.

The records are for the majority retained by the school archives at Haslemere. Besides the minute books which commence in the 1840s the most useful set of records of genealogical value are the applications from 1842 to 1877. These provide girls' names, birth dates, dates of admission, father's name and rank and surprisingly his income. There are some notes about either the parents or the child or both once the girl had left the school.

There are also a series of examination report books for 1880 to 1950 which give an insight into pupil education ability. These are in recorded in form lists.

As the school was based at Isleworth for the period 1868-1875 the local studies library also holds certain records for that period, mainly administrative in content.

The Royal Naval Free School, Devonport

The Royal Naval Free School was established at Devonport in 1831 to educate the children of seamen and retired mariners, fishermen and watermen. Around 400 children passed through the School in the first five years of its existence. There was no compulsion for pupils to join the Navy although a great number did so because of family tradition.

In 1846 entrance was opened to children whose parents were employed in the town's Royal Naval Dockyards. When this change was made the original subscription of a 1d. per week was increased to 2d. per week for dockyard labourers' children and 4d. per week for the sons and daughters of artisan employees.

In 1848 the school moved to King Street, Devonport, with the foundation stone being laid two years earlier by the First Lord Commissioner of the Admiralty. It received Royal patronage from both Queen Victoria and Prince Albert who, alongside the Admiralty and others, subscribed to the cost of building the new school.

By 1868 there were 800 pupils on the books of the school including 370 boys, 203 girls and 227 infants. Boys learned music, art, algebra, geography and history in addition to the normal subjects. Boys were also prepared for the competitive exams held for admission to the Dockyards.

One unique feature to fund the school was that collections were held on board Her Majesty's Ships where many ex-pupils were amongst the most generous of givers. Of the 8,000 pupils educated at the schools around 65% entered the Navy or the dockyards.

The records of the school are combined with the records of its successor the King Street School and are held by the Plymouth and West Devon Archives Service. Amongst the records specific to the Free School are admission registers covering the period 1899-1929 and school log books 1895-1938. Earlier records do not appear to have survived.

Training Ships

Training ships provided the Navy with a consistent intake of recruits in the form of boys and young men, many with a secure trade. In excess of 30 training ships were established in the Victorian period to feed the Royal Navy (and Merchant Navy) with young recruits. There was a range of ships from those training officers to those training pauper boys. Many of these ships were based on the Thames and around the Medway. Perhaps the most well-known was *HMS Exmouth* which was converted to a training ship in 1878 for the use of the Metropolitan Asylum Board. *Exmouth* served as a training ship until 1905, accommodating about 500 boys at any one time with a good proportion of the 'Exmouth boys' entering the Royal Navy.

The earliest training ships were administered by the Marine Society which existed from 1756. The first known training ship operated by them was *Beatty* (1786-1862) moored off Deptford. The original purpose of the Society was to recruit boys and young men for the Royal Navy from the beginning of the Seven Years War with the prime objective of minimising the number of desertions by introducing boys to sea life and provide training before they actually served at sea. The Royal Navy never fared as well as the Merchant Navy with the number of recruits, for example from the training ship *Warspite* 28,500 of its 65,000 boys went to sea in the Royal Navy during its period of service from 1876 to 1911. The Society provided poor boys with a complete sea uniform and undertook to assist them on Royal Navy vessels. Once in the service many of the boys worked as servants to the officers.

The Royal Navy's first official training ships were *HMS Implacable* based at Plymouth in 1855 and *HMS Illustrious* at Portsmouth. Their purpose was to provide a source of recruitment to the Navy and also to provide structured training in naval life, skills, and discipline to 'lads'. Up to the early 1900s another 30 or so training ships were set up, some as shore establishments. The various ships catered for boys from a wide range of backgrounds and boys typically joined the ships at the ages of 11 or 12 and completed their training when they were 15 or 16 with most securing a job in either the Royal or Merchant Navy. In order to try and instil a sense of what

Navy life was like the discipline aboard the ships was strict. Food was basic and included potatoes, biscuits and meat supplemented occasionally with fruit and vegetables. They slept in hammocks in the same way that they would end up sleeping on serving ships and those who could not swim were taught to do so. The regime included being taught basic education and also the arts of seamanship. Most of the boys left with a certificate of proficiency. The heyday of the anchored wooden hulled training ships was between 1855 and 1900 when the Royal Navy established around 15 of its own training hulks.

In order to get into the Royal Navy training ship boys had to prove physical fitness and the ability to read and write. The boys signed on for 12 years of service after their 19th birthday as well as for their training period and needed the written consent of their parents. This point was the start of their Continuous Service Record which was accompanied by a health certificate signed by two medical officers (the latter has not always survived). Boys found themselves part of a punishing daily routine and many ship's log books record the activities and details accidents, punishments etc. These can be found by ship's name in series ADM 53 at The National Archives. The most dangerous activity that boys took part in was climbing the rigging. There are records of deaths and drowning from so doing. A memorial exists in Mylor churchyard to the boys who lost their lives whilst *HMS Ganges* was based nearby before its move to Shotley.

The National Maritime Museum at Greenwich also holds a wealth of information relating to training ships. The manual of gunnery and seamanship for boy seamen is a useful guide to enable the researcher to really envisage what life was like on board a training ship. They also hold a good photographic archive and have a variety of pamphlets which relate to cadet recruitment.

Many of the independent training ships also produced recruits for the Navy and many of these were fed boys by the Boards of Guardians of Poor Law Unions although there was some reluctance in using training ships for boys in their care, presumably because of the cost of keeping them there.

In 1866 Lord Shaftesbury promoted the idea of a naval training ship for homeless boys in London. The Admiralty provided *HMS Chichester* for the purpose. The ship was moored at Greenhithe and received 50 boys from a children's refuge in Covent Garden.

Chichester's first Commanding Officer was Captain A. H. Alston RN and he was supported by schoolmasters and instructors all of whom resided on board. Alston was eventually dismissed for drunkenness.

The training ship had its own swimming pool, a water filled Thames barge which was moored adjacent to the ship. Training also included compass work, sail making, rowing and steering, knotting and splicing, knowledge about running the ship and of course the mundane skills associated with tailoring, carpentry, cooking, laundry etc. This regime was repeated on most of the other training vessels. By the end of the first year nearly 200 boys were sent for training but of the 42 who completed their training only nine actually entered the Royal Navy.

One of the Royal Navy's many bureaucratic problems was that a birth certificate or at least a baptism certificate was necessary for enlistment. Many boys who entered training ships had no knowledge of their parentage and could not provide such information. This rule was waived for boys entering from *Chichester* provided they agreed to serve for a specified period without desertion.

HMS Ganges was originally a training ship established in 1865 and later a shore training establishment at Shotley Gate in Suffolk. She was based at both Falmouth and Harwich before moving to Shotley Gate in 1905. The original hulk converted to a training school was *HMS Ganges* although other hulks had been used but retained the same name. The first intake was of 180 boys in January 1866 all of whom had been transferred from the training ship *HMS Wellesley* which was based at Chatham. A major refit enabled 500 boys to be accommodated.

Training of Boy Sailors

The status of boys recruited for the Royal Navy was protected by Admiralty regulations and within the regulations various classes were introduced for boys of different ages depending upon their progress and examinations passed. Boys under the age of 18 years were not subject to the Naval Discipline Acts but automatically became ordinary seamen on reaching their 18th birthday when they were considered an adult.

Up to 10% of the crew of an 18th century British warship would have been boys. In peacetime the boys' official role on board up to 1794 when class ratings were introduced, was generally as a servant to either the captain or other officers. Notwithstanding that the main purpose was for them to be trained as sailors. During battle most boys undertook the role of 'powder boy', generally their first experience of war. Gun powder had to be kept in certain conditions below the water line as it was dangerous to do otherwise, so the job of the boys was to fetch the powder to the gun decks to arm the guns.

Boy 3rd Class - was a boy aged 14 to 18 who served either as a waiter or steward at the port flagships or was a junior clerk or storekeeper in the naval shore based stores.

3rd Class boys were able to enter a training ship ranked as a boy 2nd class when they attained the age of 15 (subject to being physically fit). In most cases this class of boy was recruited from homes around the ports and need not have been fully resident on the ships or shore stations.

Boy 2nd Class - was a boy usually aged between 15 and 17 years and who was rated when he entered a Royal Navy training ship having been declared physically fit and of good character. It was usual for the boy's parents or guardians to sign a declaration that the boy would serve for a 12 year minimum period.

Boy 1st Class - was under training, aged between 16 and 18 years and who had completed a nine month to 18 month term under a Boy 2nd Class rating and who was able to show proficiency in seamanship. It was also a requirement that he had received at least one good conduct badge but this depended on the regime of the training ship to which he was attached.

In all cases rates of pay were enhanced by advancement.

The training ship regime for boys was regimented. The following is a typical example taken for *HMS Illustrious* c.1854. The daily toil consisted of drill, knots, splicing, boat rowing, gun and cutlass drill, making, mending and washing clothes and other elements of both education and seamanship.

5.30 am Reveille - scrub, wash decks.
6.30 am Swim (usually in the sea).
6.45 am Breakfast.
7.15 am 'Dress for deck'.
8.00am Morning evolition - drill, sail training etc.
9.00 am Assembly and Deck Inspection followed by periods of seamanship instruction.
11.30 am Decks swept and cleaned for dinner.
Noon Dinner.
1.00 pm Assembly, administration of punishments, further instruction.
3.30 pm Washing and Laundry.
5.00 pm Tea.
5.30 pm Wash down decks followed by private time.
8.00 pm Hammocks piped down.
9.00 pm Lights out.

Boys were also taken on for officer or artificer training and the ranking system was different in such cases.

Cadet - was a boy aged between 13 and 15 years who enlisted to become an officer and either trained on a training ship or at Naval College. In most cases they attended *HMS Britannia* at Dartmouth.

Midshipman - was a boy aged between 16 and 18 years and specifically serving on a seagoing ship, having passed out as a cadet before entering the ship and undergoing further training before being able to progress to a sub-lieutenant which was the lowest rank of fully commissioned officer.

Apprentice - was a boy aged between 16 and 18 years and being trained in engineering or other technical skills, usually in dockyard (shore based) schools. Their ultimate aim was to become artificers with a degree of specialism.

Midshipmen and cadets appeared in the succession books from 1699. The earliest books can be located in series ADM 6 with later records forming part of series ADM 11 from 1815. There appears to be a gap from c.1756-1815. Most of the succession books for these classes are surname indexed by subsequent piece numbers within the ADM 11 series. Between 1815 and 1822 boys also appear in the succession books, which can be located specifically in piece numbers ADM 11/23 and 24.

Records of Training Ships

Needless to say, because the various training ships were administered by different organisations the records are not held in one place so it is important to try and establish which training ship your ancestor may have served on. In some cases there is a notation contained within the Continuous Service record in ADM 188. For example it was not unusual for something like 'Exmouth boy' to appear in the occupation section of the form. However this is not always the case so it may mean looking at several records to find the information.

Initially it is worth a search of family archives in case the certificate given to the boy when he finished training has survived. The National Archives does not hold many records relative to training ships but there are some annual reports in series MT9 which occasionally name boys. Both pupils and staff will appear in the Victorian census returns which may help locate the ship and enable the furtherance of research. Some of the known training ship records are shown below but of course there may well be others. The records of *HMS Exmouth* administered by the Metropolitan Asylum Board are held at the London Metropolitan Archives and include the ship admission registers, punishment books (quite revealing!), accounts and minutes.

For *HMS Worcester* the ship's registers of boys are held by the Marine Society at Lambeth, as are the administrative records of *HMS Warspite*, although in this case the National Maritime Museum at Greenwich holds the ship's registers.

Records for the training ships under the auspices of the Shaftesbury Homes, namely *HMS Chichester* and *HMS Arethusa*, are held by the Home. The records are likely to reveal the boy's name, details of parentage if known, father's occupation, schools the boy attended and who recommended the boy to the training facility. Applications can be made for a search to be undertaken via their website: **www.shaftesbury.org.uk**

The records relating to *HMS Conway* established as a training ship in 1859 are held by the Maritime Archive in Liverpool which includes actual service records of the cadets. A database listing of the cadets giving name, dates of admission and leaving and events such as notable achievements, obituaries etc. can be searched free of charge at: **www.hmsconway.org**

Northumberland Archives hold the records of *TS Wellesley* which include the registers covering 1868-1933, log books from 1933, minute books, punishment books, Wellesley magazines and journals and a history of the ship.

The Watts Naval Training School

This school situated in North Elmham, Norfolk, opened in 1906 as a branch of Dr Barnado's in a building which was originally a Norfolk County School built in 1871. The school provided a two year course of general education followed, at the age of 14 years, by two years naval training. The school could accommodate 300 pupils and admission was open to orphan or destitute boys from age 11 to 14. The majority of boys who trained at the school then went on to complete their training at *HMS Ganges* at Shotley Gate, Ipswich, before entering the Royal Navy. The school only entertained pupils intent on Royal Navy service as Barnado's had a separate but similar facility for those wishing a career in the Merchant Navy which was called the Cotes Nautical School. The school ceased to be a Navy training establishment in 1949 although was still used as a Barnado's establishment until its closure in 1953.

63. The Watts School (taken just prior to closing).

Records which survive are held by Norfolk County Record Office at Norwich and consist of admission registers 1912-1932 and 'Jack Tar' the school magazine for certain years up to 1937.

Dr Barnado's hold the personal records of many of the pupils and these can be obtained from their archive in Barkingside subject to disclosure regulations. The records of the pupils' Navy service are amongst the personnel records of the Royal Navy.

Royal Naval Colleges

Navy officer training first took place officially at the Royal Naval Academy in Portsmouth Dockyard. The Royal Naval Academy which operated between 1733 and 1837 originally had the objective to provide an alternative means to recruit officers and to provide standardised training, education and admission which it fully achieved.

In 1733 the Academy catered for 40 recruits and provided a comprehensive syllabus of theoretical and practical experience in the dockyard and at sea which earned graduates two years of sea time thus enabling them to take the Lieutenants' examinations after four instead of the usual six years at sea. Only partially successful, the majority of Lieutenants still preferred to spend six years in sea training rather than undertake time at the Academy because recruits for officers was still by family tradition and patronage clearly based on practical experience. The Academy became the Royal Naval College in 1806. Graduates of the Academy were midshipmen ordinary, thus distinguishing them from midshipmen who served on board ships. Graduates became midshipmen after they had spent two years at sea.

The college closed its doors in 1837. Until the establishment of *Britannia* some 20 years later the only means of entry as a young officer was by sea training.

Navy officer training has been associated with Dartmouth since 1859 when *HMS Britannia* was moored on the River Dart. Prior to this there had been a Royal Naval College at Portsmouth between 1733 and 1837. The shore based Britannia Naval College, originally known as the Royal Naval College, opened in 1905 with the first intake of cadets transferring from the Royal Naval College at Osborne on the Isle of Wight.

Osborne College was established as a junior officer training college in 1903 and did not close until 1921, so officer cadets joined Osborne at the age of 13 years. before transferring to Dartmouth. They commenced their sea training when they reached 17 years of age.

When the Greenwich Hospital was closed it was converted to a training college. From 1873 to 1998 when it trained naval officers. It was frequently referred to as the 'Navy's university'. The college during its existence incorporated two other important naval training establishments - the School of Naval Architecture and Marine Engineering and the War College which was previously based at Portsmouth. In 1919 the Naval Staff College was also established at Greenwich.

During the Second World War around 35,000 men and women graduated. In 1976 training was integrated into Britannia Royal Naval College at Dartmouth, this becoming the only naval college for officer training.

Royal Naval Engineering College

The Royal Naval Engineering College was founded as Keyham College in Plymouth in 1880. This replaced *HMS Marlborough*, a hulk which had been in use since 1877. Students spent five years at the college undergoing training around the dockyard, after which they spent a further two years at Greenwich College before becoming Assistant Engineers on board ships.

The Selborne - Fisher Programme introduced in 1903 meant that engineering and deck officers received the same basic training and this led to the ultimate closure of the college in 1910. In 1902 John Fisher, Second Sea Lord in charge of personnel, had returned to the UK from the Mediterranean. Fisher felt it would be more effective for the Navy to have one system of entry and one system of training. He therefore merged all cadets' training and revised the curriculum to provide a suitable grounding for all officers.

During the First World War the college was re-opened for special entry cadet training but after the war reverted to engineer training. In 1958 Keyham College became the Plymouth Dockyard Technical College.

Gunnery Training School

The Gunnery School at Whale Island, Portsmouth was established in the early 1830s as *HMS Excellent* and has since played a vital role as the Royal Navy's main gunnery training establishment staffed by around 200 Royal Artillery instructors. *Excellent* held 600 men under training.

In 1840 the capture of the fortress at Acre secured the future of the gunnery school. The British squadron sent to capture the fortress had 120 guns at its disposal and the trained men soon achieved success. This secured the development of the gunnery school.

The gunnery practice carried out on *HMS Excellent* meant that men fired in teams over the mudflats uncovered at low tide and it is known that one enterprising local family would collect the shot from the mudflats to sell it back to the Navy!

The Gunnery School was also responsible for parade training and even today both disciplines are the responsibility of the school. Alongside gunnery *HMS Excellent* was also used as a boys' training ship with the mizzen mast kept rigged for sail training.

Passing certificates of gunners from *HMS Excellent* usually include information relative to a man's career detailing the ships on which he served and any other records of achievement whilst training as the illustrations below indicate. This personal document is dated 1902.

qualifications to serve as at *Torpedo Gunner* in His Majesty's Fleet, and we find as follows :—His Gunnery and Torpedo qualifications are as shown on the back hereof.

He appears to have served in the Ships undermentioned, viz. :— 6. *M.* 160650.

Ships.	Captains.	Entry.	Rating.	Discharge.	Character.	Time. Years of 365 days.	Days.
"Impregnable"		23 May 91	Boy 2·cl:	27 May 91			
"Lion"		28 May 91	"	22 June 92			
"Vivid"	Montgomerie	23 June 92	Boy 1·cl:	7 Mch 93	V.G.		
"Triumph"		8 Mch 93	"	18 Mch 93			
"Warspite"		19 Mch 93	"	28 Aug 93			
"Vivid"		29 Aug 93	"	30 Sept: 93			
"Nile"	L. Hammet	1 Oct: 93	"	3 Oct: 93			
"		4 Oct: 93	"	5 May 94	V.G.		
— " —		6 May 94	Ord:	26 Oct: 94		11	165
— " —	"	24 Oct: 94	"	31 July 95	V.G.		
— " —		1 Aug 95	AB	30 Sept 95			
"Victory"		1 Oct: 95	—"—	18 Nov 95			
"Excellent"	C. Bayly	19 Nov: 95	—"—	28 Nov 96	V.G.		
"Vernon"	J. Durnford	29 Nov: 96	—"—	30 Oct: 97	V.G.		
"Victory"		31 Oct: 97	—"—	14 Nov 97			
"Fearless"	A. Hingford	15 Nov: 97	"	14 Feb: 99	V.G.		
— " —	N. Yeyd	15 Feb: 99	Ldg Sea:	30 June 99			
— " —		1 July 99	S.G.2·cl:	4 May 00	V.G.		
"Vernon"		5 May 00	"	8 Nov: 02			

He produces certificates of service, ability, and good conduct from the above Captains and has served in the Navy as required by the Regulations, to qualify him to receive a Warrant as† *Torpedo Gunner*.

His service in a Seagoing Ship amounts to *4 years - 354 days*.

He produces the Educational Certificate on the back hereof.

He is in every respect a thorough practical Seaman, and is competent, if required, to take charge of a watch ; he has a fair knowledge of working and manœuvring ships, the effect of the helm, &c., and he is acquainted with the rules and regulations for preventing collisions at sea; he understands perfectly the rigging of ships according to the regulations of the Navy; he knows how to stow and secure the anchors; how to erect and secure sheers.

After full examination, we deem him to be perfectly competent to fill the station of†*Torpedo Gunner* in one of Her Majesty's Ships, subject to his passing any further examination prescribed by the Queen's Regulations.

Any further remarks }
to be here inserted. }

Given under our hands this   3 nd   day of *November* 1902.

Marge Snakeons. Navigating Officer of Her Majesty's Ship *Impregnable*

J. Delauy Gunner of Her Majesty's Ship *Graduate*

W. Jowell Gunner of Her Majesty's Ship *Crescent*

Q. Turner Boatswain of Her Majesty's Ship *Raleigh*

In the presence of

M.H. Smith Captain of Her Majesty's Ship *Duke of Wellington*

Candidate's Signature at full length *Laurence William Wright*

Date of Birth   6 th *May* 1876.

† Insert Gunner or Torpedo Gunner, according to election of Candidate.

6144

64a. Record of a Torpedo Gunner's passing certificate at the Gunnery School.

Date.	Particulars.	Captain's Signature.
1 July '95	Passed for Z.M.	L. Hammet.
26 aug '96	S.G. 1 cl:	C. Bayly.
30 Oct: '96	Diver.	M. Browning.
27 Feb: '97	Qual: S.G.Z.	A. Heneage.
15 July '97	Leading seaman	R. Neeld.
22 Oct: '97	Qual: L.Z.G.	S. Nicholson.
25 Oct: '00	Diving cert: cancelled, own request:	H. Flyd.
28 Jan: '01	R . . . . L.Z.G	C.E.M.
3 Feb: '02	2 . . . . Z.Z & completed course in Wireless Telegraphy.	Z.C.

The above to be a copy of the Notations on Parchment Certificate.

EDUCATIONAL CERTIFICATE.

This is to certify that, pursuant to an order from *the Commander in Chief* I have examined* *Lawrence W. Wright* as to his educational qualifications, and I find that he can read and write well; he has a good knowledge of the first four rules of arithmetic, simple and compound; a fair knowledge of proportion, and of vulgar and decimal fractions.

Given under my hand this 20th day of October 1902.

J.S.Mason Naval Instructor

H.M.S. *Duke of Wellington*

64b. (Reverse of previous).

234

Eastman Royal Naval Academies

These had no official connection with the Royal Navy but gained a reputation as being one of the best schools for boys who intended to join the Navy either as officers or ratings. For most of its life (1851-1923) the Academy was based at Winchester, Hampshire although its origins can be traced back to Portsmouth (Southsea).

In 1838 the Royal Navy introduced entrance examinations which encouraged the development of schools which specialised in preparing boys for the service, Eastman's Royal Naval Academy being amongst the earliest.

The school curriculum had a nautical flavour with subjects such as navigation and knot tying being taught alongside basic subjects, which at the time included Latin, English Literature and sports such as boating and gymnastics. In 1870 there were over 900 pupils who entered the services, most joining the Royal Navy.

It was one of the schools that held the accolade of being accredited by the Royal Navy as an examination centre for Navy entrants. Another Eastman Royal Naval Academy ran on the same lines opened in Wallington, Hampshire in 1881.

Unless any reader can enlighten us to the contrary there are no surviving records of either school deposited within the archives.

Records of colleges, schools and academies

The main records can be located at The National Archives and form part of ADM Division 23 with the records of the Royal Naval Colleges and the Council of Naval Education being found in series ADM 203.

This series includes in-letters of the Royal Naval College, Greenwich, examination results, and minutes of the Board of Studies; papers of the Council on Naval Education, 1877 to 1904; and papers relative to the inspection of Greenwich Hospital School, 1883 to 1904. It also contains lists of officers, masters and cadets.

Reports on candidates for admission to the Academy and the progress made of the cadets can be found in series ADM 1 for which there is a nominal list by name at The National Archives reading room. The detail found within the record includes, name, age, birth date and place, subject listing and report of progress, discharge date and reason and also remarks made by both the headmaster and governor - in effect a 'school report'.

Details of scholars warranted to the Academy between 1733 and 1756 which is surname indexed can be found in series ADM 6 and a listing of candidates for the college between 1811 and 1836 is found in series ADM 11. For a very limited period 1813-1815 there are copies of baptism certificates for college candidates some of which also include correspondence from parents. These can be located in series ADM 7.

The Navy List also has a list of officers studying at the college for the period 1875-1923 but some listings for the earlier period back to 1848 can only be found in series ADM 11.

Candidates who trained on *Britannia* between 1857 and 1888 can also be located in ADM 11 and these provide date of birth, date of entry to the college and the date of discharge indicating which ship. Records of examination results exist in ADM 6 for the period 1877-1902. These lists include name (often just surname and forename initials), date of entry to Britannia, marks achieved in the various subjects with a total in the end column. Series ADM 11 also contains lists of other officers on more specialist courses such as torpedo training, engineering etc.

Royal Naval College Final Examination

The following examples are taken from the 1885-1886 final examination lists and names are listed in order of merit. Published lists give the following information:

Name.
Index Number.
Rank.
Date of commencing college course.
Division in Mathematics.
Columns then for marks in each subject.
GROUP A.
Mathematics (Pure and applied).
Physics (Lectures and practical).
Chemistry (Lectures and practical).
Steam and the steam engine.
Theory of navigation.
Practical navigation.
Marine surveying.
Naval architecture.
Compass correction.
Permanent fortification.
Field fortification.

Military surveying and drawing.

Military tactics.

French.

German.

Freehand drawing.

GROUP B.

Naval history.

International law.

Minor tactics.

Meteorology.

Practical astronomy.

Total.

Indications are also given if the student was awarded a prize in any subject.

There are various lists of cadets studying at the Royal Naval College in Dartmouth for the period 1931 to 1964 deposited in series ADM 203. A small collection of these lists is also contained in the Royal Navy Tracts Box in the Upper Library at the Society of Genealogists Library primarily for the mid-1930s.

A list of officers who qualified in gunnery between 1833 and 1842 exists in series ADM 6 which is surname indexed. Of more significance is the set of service records maintained by the Gunnery School for the period 1838-1898. There is also a separate index of gunners covering the records which form part of ADM 196. These records give the name and date of birth of the officer and career details (up to around 1902) including ships and remarks about conduct, knowledge and ability.

18th century drawing of the first Marshalsea Prison, 1878. Public domain image.

CHAPTER NINETEEN

Royal Navy Courts Martial and Tribunals

T he ancient maritime laws that feature in the Admiralty Black Books back as far as 1336 are the basis of Royal Navy discipline, later determined by statute. Before the mid-1600s naval discipline was basically under the auspices of the captain of each vessel without any uniform system of administration. In such times disciplinary offences were punished in accordance with an individual Captain's personal code of conduct.

The system changed in 1652 when the Admiralty introduced a standard code and also the Articles of War allowed fixed punishments and/or penalties for certain less serious offence. Articles of War were also enforced during peacetime and as such became incorporated in the statutes of 1661, 1749 and 1886 known as the Naval Discipline Acts and by which all naval tribunals and Courts Martial had to adhere.

In accordance with the Articles of War whenever a ship was lost there had to be an automatic Courts Martial. In this regard there is a published list 'The Lost Ships of the Royal Navy 1793-1900' available in The National Archives library which lists the ships, the date of the court and TNA reference to give quick access to the documents without further recourse to indexes and finding aids.

The Royal Navy system of dealing with discipline was unique and serious offences could even be dealt with by passing the death sentence. Statutes governed all Navy discipline. Trivial offences did not go before a Tribunal or Courts Martial. Both social and naval offences were dealt with in the Courts Martial system including:

Naval Offences

Examples include Desertion and being absent without leave; Mutiny; Brutality; Conduct unbecoming of an officer; Loss; collision and grounding of ships and submarines; Neglect of duty; Disobedience to orders; Sedition etc.

Social Offences

Examples include Alcohol (Drunkenness) and drug related offences; Embezzlement, Theft and Plunder (which sometimes involved the whole crew of a ship); Disturbance of the peace, Fighting and striking an officer; Self-mutilation, etc.

In some cases multiple offences formed part of the same case against both men and officers.

The judicial process began with a formal letter of complaint to the Lords Commissioners of the Admiralty for offences within home waters or to the Commander in Chief of Foreign Stations. The regulations and instructions required the information to be precise and cover three essential points:

- The charges.
- A clear explanation of the crime or offence detailing time, place etc. of each transgression.
- Details of how the offence had been perpetrated.

In some cases a Court of Inquiry was then held to determine the validity of the complaint letters. This was a less formal setting that an official Courts Martial. Between three to five tribunal members gathered evidence and testimonies which were not taken under oath and the sole purpose was to determine if court action was necessary. The Commander then determined the action to be taken and if necessary issued the orders for the formal Naval Tribunal or Courts Martial to be convened.

The courts had to follow a rigid procedure and each accused was entitled to the protection of the regulations in order that a fair trial was given.

The second or third ranking officer of the station usually became the President of the Court and between five and 15 officers formed the panel which was convened on the day of the trial for that specific purpose. The procedure made sure that:

1. Account for all qualified justices being present and that they sat according to seniority. The Judge Advocates had to be well versed in the laws and regulations relating to naval tribunals.
2. The witnesses and any audience were then admitted to the room.
3. The accused was then brought to court by the Provost Marshall (RN Police).
4. The order for the trial and the warrant appointing the Judge Advocate were actioned.
5. All parties swore their respective oaths.
6. The letter of complaint was then read out.
7. At this point all witnesses were ordered to withdraw from the court.
8. The trial then began with prosecution and defence cases and witnesses were interviewed and cross examined. The naval Disciplinary regulations determined the number of witnesses for each side dependent upon the severity of the case.
9. The accused would then enter his defence.
10. The court was cleared whilst the case was deliberated on by the panel.
11. The verdict was then ratified - sentences for some offences were pre-determined by the Articles of War (the procedure could be slightly different if a commissioned officer or Warrant Officer was the accused as opposed to a rating).
12. The decision of the tribunal was put in writing and signed by each member of the panel in order of seniority.
13. The court was re-convened and the Judge Advocate announced the findings. Those found to be innocent with no case to answer were immediately freed and exonerated and those convicted were handed to the custody of the Provost and their record marked accordingly.

Perhaps one of the most common aspects relating to Naval Discipline relates to the vast number of ratings who, over a period of time deserted (indicated by 'R' or Run on many records). It is thought that desertion rates amongst ratings often ran as high as 25%. The peak of desertions seems to have been during the press gang period. Between 1755 and 1763 around 38,000 men deserted the service and into the 19th century it is estimated that around 2,000 men each year deserted. Men who deserted gave up their right to pay, medals, 'prize money' and pension.

Information relating to deserters can be located in various sources. After about 1875 it is worth searching the *Police Gazette* as all such people are listed giving valuable information including name, date of desertion, their rating, age, physical description and details of their ships. You may even be lucky enough to find a photograph of the deserter as these are included in some instances.

ADMIRALTY.

Description of Deserters from Her Majesty's Sea Service.

Subject to the Admiralty Regulations (Police Gazette, 28th April, 1885) a reward at the discretion of the Captain of the Ship of not exceeding apprehension, within two years, of Deserters or Absentees (except when apprehended within the precincts of a port or place where there is a Naval Establishment.) Expenses will also be paid in accordance with these Regulations.

65. *Deserters from the Royal Navy as recorded in the Police Gazette or Hue and Cry.*

Ships' musters provide information in the form of the 'Run' annotation and the musters are the main source of information before the *Police Gazette* recorded the deserter. Please remember that no musters exist after 1878. The *Police Gazette* for 1828-1845 can be searched in series HO 75 and some later ones exist in series ME PO6 although it is not a complete run in this series. Some information can also be located in the Admiralty Digests but this is not the best source as they are complicated to use and also they will not record all deserters. However one advantage is that they sometimes list all the deserters from one ship. Often men deserted in groups. Records of Courts Martial as described below are also a useful source for those deserters who became subject to naval discipline.

Many Royal Navy personnel deserted in Australia and a database exists on **Ancestry.com** giving the name, ship, reference to the pre 1862 *NSW Government Gazette* or *Antipodean Police Gazettes* after 1862, and a physical description including place of birth. An example entry is shown below:

ADAMS, HMS Pearl p287, From, Sydney, on the 30th October, 1875:-Ord., 1st
Alfd. 6.10.1875 class, born on the 26th November, 1856, at Gosport, Hants, England, 5' 8½', brown hair, grey eyes, fair complexion. Former ship 'Adventure'. £3 reward.

Records of Courts Martial

The essential information for finding the records of a Courts Martial are the date the case was heard and the name of the accused as most records are organised chronologically. Many cases took place some time after the offence was committed.

Records of the Courts commence in 1680 and the content of Courts Martial records varies from a brief summary of the case to full transcripts and minutes. Some records from the mid-19th century to the early 20th century have not survived. As you research the case papers you may also be lucky enough to find as part of the papers the service records of those accused alongside other official documents used as evidence such as casualty lists, extracts from ships' log books, Warrant Officer accounts and the like.

Indexes and finding aids

Many of the official Courts Martial records are found within series ADM 1. If you do not have a date for the hearing then it may be possible to find the reference for the case by using the name of the accused in Discovery together with the key words Courts Martial and restricting your advanced search to ADM 1. The Discovery catalogue allows direct access to the reference for cases heard between 1680 and 1702. Not all cases are individually listed so you may have to revert to one of several finding aids and indexes which are available at The National Archives. The indexes to series ADM 1 are found in ADM 12 (how to use these records is discussed later in this book). Using ADM 12 enables the date to be located. There are two types of registers in ADM 12 and you should use the one arranged by initial letter of the surname or the ship's name. They are organised by year so you may have to search over a span of years before you locate the case if you have no idea of the date. Once you locate the name sufficed by the letters CM (Courts Martial) or the sub-series 'Ct Mar' then you can use the reference to find the actual files in series ADM 1. The indexes in series ADM 12 allow searches to be made up to 1958 but of course some records will be the subject of closure.

Registers - lists of trials

Series ADM 194 consists of the Courts Martial Registers covering the period 1812-1978. These registers cover mainly Courts Martial of the Portsmouth and Plymouth Divisions. Pieces ADM 13/103-104 which are more of an index also contain registers of Courts Martial of Royal Naval Officers and ratings, 1812-1815, and of Royal Naval Officers and Warrant Officers, 1857-1915, which may overlap with ADM 194.

In the registers you would expect to find information giving brief details of the trials, arranged chronologically and including the number of the Courts Martial, date of the trial, name, rank, ship (serving with when the trial took place), nature of the charge(s), whether proved or not and details of the sentence imposed (or acquittal).

Courts Martial Papers

Series ADM 1 which is a huge series of Admiralty and Secretariat papers contains the records of Courts Martial covering the period 1680-1839 and 1845-1910. There are no records from 1840 to 1844. These are the minutes of proceedings and the sentences of Courts Martial held both at home and abroad. Pieces ADM 1/5253-5263 are listed by the name of accused on Discovery. Most of the records are handwritten sheets normally of around 10 pages depending upon the complexity of the case. A few are however written in shorthand.

For some reason records have been extracted from ADM 1 (specifically pieces 116, 137 and 167) for the period 1890-1965 and included in series ADM 156. They comprise records of Courts Martial of officers and men of the Royal Navy, the Naval Reserve and Auxiliary Forces.

Naval Courts Martial and Boards of Enquiry Reports of a sensitive nature for the period 1892-1951 can be found in series ADM 178. Because of the sensitive nature of the content access restrictions may apply.

There are also other classes which include various papers relating to Navy Courts Martial outside of the main series and not altogether indexed. Registers and returns of cases conducted on the Nore Station (Chatham) between 1848 and 1863 are in series ADM 153 and those for the Mediterranean station between 1863 and 1874 are in series ADM 121.

Marshalsea Prison Admiralty Side

Within the Marshalsea prison in Southwark (most noted as a debtors prison) there was an Admiralty division which housed prisoners sentenced to imprisonment under Royal Navy Courts Martial for mutiny, desertion, piracy, and what was referred to as 'unnatural crimes'. The premises occupied by the Admiralty division were pretty dilapidated and formed part of the old borough gaol. Because of the state of the cells and the attempted and successful break outs of naval prisoners, they were often housed in the infirmary which was more secure.

The naval prisoners were supposed to have a separate exercise yard in order to prevent criminal and civil (debtors) prisoners from associating but layout plans for the Marshalsea suggest that this was not the case.

The records for the Admiralty prisoners for the period 1773 to 1843 are maintained in separate admission and discharge records found in series PRIS11. The records give details of the man, his quality, age, details of the crime/charges, where court martialed and the date, the terms of the sentence and also when and under what conditions the discharge took place.

Digests of Convictions (Black Books)

The black books run for the period 1741-1815 and comprise three volumes of digest of convictions of officers at Courts Martial and can be located in series ADM 12/27 suffixed by the letters B-D. They are arranged chronologically and are a useful supplement to the case information previously discussed. The three volumes are indexed by initial letter of the surname in ADM 12/27E. The information is in summary format and provides date of the Courts Martial, brief outline of the charge and details of the sentence.

A similar document for Warrant Officers covering the same period can be found in ADM 11/39

Although not directly concerned with matters of the Courts Martial the High Court of Admiralty (Admiralty Sessions) does contain some records relating to Courts Martial, between 1802 and 1857, namely warrants for the arrest and imprisonment of both officers and ratings in regard to breaches of either naval or criminal law and can be located in a warrant entry book which cover the period 1811 to 1857 and are contained within series HCA 55 in series 1 and 2.

The actual Entry Book of warrants from Lords Commissioners of the Admiralty and relating to the apprehension and transfer of persons and the execution of sentences imposed by the Courts Martial can be found in HCA 38/39. It is surname indexed and covers the same period as above.

Liberated naval and merchant seaman POWs at Marlag und Milag Nord at Westertimke, 29 April 1945. Public domain image.

CHAPTER TWENTY

Royal Navy Prisoners of War

T
here are no comprehensive records relating to Royal Navy prisoners
of war and many of those which do exist contain little information.
There are specific records in the ADM classes but information can
also be found in the Foreign Office records under the departmental heading
of Prisoners of War and Aliens Department. Prisoners of War were taken
from all the divisions of the Navy so it is more than probable that such a
notation will exist of their personnel record and this is often the only record.

Prisoners of War have existed since the time of the American Revolutionary
Wars. Perhaps the most notable set of records existing for captures pre 1793
are those found in a nominal roll of POWs for 1779-1780 in series ADM
103. The list relates to POWs held in various French towns and of course like
many of the records in series ADM 103 are written in French! There is also
a series of policy papers mainly relating to the exchange of prisoners in
series SP 42 but few actually mention names.

Research becomes a little more complex for the period between 1793 and the
outbreak of the First World War and this is particularly true of the
Napoleonic War period when of course many of the Royal Navy personnel
were taken prisoner by the French.

The records in ADM 103 comprise volumes which are registers of prisoners incarcerated in either prison ships or depots and taken between 1793 and 1815 during the wars with France and created by the Prisoners of War Departments of the Sick and Hurt Board (to 1796) of the Transport Board (1796-1817) and of the Navy Board, Transport Branch (from 1817). They relate to British and French prisoners as well as the exchanges which took place between both countries. In most cases they will show the places of birth, physical description and the disposal of the prisoners.

The registers cover two distinct sequences for the wider period of 1755 to 1831. One sequence covers registers of home and overseas prison ships and depots arranged alphabetically by location and then ships' names. The other series is arranged alphabetically by nationality and also includes details of any parole prisoners or registers of deaths. It was not only British prisoners that were captured as there are records of both American and Spanish prisoners within the registers.

There is little information on Royal Navy POWs between 1831 and the start of the First World War. For the world wars information relating to Royal Navy prisoners of war can be accessed using the Indexes in ADM 12 (using code 97) as detailed above. There are however a couple of exceptions. The prisoners held at the Gressen POW camp from the crew of *HMS Crusader* and *HMS Maori* can be found in series ADM 1. The Navy List of 1917 (confidential edition) also contains a list of officers from the Royal Naval Air Service held as prisoners of war.

Those officers from all branches of the Royal Navy (including volunteers and reserves) who were held as POWs between 1914 and 1917 are listed by name, rank, camp and date of capture, provided they were held for more than 18 months, in series FO 383.

The International Committee of the Red Cross holds records of all known prisoners of war for both world wars. The documents are currently undergoing digitisation (project due to be completed for the First World War period towards the end of 2014). The archive, established in 1914, is a valuable resource for persons tracing their POW ancestors in the Navy (Royal and Merchant) as the Red Cross collected, analysed and organised information received from detaining powers on individual prisoners numbering around six million cards. It fulfilled a valuable role in being able to provide information to next-of-kin and enable family links to be maintained.

Once completed a digital copy of individual records will allow quicker and easier retrieval through the internet. Details of this will be forthcoming at some future point. The minimum information required for a search is a name, date and place of birth, nationality, military status but if you can provide additional information then such items as rank, service number, parentage are also useful.

Minimal information is also held on Second World War POWs. There is a published source which should be the first place for research 'Prisoners of War, Naval and Air Forces of Great Britain 1939-1945' available in the library of The National Archives. Some War Office records provide details of Royal Navy personnel (both officers and ratings) in series WO 392 relating to those held in camps in Germany or its occupied territories and those held by the Japanese.

The records for those held in Germany give name, where held, camp number, POW number and Royal Navy service number. In the Japanese camp listing the information provided also includes date of capture and liberation and information on death (if applicable). In comparison to the army and air force the number of POWs amongst Royal Navy personnel was relatively small.

In Germany there were separate camps for Royal Navy personnel known as Marlag divided into two parts, one for officers the other for ratings. However in 1942 the ratings were all sent to Stalag VIII-B in Lamsdorf.

Marlag contained 29 huts sleeping between 14 and 18 men in each. It had its own Post Office and POWs were allowed to send two letters and four postcards each month but there was no restriction on the number of letters they could receive all of which were subject to censorship.

Sailors using holystones aboard HMS Pandora, c. 1913. Public domain image.

CHAPTER TWENTY-ONE
Admiralty Digests and Indexes

O ne of the most underused sources of genealogical information outside of Royal Navy service records is the information contained in a class of documents known as the Admiralty Indexes and Digests (which includes Secretariat papers). They are not the easiest sets of records to research but they cover many aspects of naval administration and are split up into four basic classes with an index in series ADM 12. Because of the way in which the records are organised you will need to understand and use the indexes to find relevant information although there are indexes and digests for each year. Throughout its history the Admiralty used various codes and abbreviations as well as changing its filing system on more than one occasion. The basic difference is that the index relates to ships and people and the digest relates to subject.

The digests and indexes in ADM 12 mainly relate to:

Letters received by the Admiralty in series ADM 1 (Admiralty in-letters) covering 1793 to 1913. ADM 1 actually includes Admiralty correspondence from 1660 to 1976.

They can also relate to:

- Letters sent by the Admiralty in series ADM 2 (Admiralty out-letters).
- Admiralty Minute books in series ADM 3 covering 1657 to 1881.
- Case files - series of letters etc collected together into a single file - in series ADM 7.
- Supplementary Admiralty records in series ADM 13.
- Official History of the First World War in series ADM 137.

The Digests are summaries of information in the various documents and they are essentially the basis of the indexes. Sometimes the Digest is the only reference to the existence of a document or letter as over time the Admiralty may well have disposed of its correspondence and this is more noticeable from the mid-1800s onwards. Separate records exist for the records of the Navy Board in ADM 106.

In order to understand how to use the ADM 12 series some background information is needed.

The documents received by the Admiralty were divided into separate classes namely Public Offices, Letters from each rank of flag and commissioned officers, Miscellaneous (often referred to as promiscuous) and Admiralty Board minutes. As the clerks in the record office read them they decided whether the record should be indexed by the name of the person or the name of the ship. There were around 104 subject headings (codes) and the list can be located in the reading room at The National Archives. It was at this point that the system of cross referencing operated. The correspondence from officers and in the miscellaneous sections were sorted into alphabetical order and the rest were kept in chronological order. Each was allocated a number and this is the important piece of information to step from the index and digests to the original record.

Originally each year was covered by an alphabetical index to persons and ships and a digest, which combined a summary and a subject index of the papers. They provide cross references to each other and also point to the location of the original papers. However a further stage is needed to translating the references to find the correct document at The National Archives. In some cases there is more than one type of index in use. During the First World War Two clerks worked on the indexing and digests and each had their own volumes, as such both volumes need to be consulted to locate relevant information.

The Indexes

These contain entries by the name of the person who authored the letter, Royal Navy ships (annotated in red ink), Merchant Navy or foreign registered vessels (annotated in black ink). The indexes also refer to people mentioned in the letters as well as the author.

In each book until 1859 there are four columns, none of which have headings but they relate to the following (running from left to right) - column one - Marines, column two - Ships, column three - officers and ratings and column four - Promiscuous.

After 1859 the number of columns is reduced to three all of which are labelled thus: column one - Naval & Marine Officers, column two - Ships and column three - Promiscuous.

Each main column, whether labelled or not, was then sub-divided into three smaller columns - the original date of the correspondence, the ADM 1 reference and subject column. If more than one number is included then there may be more than one reference in the digests to which the letter refers. From 1860, an extra column was included in the index volumes showing the date of any correspondence generated by in-coming letters and reports and including the code-letter of the Admiralty branch originating the action. This information is important when locating the out-letters.

The Digests

Not all correspondence found in the indexes warranted inclusion in the digests. If an item was included then it was placed under one of the 104 subject headings. The codes were revised on several occasions and there are separate tables for 1800, 1843, 1909, 1935 and 1963.

It is necessary for you to understand how the digests can be accessed to provide you with the appropriate information about your ancestor. Initially to use the index you will need to know the name of a ship or the name of a one of the officers on a ship. Some references also relate to ordinary seamen. There is a slightly different technique depending upon the years to be searched and also whether you want an index or the digest.

Locating a Document

For the majority of index searches up to 1913 if you follow the procedure outlined below you should locate a relevant entry:

1. Browse through ADM 12 using Discovery to the index for the year(s) and person or ship. This will provide you with the reference of the document which covers your search criteria.
2. You will then need to order that original document and find the entries in the index which relate.
3. You will then need to note the abbreviation(s) which are sometimes just a single letter followed by a number in the 'How and where to be found' column. You will need to refer to the abbreviation table in order to find out what it means as this becomes your key word or phrase for the following step.
4. Use the advanced search facility in Discovery to search ADM 1 by using the keyword or phrase and restricting your search to the relevant year. It may mean that you have to refine your keyword search as it may not always work.
5. Consult the original ADM 1 document.

For the majority of Digest searches up to 1913 if you follow the procedure outlined below you should locate a relevant entry:

The ADM 12 index volumes contain cross-references to the digest volumes, where you can inevitably locate a summary of the ADM 1 correspondence which is sometimes enough information to make an actual ADM 1 search unnecessary.

1. Locating the entry in ADM 12 is basically the same as shown for an index search only this time search for a Digest entry rather than an index entry.
2. Note the number found in the Subject column and use this to find the digest volume and the year. You may find that the ADM 12 reference relates to a range of numbers in which your specific number is included.
3. Obtain the original ADM 12 document.
4. Locate the entry (sometimes noted as a 'cut') in the volume that corresponds to the reference number you previously located and be aware that there may be multiple entries which relate to the same reference.

You can often use the digest volumes as the subject index to ADM 1 and thus avoid using the indexes. Doing this gives no guarantee that the original ADM 1 document actually exists and all you can rely on is the digest summary.

1. Look up your subject in the Alphabetical Index to Admiralty Digest Headings and make a note of the number code and then use Discovery to search ADM 12 for the appropriate digest volumes as shown earlier.
2. Order the document and find the entry as shown in the Digest headings.
3. Follow the remaining procedures as shown above.

As the majority of the ADM 12 Indexes etc. relate to documents in classes ADM 1 and ADM 2 the following is a summary of what they contain and how useful they will be once the appropriate record has been located in ADM 12.

Some of the indexes in the earlier pieces of series ADM 12 relate to documents generated before the Index and Digests began in 1793. As such it is not always possible to relate them directly to the documents in ADM 1 although with some perseverance it may be possible to locate them. If not the only information available will be that contained in the ADM 12 narrative.

There are some other smaller indexes which are available in the research room at The National Archives and which appear to have been compiled for specific subjects or specific piece numbers by individuals and not always totally clear but they include:

- Correspondence from unemployed admirals ADM 1/577-580.
- Orders in Council ADM 1/5246-5252, ADM 1/5138-5168, ADM 1/5170-5181, ADM 1/5189-5190, ADM 1/5198 and ADM 1/5201.
- Correspondence from the Navy Transport Department ADM 1/3729-3774.
- Correspondence about Ireland ADM 1/3988-3991.
- Leeward Islands admirals' despatches ADM 1/312.
- Correspondence from Secretaries of State ADM 1/4080.
- Correspondence from the Royal College of Surgeons up to around 1817.
- Miscellaneous letters and reports ADM 1/5114-5124.
- Petitions ADM 1/5125-5137.

What does ADM 1 contain?

From an organisational viewpoint the records in ADM 1 relate to a number of groups for a range of years. All of the contents are arranged into four basic groups according to the author:

- By their rank.
- By the first letter of the surname.
- By the area of the world from which the letter or report was sent.
- By the name of the naval station from which the letter was sent.

Unfortunately these groupings do not remain consistent throughout the series and they also vary according to different periods.

Sometimes, because of shortcomings in the catalogue system searching ADM 1 even using the ADM 12 Indexes is far from straightforward and requires patience and gaining familiarity with the series. It is worth persevering as the records contain a wealth of information. You may even end up having to just browse through the year or name ranges to find your record.

ADM 1 is a series which contains the official correspondence sent (in letters) for the information of the Lord Admiral or the Lords Commissioners and includes correspondence to, from and within all the departments of the Admiralty from c.1660 to 1976. Minutes were also noted on the in-letters and from around 1870 minute sheets were added to important letters when they were received as a matter of course. Sometimes the copies of relative out letters were placed with the in letters (although ADM 2 is the main class for such a series) but in doing so 'files' were composed.

From around 1832 the centralised nature of the naval affairs changed and the papers in ADM 1 began to appear as secretary papers. For the 20th century most of the papers are internal correspondence within the Admiralty as opposed to those just relating to in-letters.

To add slightly to the confusion the organisation of ADM 1 differs depending on the period and the series has therefore been sub-divided. Up until 1839 the series is organised into groups according to the source of the incoming letters. Between 1840 and 1913 the series is organised into year groups and also within each year into the same groups that existed for the pre 1839 series.

For later series records see the section on 20th century operational records.

Captains' and Lieutenants' letters

One of the valuable resources in series ADM 1 is the Captains' letters. The letters written by captains contain a variety of information and if your ancestor was indeed a Royal Navy Captain they are likely to be of interest. It is unlikely that they will contain genealogical information but will be useful when tracing their careers. The name index to Captains' letters for the period 1698 to 1792 is in ADM 10 and from 1793 to 1815 (some extend to c.1839). There is a separate index in The National Archives reading room but for some reason it does not extend beyond the surnames beginning with the letter P. The volumes do, however, give the ADM 1 reference.

The example below would be extremely useful in genealogical research.

Transcript ADM 1/1842 - Captains Letter from John Gibson dated 1795:

Bowman, Crediton Feby 95

Sir

The Reverend William Radford curate of this parish having informed me of his intention of making application to the Lords Commissioners of the Admiralty for employ in His Majestys Navy as a Chaplain, having known him some time I have taken the liberty through you to offer them my testimony in his father as he is a young man of good morals & very liberal education, seems well adapted for the employment he solicits -As I think he would be an acquisition to the service I have been the more induced to render him any assistance in my power. Should their Lordships approve of him it will be confirming an obligation on their & yours.

Jn Gibson Capt R.N.

Philip Stevens Esq.

Within ADM 1 the letters are grouped together in a series namely A-H, I-Q and R-Z arranged by the initial letters of their surnames. They include both officers at sea and those employed ashore and are particularly useful for those on half-pay and also for those employed in the Impress Service. Some captains' letters are summarised in the similar series for Commander in Chief letters. The letters also relate to post-captains, masters and commanders and in some cases Commodores who were in positions of command. Up to 1705 the letters from can also contain those from acting-captains of H.M. ships. In the ADM 12 indexes the Captains' letters have a reference commencing 'Cap' followed by the first letter of the surname.

Lieutenant's Letters exists from 1791 to 1839 arranged by the initial letter of each officer's surname. Letters which were written before 1791 have been destroyed in various Admiralty re-organisations. The series consists of letters written by Lieutenants to the Secretary of the Admiralty and includes Lieutenants who were in command of vessels but not reporting to a senior officer. However, most of the letters in this series are from Lieutenants on half-pay or employed in shore establishments. The series also includes some letters from sub-lieutenants although they are few and far between. In the ADM 12 indexes they are referenced by the letter 'L' followed by the first letter of the surname.

What does ADM 2 contain?

The series contains Admiralty out-letter books and includes information on commissions and warrants appointing sea and naval officers, and other out-letters, principally the 'Lords' letters' and routine correspondence.

'Lords' letters' were formal letters signed by the Lord High Admiral, by the lords commissioners of the Admiralty, or by the monarch holding the office of Lord High Admiral. Routine correspondence was that which did not require the signature of the Lord High Admiral or the Admiralty Board and which were normally written and signed by the Secretary.

The records only exist in this series up to 1859 and most of the individual volumes contain their own index.

CHAPTER TWENTY-TWO
Royal Navy operational records

There is a tremendous amount of information contained in the operational records of the Royal Navy which can provide background details of a man's life at sea. This is particularly true for late 19th and to mid-20th century service. We have already dealt with the majority of records of genealogical value including service records and pensions but details of their actual vessels etc. will enable you to put the flesh on the bones of your ancestor's life in the Navy.

The most important source of information on all the activities of the Navy is the correspondence of the Admiralty Board, primarily in series ADM 1 but there is other information which will help you flesh out the bones.

Log Books, Journals and Ships Histories

Types of Ships

The main fighting vessels of the Royal Navy were referred to as 'Rated Ships of the Line' and were rated according to their size and number of guns carried. The rating criteria varied over time. Frigates were smaller ships of the line (normally 5th rate). These frigate ships were used for armed escort duties, patrols and communication purposes. Sloops were even smaller and were frequently used for coastal and inshore duties with the object of disrupting enemy shipping. The next class consisted of an array of specialist and support ships. Specialist ships included bomb ketches and fire ships but the support vessels were often older ships of the line retired to become floating command centres or hulks and were usually located on Navy bases or in river estuaries.

If you want to find out details of the ships used by the Navy then you should consult 'Ships of the Royal Navy' as this covers all vessels commissioned since the 15th century. The details given relate to name (and any change of name), place it was built, launch date, armaments, when and where it served and what happened to it e.g. sunk, sold, decommissioned etc. The book includes details of the ships requisitioned through time into Navy service even if they were not built as such.

Ships' Logbooks

There are various sources that will enable you to trace the locations and movements of ships and the weather they encountered on their voyages alongside the 'gems' which indicate the tasks performed by the crews, discipline as administered on board and of course not reaching the Courts Martial, losses and damage and the health and welfare of the crews.

The records of most use fall into three basic categories:

Officers' Log Books - Admirals journals cover the period 1702-1916, Captains' log books covering 1669 to 1852, Master log books covering 1672 to 1871 and the Lieutenants' Log Books which in many cases where they survive are the most useful. Although some exist in amongst other classes the majority of surviving log books are held by the National Maritime Museum.

Ships' Logs - these in many cases superseded the above but in some instances ran alongside them. Many can be searched up to around 1967.

Medical Officers' Journals - these run from c.1785 until around 1963 and are possibly the most useful for searching for names and details of individuals.

Admirals' Journals in series ADM 50 exist for the period 1702-1916 and contain formal records about navigation, meteorological information, Admiralty orders and other official business. Up until 1854/1856 they are organised alphabetically under the personal name of the Admiral but the later journals are organised by the station or squadron where the Admiral was based at the time.

Captains' Logs in series ADM 51 exist for the period 1669 to 1853 and were kept by the captain of each ship on a daily basis. These are more interesting to family historians as they contain details of the employment and ship's company and as such provide a full picture of the daily routine on board. Some log books also include a list of crew. They are listed alphabetically and then chronologically for each ship.

Amongst this series you may also come across a few Lieutenants' Log Books.

Masters' Logs in series ADM 52 cover the period 1672 to 1840 and were completed specifically by the Sailing Master providing a record of the ship's course and position, together with information about the employment of the crew and records of any punishments administered. The Logs often contain sketches and/or maps of uncharted land or harbours that had not previously been visited. These were then circulated to other ships to act as navigational aids.

The series is again listed alphabetically and chronologically under each ship.

Lieutenants' Log Books are mainly held at the National Maritime Museum in series ADM/L covering the period 1673 to 1809 and comprise over 5,000 volumes. Occasionally such logs can be found in the other log book series of records found at The National Archives. The Lieutenants recorded details of weather, navigation and the routine on board their ship. They are particularly useful for records of incidents which occurred on board. From around 1800 fairly standard printed formats began to emerge but it was not until 1805 that the Admiralty laid down a specific format. Each year the logs were deposited at the Admiralty Office together with a certificate stating that the officer had complied with all instructions and had not been absent from his ship.

Receipt of the log book meant that the Lieutenant could be paid. The log books were bound into volumes according to the name of the ship (not the name of the Lieutenant). In some cases ships with the same initial letter of their name were bound together by year. In some cases Captains' Logs are also bound so it may be necessary to research in both repositories for a full picture.

A detailed index of the logs is available via the Maritime Museum Archive catalogue and also in the search room.

Ships' Logs in series ADM 53 cover the period 1799 to 1985. These were maintained by the Officer of the Watch and exist for every ship of the Royal Navy when it was in service (hence there may be gaps in the records when ships were out of commission for refits etc.) thus providing a daily record of the ship's movements and position, orders received and more importantly details relating to the employment of the ship's company, deaths on board and the warrants issued to enable disciplinary action to take place. They also include records of visits to the ship by dignitaries or foreign officers.

The lists for ships' logs are not always obvious but most reflect that the returns were annual and they are arranged generally alphabetically by name of ship. Some are out of sequence for the war years however, whilst all ships logs exist for 1939 and early 1940, the majority of logs for ships smaller than cruisers have not survived for the remaining years of the Second World War.

There is also a supplementary series of ships' log books in series ADM 54 covering the period 1808 to 1871 so both classes need to be searched.

There are also odd pieces within other Admiralty records that contain log books for certain ships and these can be ascertained by using Discovery and typing in the search field the name of the specific ship. Such records are known to exist for *Phoenix*, *Lincoln* and *Young Lady*.

There is also series of log books from Portsmouth based ships authored by different officers including Lieutenants (where these are not in the NMM) and importantly by Midshipmen covering the period 1757-1992.

Logs and Journals of Ships on Exploration in series ADM 55 cover the period 1757 to 1861 and also for some reason 1904 and relate to both navigational logs and narrative accounts of naval officers (captains, lieutenants, masters, mates, boatswains and assistant surgeons) involved in the various voyages of exploration. They tend to be concerned with specific areas including the Pacific, Arctic, Antarctic, Australia, the Americas, China, St Helena and the west coast of Africa,

Charles II founded the Royal Society of London to encourage scientific knowledge of astronomy, biology, geographical exploration, navigation and seamanship. In 1714 the Board of Longitude was created and offered a prize for solution to discovering longitude at sea. The problem was solved by John Harrison's chronometers.

In 1782 signalling with 28 flags using a numbered code was introduced and this was further developed in 1796 by the introduction of semaphore. 15 semaphore stations were inaugurated between London and Deal, with a further ten stations being set up between London and Portsmouth. In 1795 lemon juice was introduced to prevent scurvy on board ships and in the same year the Admiralty's Hydrographic Department was established. The first Admiralty chart was issued in 1801 and from 1819 the Admiralty also sold its charts to the Merchant Marine. Since then navigation has operated entirely on British Admiralty charts. The 19th century saw the beginning of Arctic exploration.

The CORRAL project has digitised ships logbooks specifically for those ships employed in voyages of scientific discovery and those in the service of the Hydrographic Survey together with coastal and island records contained in UK Colonial documents. This project is mainly concerned with meteorological data back to the 18th Century but the digitised data may be a useful insight into a voyage. The records are available online on the British Atmospheric Data Centre website and records are extracted from the following classes:

- ADM 51 - Captains' Logs, 1669-1853.
- ADM 53 - Ships' Logs 1799-1985.
- ADM 53 - Flying Squadron: Ships' Logs 1869-1872.
- ADM 55 - Supplementary Logs and Journals of Ships on Exploration, 1757-1861 and 1904.

Medical Journals and Surgeons' Logs in series ADM 101 and MT32 cover the period 1785 to 1963. Surgeon Superintendents' Journals of Convict Ships in the latter class cover the period 1858-1867 and contain regulations, lists of names, dietary and medical reports and are arranged by ships names.

Since establishment the medical officers of the Royal Navy were separated into either surgeons or physicians. Every serving ship had either a surgeon or assistant surgeon, who would have to treat patients, perform surgical procedures and prepare medications. The more senior ranking physicians would usually only work on a capital ship or be in charge of a land based hospital.

The main series in ADM 101 are by far the more informative and are a valuable resource for family historians as they list names of sick (and others who may have come to the surgeon's attention) among passengers, convicts and crew. These frequently include details of those who did not recover and never reached their destination. They also offer information about life on board ship including such occurrences as drunken debauchery, gunfights, mutiny, being killed by lightning, bitten by a shark, sexually transmitted disease, the significance of scurvy amongst the ships' company and one strange case of blood-letting which resulted in the 'rapid procession to fatal termination'- what a good description for someone who was obviously left to bleed to death whilst under medical care!

They comprise journals returned by the surgeons of HM ships, some of the naval hospitals, and those relating to Naval Brigades and shore parties. The series also includes journals of the naval surgeons or assistant surgeons assigned to both convict and emigrant ships. These journals provide a fascinating record and account of the treatment of both medical and surgical cases arising within the ship's company (both passengers and crew) including a copy of the daily sick list and general comments on the health and activities of the ship's company. Some contain information relating to discoveries of cures etc. which happened either by accident or design as serving medical officers had to submit detailed records of the health, treatment and survival rates of the ships company.

The log books contain details of the individual patient (name, age, rating/quality), nature of the disease, illness or wound, account of the medical treatment administered which frequently detailed daily progress. Many of the journals also include intricate drawings, charts or diagrams which detail the injury etc.

Ancestry.co.uk has a series of medical journals of 19th century ships searchable by name but covering mainly the records of some convict ships for the period c.1817-1857. The database contains indexed images of medical journals which include names of patients and other passengers and crew aboard. The collection consists of around 670 journals the majority of which are from those ships bound for Australia. These journals relate to both male and female patients and give names, ages, rank or status aboard (including prisoners treated as well as crew), medical information including dates of illness, notes on symptoms and treatment. The records are also extremely useful for information relating to those who died as a result of disease or injury.

The journals generally also offer an interesting insight on contemporary treatments and medical practices, as well as stories of life aboard ship.

The National Archives also makes some of the ADM 101 records available as part of the digital microfilm project.

Because of data protection etc. some of the 20th Century journals are held by the Admiralty Library on HM Naval Base, Portsmouth.

Submarine Logs in series ADM 173 cover the period from 1914 to c.1982 which are effectively a comprehensive record of navigation, the firing of torpedoes and depth keeping information. Little information is contained about actual crew members but occasionally there is a 'gem'. Unfortunately they contain a number of abbreviations which were not standardised throughout as they were invariably maintained by an officer or crew member of the submarine's company. When the submarine was lost so, unfortunately were the current log books of the time.

Ship Photographs and Histories

For many finding out about the ships on which your ancestors served is as important as finding out about an individual's career. At The National Archives there is a series of photographs of Royal Navy ships in series ADM 176. The series comprises over 1,000 photographs of ships in commission between 1845 and 1945. Some are mounted and some are un-mounted and each series is arranged alphabetically by the name of the ship and can be searched individually using Discovery. Each piece for a particular ship may contain more than one photograph. Both the National Maritime Museum at Greenwich and the Imperial War Museum have unbridled collections of naval ships' photographs for the World Wars.

There are also various sources on the internet which give access to photographs of ships mainly from the 1880s to the 1950s. **www.ShipPhotos.co.uk** and **www.navyphotos.co.uk** are useful websites and contain good quality photographs not just of the ships themselves but sometimes crew or memorial photographs. There is a particularly useful section on the photographs of the trawlers used by the Royal Navy which were either seconded or purpose built.

Researching the history of a ship can also be fascinating. The main source of information with regard to the building and maintenance of a ship can be accessed at The National Archives.

Series ADM 180 covering the period 1620 to c.1914 comprises registers of all naval vessels and gives details of their construction, launch, refitting, their armaments, number of crew etc. The series comprises the Progress Books which are arranged by years and then for the types of ships often identified by their rate or by 'steam vessels', 'smaller ships and boats' etc. The second part of the series relates to List Books.

For those wanting more in-depth history, classes ADM 135 and ADM 136 will be of interest as these are reports and papers relating to the maintenance history of the ship from construction to disposal. The records generally cover the period from 1807 to 1962 but not all ships' maintenance books exist as series ADM 136 appears to include information for only those considered to be famous or of significance in naval history. They are organised by date of launch. Research into ships' histories may also be supplemented by correspondence and information from the Office of Surveyors of Ships found in series ADM 95.

The National Maritime Museum at Greenwich also has microfiche giving warship histories from c.1650 to 1950. The information contains launch date, size, number of guns, crew complement and brief 'ship's career'. In many cases this is a brief description and sometimes a duplication of information in series ADM 180 albeit that it is not as comprehensive. There are also various published books available detailing ships' histories.

Ships' Newspapers

Many Royal Navy ships unofficially published their own newspapers and magazines. The earliest newspaper was published in 1857 and they run to the present day supplemented by 'Navy News' which was founded in 1954. Copies of various papers can be located amongst the collections of maritime archives including the National Maritime Museum, Royal Navy Museum etc. A search of the respective repositories' catalogues will provide more information and coverage.

The newspapers and magazines are generally light-hearted with articles covering humour, short stories, verse, serious articles, ship's news and gossip. Most are illustrated albeit crudely in some cases. The majority of newspapers were given their own name branding such as 'The Rocket' which was the paper of *HMS Minotaur*, 'The Magpie' for *HMS Sierra Cordova* and 'The Young Idea' for *HMS Chesapeake*.

Some magazines relate only to one voyage and are in the form of a newsletter type log or diary but if your ancestor was a crewman (or sometimes a passenger on a Royal Navy Ship - or in the convoy) they would be of interest in fleshing out the bones of your ancestor's career in the Navy.

The Royal Naval Museum, Portsmouth holds several runs of ships' magazines between 1882 and 1982 but these are mostly associated with Portsmouth based ships.

Naval Operational Records of the Two World Wars

The most important operational records for the Second World War can be found in classes ADM 1 and ADM 116 at The National Archives. Documents are arranged by subject. The official history of the Navy during the war is included in series ADM 199 which actually covers the period from 1922 to way after the end of the war and looks at the way in which all operations were executed. Most of the information has been compiled from the information in ADM 1 and ADM 116 but its use is slightly difficult as it does not appear to be in any specific order. The records included cover such subjects as: damage to ships, war diary summaries, information on submarine and U-boat matters, Operation Neptune, action reports of the Fleet Air Arm squadrons and daily naval events, to mention but a few.

As the main source is again ADM 1 it is necessary to understand how to access these records for the Second World War period.

As previously stated the ADM 12 index and digest volumes run until 1974. However, for the Second World War period the indexes become less useful as finding aids.

The best way to consult documents in ADM 1 for the war periods is by searching 'Discovery' and using a series of keywords or by using the subject index which is available whilst at The National Archives before ordering the appropriate ADM 1 document.

For the specific years of 1938 to 1945 you can also find Admiralty code numbers in ADM 12 and then search using the code number in place of a keyword. The codes relate to both ADM 1 and ADM 116 classes.

Between 1938 and 1952 the documents in ADM 1 are arranged by series. Which index to use depends upon which series the documents are in. Series I uses the 1963 Alphabetical Index to Admiralty Digest Headings and Series II the 1935 version.

If you wish to consult the Official History in ADM 199 you will need to find War History (WH) case numbers in ADM 12 and, using the subject key in the printed version of ADM 199 available only at The National Archives, locate the appropriate ADM 199 piece number. If you come across any other form of index to ADM 199 then it may not contain the correct and modern piece references.

A couple of other very useful sets of records relating to naval convoy operations in the Second World War can be found in ADM 217 and ADM 236/ADM 237.

ADM 217 relates to the operational records of the Western Approaches Command. The series includes reports from officers and is indexed by convoy and also by the ships of the senior officers. However, it does not appear to be complete.

To some extent the information in ADM 236/237 supplements and compliments the information which can be found in ADM 199. Again this series seems to not give the full picture but the convoy information is well worth a search if your ancestor served on any of the convoys. They include Reports of Proceedings, Commodores' Reports and other papers. ADM 236 is specific to submarine patrol reports mainly from the Mediterranean area. There is an index of convoys available for consultation at The National Archives.

For the First World War the main resource has again to be ADM 12 but the records are arranged differently to that of the pre First World War period and of the Second World War.

For the ADM 12 index and digest volumes for the years 1914-1919 there are two sets of every index and digest, with references suffixed by the letters A and B. Both will need to be consulted to find information relative to a particular name or subject. For the First World War period many ADM 12 references exist to series ADM 137 which is primarily concerned with records compiled by the Admiralty Historical Section in the form of an official history of the war.

There is a slight short cut which can be taken using the Discovery catalogue. Direct searches of both ADM 1 and ADM 137 can be made using keywords but the project of indexing the official history in series ADM 137 is so far incomplete that it is not always successful necessitating a search of ADM 12 also.

Because ADM 12 is arranged differently for the 1914-1918 period you will need to search as follows:

1. Browse through the catalogue to the appropriate index or digest for the year(s) and person or ship in question. You will need to use the Alphabetical Index to Digest Headings to obtain the appropriate digest code.
2. View the original ADM 12 document and find the entry for the person or ship. Note carefully the reference as there are three possible categories in which the record could lay and case numbers (particularly relevant to series ADM 116, Admiralty papers for which the reference is both a letter and number) or the Admiralty date reference.
3. Your next step for ordering the actual document depends on what type of reference you have located.

Confidential Navy Lists

The published Navy Lists for the duration of both wars did not include sensitive information but there was a series of Lists also produced referred to as the Confidential Navy Lists which are in series ADM 177. They contain complete information for officers and ships which was systematically omitted from the published editions.

Running alongside the Confidential Navy Lists for the Second World War are the 'coloured' lists which detail specific aspects of the Navy during the war years which were issued on a more frequent basis than the Navy List. For operational research these should also be referred to.

The Red List in series ADM 208 related to port locations of what was classed as minor war ships or vessels in home waters.

The Pink List in series ADM 187 relates to port locations of all ships and air squadrons in commission. This was the most frequently published with a couple of issues every week.

The Blue List in series ADM 209 recorded shipbuilding during the war and was published each month.

The Green List in series ADM 210 related to various landing craft utilised in home waters.

Official History of the War - ADM 137

If you want to undertake research on Navy operations in the First World War then you should consult the five published volumes of the Official History which in themselves can provide in depth information on operations. The index also allows you to trace individual ships.

Those who compiled the official history did so from various records, namely the 'cases' from the Admiralty Secretariat papers, the records of the Grand Fleet and some other naval commands and the Naval War Staff records. The record was compiled from the operational reports, signals and other telegraphic information received from convoys, ships, squadrons, naval stations used in the war period and from the German naval blockade.

Ship Losses in the Two Wars

If you wish to find details of ships lost in the two world wars there are various online sources which can be used as well as official records. Part of series ADM 242 which relates to war losses covers ships lost in World War One. There is a card index in The National Archives covering such losses during the period 1914 to 1919.

A database also exists online at **www.roll-of-honour.net/royalnavy** which details the following information: class of vessel, name, tonnage, launch or completion year, date of loss, how and where lost and other information. For brief information it is worth consulting this data.

For losses of Royal Navy ships in the Second World War consult **www.navy-history.net** which details similar information for all World War Two losses and does include the Merchant ships which were part of convoys that were scuppered.

Wartime Naval Intelligence

ADM 223 relates to the Naval Intelligence Division and covers the period 1914-1978. It covers Admiralty Intelligence papers and includes information relating to foreign (mainly German) naval communications and signals as well as intelligence reports from Japanese and Mediterranean waters, The class is particularly useful in regard to U-boat attacks on convoys, minesweeping and enemy shipping movements. The series also includes photocopies of documents referred to in the official history of the intelligence services as well as a small series of message logs from the First World War.

The Disposition and Movements of HM Ships

Because of the world wide deployment of Royal Navy ships and personnel, the Navy established stations and shore bases in various countries and as such it is reasonably easy to find the disposition of any serving ship.

You should be able to discover the station, movements and sometimes employment of HM ships by reference to either ADM 7 or ADM 8. In order to find details of a ship it is usual to have some idea of where your ancestor was on a given date. You can then use the above series of documents to establish the names of the ships in the locality and then search in the musters for your ancestor's record. Ships movements can be determined from 1648 although in the early days records are not always comprehensive.

The following is a summary of available records for ships establishments:

- ADM 7.
- Abstracts of Ships' Journals 1736-1795.
- Board Room Journals 1796-1829 (later journals 1842 to 1880 are in series ADM 13).
- Daily Returns to the First Lord 1812-1830.
- Miscellaneous Muster Books 1741-1759; 1772-1804.
- Stations of Ships 1696-1822 (some gaps).
- ADM 8.
- List Books 1673-1893; 1903-1909.

The most useful collection of documents detailing a ships whereabouts are the List Books in series ADM 8 covering the period 1673 to c.1910. The list books consist of monthly returns compiled in the Admiralty Office and are known as 'The Present Disposal of His Majesty's Ships and Vessels in Sea Pay'. These each show the location of a serving ship and the names of the officers.

Unfortunately these lists are not indexed, but it may be useful to employ two resources, firstly the Commissioned Sea Officers, 1660-1815 as officers service is extracted directly from the List Books. Use the Navy Lists after 1815. From 1855 the List Books were printed, and included additional information about the ships.

The List Books are returns only of ships in commission and are arranged roughly geographically. They include the names of the Captain (some Lieutenants are named in the pre-1810 lists) and show their crew complement and their rate usually when they were commissioned or when they had last docked. Supplementary to this series there are also a series of Muster Lists covering some ships for the period 1741 to 1759 and 1772 to 1804 available in series ADM 7. These are over and above the records of musters shown earlier.

Losses of Warships

Records exist of the losses of ships of the fleet from about 1700 onwards. Information can generally be located up to around the mid-1800s in series ADM 1. These are mainly reports of the losses given by captains or flag officers under whose command the vessels were. Most records provide accurate information about the position the ships were in at the time of the loss.

From around 1850 series ADM 116 referred to as 'cases' for which there is a subject index at The National Archives also contains some information although this is not comprehensive. Other series in ADM also have information regarding shipwrecks. One of the most useful series is ADM 106 - letters to and from the Navy Board. This series is particularly informative where ship losses occurred which resulted in salvage attempts. In most cases but particularly for events occurring before the early 1820s you will need to know the date and location of the loss.

If the loss occurred during the First World War then there are loss reports in series ADM 137 which also records enemy losses and details of any merchant vessels which formed part of a Navy escorted convoy. Records in this series were those used to compile the official history of the war. Similar records of losses in the Second World War can be found in series ADM 199.

If you are lucky enough to locate a surviving log of any of the ships wrecked or lost then these will often provide first-hand information of the circumstances leading to the loss. You will need to research classes ADM 51 - ADM 54 which are generally arranged in alphabetical order by the name of the ship. Clearly if the log books went down with the ship then few records will exist. Again however there may be surviving Lieutenants' logs or personal diaries of crew members which may provide useful information.

There will of course be the records of the Courts Martial which were held where there were surviving captains or other officers held accountable for the loss as it was the norm for the courts to undertake official enquiries of wrecked or lost ships although few seem to exist where the loss was as a result of wartime action. (See section on Courts Martial and also information concerning ADM 1 above.)

Admiralty Charts

In connection with the loss of a ship you may also want to search available maps and charts, particularly if the loss occurred in coastal waters or on set convoy routes. Using an Admiralty chart is the equivalent of using a contemporary map as we undertake our general family history.

Admiralty charts produced by the British Admiralty are maps which aid navigation at sea. Its first chart was published in late 1800. They exist for seas and coastal areas in all parts of the world.

As a tool for navigation the scaled charts mapped coastlines showing water depths and tidal marks. Many also record the position of wrecks as well as other information. They record navigational hazards such as reefs and wrecks, and navigational aids, such as lights, buoys and beacons. Many also show longitude and latitude.

Because they had to remain accurate the charts were continually updated and any obsolete charts were systematically destroyed because of potential navigational hazards. Dates of the original survey and re-compilations were recorded. Some Admiralty charts contain detailed charts of harbours and also show names of coastal features some of which no longer exist.

At The National Archives, Admiralty charts are included with many different documents. The best set of records are held by the Hydrographic Office in Taunton, Somerset, which holds virtually a complete set of printed Admiralty charts and associated records.

The British Library also holds perhaps the largest collection of Admiralty charts in its map department as well as those where the East India Company carried out the charting and marine surveys within the Indian Ocean and China Sea between 1779 and 1858. Some of the EIC charts are also at Taunton.

The National Maritime Museum at Greenwich has a collection of around 100,000 sea charts and maps dating from the medieval period to the present day although the collection is not all British.

Royal Navy Stations (and Associated Fleets and Squadrons)

When not with the home fleet, many ships were stationed around the world. The majority of records relate to correspondence and orders or memoranda specific to the stations. The records which exist seem to vary significantly in their style and the time periods for which they survive. Stations were the geographical divisions from which the Navy administered its worldwide responsibilities. They were normally run by a Commander in Chief and his staff. Ships were assigned at different time to various stations. Details of the ship assignments can be established through the annual Navy Lists and the above mentioned records.

There were various home stations, supported by the home fleet, namely:

- Channel - records exist between 1867 and 1907 in series ADM 144.
- Ireland - records exist between 1816 and 1912 in series ADM 149 indexed in ADM 150.
- Nore (Medway) - records exist from 1805 onwards in series ADM 151 indexed in ADM 152.
- Portsmouth - records exist from 1880 onwards in series ADM 179.
- Plymouth - records exist from 1859 onwards in series ADM 130.

The foreign stations are perhaps of much more importance for family historians as they place your ancestor in different parts of the world at different time periods. Whilst most of the records relate to correspondence and orders there is some information about personnel over and above that which can be found in normal service records.

North American & West Indies stations - records exist from 1810 to 1913 in series ADM 128 indexed in series ADM 129. The station existed from 1745 until 1956. Until 1818 The North American Station and the West Indies Station were separate entities. The support squadron was also formed in 1745 to counter French forces in

North America. Its prime headquarters was the Halifax naval yard in Nova Scotia which was commissioned in 1759 and was the main base during the Seven Years War and the War of 1812. In 1818 the squadron shifted to the Bermuda Naval Dockyard which had been a base since 1795 and continued until 1951. Halifax continued to be used only as the summer base for the station.

Pacific station (known as the South America Station until 1837) - records exist from 1843 to 1858 in series ADM 172 indexed in series ADM 173. The station was established in the early 19th century at Valparaiso, Chile to support British interests along the eastern shores of the Pacific. In 1842 Esquimalt Dockyard was established.

In 1855 three Crimean huts were built at Esquimalt to serve as a hospital intended to receive wounded from the Crimean War and these huts formed the first shore establishment at Esquimalt which became the station headquarters in 1865.

A dock was commissioned at Esquimalt in 1887. The station closed in 1905 and subsequent to that the responsibilities were divided between the China, Australia and North America and West Indies Stations.

Australia station - records exist from 1855 to 1896 in series ADM 122. Following the establishment of New South Wales ships based in Australian waters came under the control of the East Indies Station. In 1848 an Australian Division was formed which became an independent station in 1859.

The Australia Station included Australia and New Zealand and extended to the south sea islands of Samoa and Tonga, to the western edge of the Indian Ocean and to the Antarctic Circle. The area covered by the station was subsequently extended in 1872 and again in 1893 to cover a quarter of the Southern Hemisphere. Just prior to the First World War the station was handed to the Royal Australian Navy. However, in 1921 the area around New Zealand was restored as part of the China Station.

China station - records exist from 1828 onwards in series ADM 125 indexed in series ADM 126. Between 1831 and 1865, the China Station as well as the East Indies Station were combined and known as the East Indies and China Station. Subsequently the China Station, established in 1865, had responsibility for the coast of China and its navigable river deltas, as well as the western part of the Pacific Ocean which included the Dutch East Indies. The later formation of large naval bases at Singapore, Hong Kong and Wei Hai had an impact on the station. Ships based on this station were white with dark funnels which were not the usual Navy colours.

East India station - records exist from 1808 in series ADM 127. The East India Station which was established in 1865 covered parts of the Indian Ocean from the border with the Australia Station and included the Persian Gulf and the Red Sea mainly to protect Britain's trading interests.

The East Indies Station had bases at Colombo, Trincomalee, Bombay, Aden and Basra. In response to increased Japanese threats, the separate East Indies Station was merged with the China Station in December 1941 to form the Eastern Fleet.

West Africa and Cape station - records exist from 1797 onwards and include the Cape and West Africa Station divisions in series ADM 123 indexed in series ADM 124. The Squadron based at the Africa station had the task of suppressing the Atlantic slave trade by patrolling the coast of West Africa. In 1819 the naval station in West Africa was known as Freetown and was the capital of Sierra Leone, the first British colony in West Africa. From 1821, the Ascension Islands was also used as a supply depot, later moving to Cape Town in 1832.

The West Africa station was considered by personnel to be one of the worst postings as it suffered from a high level of illness from the various tropical diseases. Many of the Royal Navy surgeons developed cures for such diseases while assigned to the station.

The station was considered the most active. At the height of the slave trade up to 1860 its squadron successfully captured 1,600 slave ships and freed around 150,000 Africans, many settling in the Sierra Leone protectorate.

The Cape of Good Hope station was established in 1857 and covered most of the southern part of the Atlantic Ocean. In 1865 it was combined with the East India station but because of strategic requirements at the time was reestablished in 1867. In 1870 it absorbed the former West Africa Station and squadron and formed the South Atlantic Station in 1939.

Atlantic station - records exist between 1902 and 1910 in series ADM 145 indexed in series ADM 146. Part of the Channel Station and fleet were re-styled in the lead up to the First World War but was disbanded for the duration of that war reforming in 1919.

Mediterranean station - records exist from 1843 to c.1968 in series ADM 121. The station was established at Gibraltar (captured from the Spanish in 1704). Though the British had maintained a naval presence in the Mediterranean before then the capture of Gibraltar enabled the Navy to establish its first naval base there. The station also used Port Mahon, Minorca as a naval base for a short period. After 1800, throughout the Napoleonic Wars and thereafter Malta was the pre-eminent naval base of the Mediterranean station. In the latter part of the 19th century the Mediterranean Fleet was the largest squadron of the Royal Navy and protected the vital trade routes to the Far East.

CHAPTER TWENTY-THREE
Royal Navy Dockyards and Victualling Yards

R oyal Dockyards provided the Royal Navy with the shore support facilities it required to build, repair and maintain the fleet. Central to any Royal Dockyard were, as the name suggests, their dry docks and it was the provision of these expensive structures that set the Royal Yards apart from their civilian counterparts until well into the 19th century.

In the 17th century and throughout the 18th there were six main Royal Navy dockyards in England at Chatham, Sheerness, Portsmouth, Deptford, Woolwich and Plymouth, supported by a number of out-ports around the coast of England and also overseas dockyards in Gibraltar, Halifax and Jamaica. Yard Officers were appointed by the Board of Admiralty but administered by the Navy Board, under the direction of a yard commissioner. The majority of the employees at the yards were civilian staff.

By the mid-18th century the Royal Dockyards became 'well-oiled machines' and were amongst the largest industrial organisations throughout the world employing thousands of skilled workers in a wide number of trades. The high level of skills provided in the Royal Dockyards was essential to the Navy's success at sea.

The main personnel employed at each yard included the Master Shipwright; responsible for workmen and construction/repair and refitting work; the Master Attendant, who managed the ships in dock and organised the maintenance of the ships in Ordinary; the Clerk of the Survey (abolished in 1822) who checked and kept the stores and received and issued materials; the Clerk of the Cheque who was effectively the dockyard accountant but also mustered the workmen. Where a ropeyard existed there was also a Clerk of the Ropeyard (abolished 1822) who had much the same role as the Clerk of the Survey but specific to the ropeyard (see later).

Before 1832 all the Royal Navy dockyards were run by naval officers who were civilian employees of the Navy Board and not sea officers. There was movement of staff between the two services, so if you are researching a man's career, especially one of the skilled men, you should look at records of the dockyard staff and also the Royal Navy personnel records.

In 1832 the Navy Board was abolished and all yards and establishments, except gun wharves, were amalgamated under the direction of the Admiralty although the victualling yards remained virtually independent. The senior officer was a serving sea officer known as the admiral or captain-superintendent and who was sometimes also the port admiral, or flag officer.

Overseas dockyards and British out-ports were administered with the same organisation, albeit that they had fewer facilities and personnel. All of these were supplied by the main dockyard at Deptford.

The Royal Dockyards and various other Naval establishments, both in United Kingdom and overseas, trained apprentices to become skilled tradesmen. Although all personnel entered the dockyards in this way a large number completed their training in the dockyard environment. It was also an occupation where generations of the same families worked and where much of the work in dockyards was undertaken in difficult conditions.

A *Shipwright* was involved in the building, repair and alteration to ships' structures, ships plating, welding, the fitting out of compartments, fitting of deck coverings, gratings, ladders, benches and stowage, the manufacture of dinghies and wooden small craft including masts and spars and in fitting out the ships.

A *Ship Fitter* was involved with the mechanics of the ship responsible for capstans, winches, rudders, steering gear, submarine hydroplanes, gun rings and tank testing,

An *Engine Fitter* maintained, changed and installed engines, steam gear and turbines and was responsible for lubricating oil, diesel, missile launching equipment, propellers and all shafting on the ship shafts.

The *Boilermaker* manufactured marine boilers, steam pressure etc, fabrication, steel work, tube bending and boiler testing.

The Smiths - blacksmith and others were responsible for forging of molten metal for such items as chains, springs, shackles, galley ranges and ovens and anchor cables (after steel replaced the ropes). A coppersmith was responsible for high pressure pipe work and systems.

A *Patternmaker* made patterns from wood for casting of engineering items.

The *Iron Founder* was charged with the preparation of casting moulds and pouring molten metal to produce castings.

The *Joiner* was more than a carpenter and usually included the job of block maker. He was also responsible for all 'second fixings' on the ship and for polishing, varnishing, treating wood with preservative, upholstery and any 'wheelwright' work.

A *Block Maker* made all forms of blocks for lifting equipment, spars, sails, yards, masts, moorings etc.

The *Painter* was responsible for all decorative and artistic paintwork on board the ship including figurehead, mouldings etc, the preservation of decoration of the ships, tenders and boats, ornamental gilding, graining, marbling, signwriting and the ship's crests and any other artwork.

A *Rope Maker* was responsible for the manufacture of ropes and for their installation in conjunction with the caulkers and riggers.

The *Caulker* had a very specific role - that of caulking the wooden planks in the hull with oakum to maintain water tight holds. On board ship he was a lower class Warrant Officer and usually worked alongside the carpenter in the dockyard.

A *Sail Maker* was responsible for the manufacture and repair of sails, boat covers and the making and repair of both national and signalling flags.

During the late 19th century and throughout the 20th century other trades associated with electrical installation, welding, modern armaments, hydraulics and air-conditioning were also employed. Many of the above trades disappeared between the wars.

In the early 1840s, the Admiralty, recognising the need to improve the technical education of Naval Dockyard Shipwrights, established apprentice schools, the first of which opened at Chatham in 1843. Schools were also established at Portsmouth and Plymouth in 1844 and at Woolwich, Deptford, Sheerness and Pembroke in the following two years. Initially the schools aim was to improve the technical competence of the shipwright apprentices and to help the most able to qualify as Naval Constructors but the teaching at the schools expanded as the move from wood to steel ships evolved. After the Second World War the role of the Royal Navy worldwide was reducing. As dockyards closed around the world it meant the demise of the schools which had occurred by the early 1970s.

The specific records relating to apprentices at dockyards can be located in series ADM 12 using code 41.16. Naval Dockyard personnel who passed examinations are arranged chronologically from 1876 in the 'B' series binders of series CSC 10 at The National Archives. Other records and information can be located through the pay records etc. as detailed below.

There are many reasons why your ancestor may have worked in a naval dockyard and the following outlines the history and development.

Portsmouth Dockyard

The dockyard was established in 1495. At the end of Henry VIII reign it was neglected until the start of the Civil War. Various expansion took place which made Portsmouth an important dockyard from the mid-18th century having doubled in size. Further expansion took place in the 19th century and the dockyard remains in operation today. For the last 500 years, the dockyard at Portsmouth has been one of the Navy's most important assets without which the Royal Navy could not have existed. The Dockyard also had victualling and armament yards, first in Portsmouth and later expanding around Gosport. It is said that the Dockyard developed its own culture and language. The Dockyard plans reveal the expanse to include three basins, 17 dry docks, various berths and many different buildings which have been constructed in the last 300 years.

The dockyard has its own heritage trust which holds in its archive the original Dockyard Rate Books which were the registers of employment. These provide details of all the employees who worked in the dockyard or in the other Admiralty Establishments in the town. The records consist of around 200 volumes running from the mid-19th century until around 1950/1955 for which an index is in preparation.

The entries contain a wealth of information including name, date and place of birth, height, Certificate from the Civil Service Commissioners, details of service (which includes capacity, location of yard employed in, pay, period of employment, cause of discharge), pension paid and a general remarks column.

The records of the dockyard at the Royal Naval Museum include Records of the Sawmills at Portsmouth Dockyard 1789-1853. Some records of the activities of the Portsmouth and Gosport Victualling Yards 1718-1871 and the Medical Department. at Portsmouth Dockyard 1810-1815 and 1850-1955. Account books of the Portsmouth Victualling Yard including Monthly pay book of labourers 1721-1728, pay books 1736-1744 and staff records for the period around 1820.

The Medical Department records include: case books 1866-1918, hurt books 1873-1877, 1899-1926 and 1941-1943. accident books 1912-1916 and discharge books 1940-1943. Some may be subject to restricted access.

Plymouth Dockyard

Plymouth dockyard latterly, known as Devonport dockyard, was founded in 1690. In the 18th century its prime role was to maintain the Western squadron whereas in peacetime it built and repaired many of the Royal Navy's fleet of ships. It was one of the first yards to bring into operation a steam yard in about 1844.

Chatham Dockyard

The dockyard came into existence in the reign of Elizabeth I in 1567 and was important because of its location. It was the largest naval dockyard in the late 1600s only to be superseded both by Plymouth and Portsmouth. In 1662 the dockyard moved to a new site. By the 1860s and for around 20 years Chatham had established itself as a building yard because of the navigational difficulties resulting from the silting of the Medway on which it stood. Four new dry docks were built mainly by convict labour and were instrumental in completing the building of two new ships each year. Between the two world wars Chatham built submarines. When Deptford and Woolwich dockyards closed in 1869 Chatham resumed its importance as a dockyard and remained open until 1984, subsequent to which the dockyard has become a heritage site managed by the Chatham Historic Dockyard Trust.

Staff and volunteers at the Royal Dockyard Library have started a project to create a database of all the named individuals in their records which is a valuable resource for family historians. The ultimate aim is to make this available online but the staff are happy to assist researchers in the meantime. The trust also manages a valuable reference library covering Royal Naval history and biography, warships, shipbuilding, models, life at sea and associated subjects as well as books, drawings, documents and archive material specifically relating to Chatham Dockyard.

Deptford Dockyard

Deptford dockyard was established in 1513 and was the Navy's leading dockyard in the 16th century. Like Chatham its use was restricted to ship building and as stores supplying all the other yards and fleets abroad because of difficult navigation on a silted River Thames. The yard expanded rapidly throughout the 16th and 17th centuries and for a while was the Navy's main victualling depot as well as the headquarters of naval administration. It built and maintained warships of the fleet for over 350 years. The dockyard was largely inactive after 1830. Though shipbuilding briefly returned in the 1840s the Navy closed the yard in 1869. The victualling yard continued in operation, dedicated to the manufacture and storage of food, drink, clothing and furniture for the Navy, until its closure in 1961.

Deptford concentrated on building smaller warships. By the late 1700s it had five slipways for building warships, and by 1807 was also served by one of the first sheer hulks used by the Navy. A sheer hulk was used in the days of sail as a floating crane, primarily to place the masts of a ship under construction or repair. These masts were known as sheers, hence the name. The lower masts were the largest single timbers on a ship, and erecting them would have been extremely difficult without the use of a sheer hulk. Some of the other dockyards had land based masting sheers.

After 1820 maintenance work was all that happened at Deptford and within ten years only shipbreaking was undertaken at the dockyard resulting in the yard virtually closing down between 1830 and 1844 when small-scale warship construction resumed. This continued until the yard was closed completely.

Pembroke Dockyard

Pembroke dockyard was established 1815 having moved from Milford Haven, which had been a small building yard administered by the Navy since 1800. In 1930 the yard was used only as a store and fuel depot.

In 1809 a naval commission recommended the formal establishment of a Royal Navy dockyard at Milford Haven. In 1816 the first two ships built at the dockyard were launched. Until 1922 when the dockyard closed Pembroke built a further 263 Navy ships. It was at Pembroke that five Royal Yachts were built and fitted out over the same period.

As the dockyard became strategically important the town of Pembroke Dock became a military garrison town with a contingent of the Portsmouth Division of the Royal Marines barracked there subsequent to which the town barracks were home to many army regiments defending the dock.

Harwich Dockyard

In the 1660s Harwich became an important naval base and dockyard. The yard was especially important during the Dutch wars. The Navy Yard actually closed in 1713, but naval ship-building continued on the site under private ownership until 1829. During this time it also served as a small refitting and storing base. The Napoleonic Wars brought further defensive measures to Harwich. In the 1890s Beacon Hill fort was built which played an important role as a naval base for coastal forces during both World Wars.

Sheerness Dockyard

Sheerness was located on the Isle of Sheppey in the Medway estuary as an extension of Chatham and was initially established in 1665 primarily to store and refit ships. It became a construction yard after a second dry dock was built in 1720 for building fourth and fifth-rate ships. Following the Napoleonic Wars the yard was completely reconstructed (between 1815 and 1826). In 1854 a steam yard was established. It became a major employer on the Isle of Sheppey until its closure in the late 1950s.

The origin of Sheerness was a fort built in the reign of Henry VIII preventing enemy ships from entering the Medway and attacking the Chatham Dockyard. In 1797 Sheerness witnessed one of the few mutinies by discontented Royal Navy sailors. The dockyard suffered as a result of its location in that there was low quality housing and a poor water supply which resulted in a lack of workers, thus slowing down ship construction. Blue Town was subsequently established by the Navy for accommodation.

Woolwich Dockyard

Woolwich Dockyard was one of the earliest to be established in 1512 followed by a separate ropeyard which was established in 1610. The Dockyard gradually declined owing to limited facilities and the Thames silting up. By the start of the 19th century the main activity at the Dockyard was the fitting out of vessels built at nearby Deptford and refits of some of the smaller ships originally built at the Nore. In 1839 a steam factory was established at Woolwich. The ropeyard closed 1835 and the yard in 1869.

Cork Dockyard

The dockyard which was adjacent to the naval base and known as the Royal Alexandra Yard with its basin and dock opened in 1822. The Dockyard was located on Haulbowline Island in the mouth of the river. It was handed back to the Irish Free State in 1923.

The British Navy also had dockyards in other countries worldwide some of which were associated with stations. Royal Navy dockyards were established at Gibraltar, Malta, Halifax, Jamaica and Bermuda.

Bermuda Dockyard

1809 saw the establishment of a Royal Naval dockyard at Ireland in Bermuda which ultimately became the largest dockyard outside of the United Kingdom. The Royal Navy established the Dockyard and victualling yard for strategic reasons after the American War of Independence which resulted in Britain not having an operational dockyard between the West Indies and Halifax, Nova Scotia. It was part of the North America and West Indies Station. The dockyard closed in 1951.

Jamaica Dockyard

Port Royal in Jamaica was established as early as 1675 although it was from 1735 that the yard became important as a dockyard. In Queen Anne's reign a hulk was established there allowing the construction of other accommodation including two wharves. The yard's wharfage and storage capacity was subsequently increased in the mid-19th century. The yard closed in 1905.

Halifax Dockyard

The yard in Halifax Nova Scotia was established in 1759. By 1774, it had two wharves for refitting ships. These remained largely unchanged until the mid-19th century when a graving-dock, coaling facilities and torpedo boat slip were added, In 1887 it had its first dry dock. It remained in the hands of the Royal Navy until it was handed to the Canadian government in 1907. During its existence the yard played a vital role supplying the entire Royal Navy with masts and spars.

Antigua Dockyard

English Harbour, Antigua was used as a Naval Dockyard from 1725. Its usefulness was improved by additional development in 1743 using slave labourers from nearby plantations. It became Nelson's principal base in the West Indies during the Napoleonic Wars after which it gradually became run-down ultimately ceasing to be used from 1889. Many of the dockyard buildings were constructed between 1785 and 1794.

Malta Dockyard

The first dry of four dry docks at Malta Dockyard was built in 1848 which was also a strategic supply depot and arsenal. It was a prominent and strategic dockyard during both the First and Second World War. Malta dockyard was closed in 1958. During the Second World War the dockyard employed over 13,000 men. It was also one of the few dockyards abroad to establish a dockyard school as early as 1858.

It also had its own Royal Dockyard Battalion of Artillery of about 300 men to defend the Malta Dockyard and was established in 1853 from civilian volunteers in the employment of the naval department at Malta. The Artillery was under the command of the Admiral Superintendent of the Dockyard. The Malta Dockyard Battalion of Artillery consisted of three companies of 100 men each. These were the Dockyard Company, the Factory Company and the Victualling Yard Company. The artillery officers were appointed by the superintendent with Admiralty approval. The men were trained on Saturday afternoons to become gunners.

Victualling Yards

In the United Kingdom there were two major victualling yards, one at Plymouth and the other at Deptford. As with all victualling yards around the world they were closely associated with the adjoining dockyards.

The Navy's original victualling yard was situated in East Smithfield and operated from that location between 1560 until 1785 when it moved to Deptford. The Deptford victualling yard was the headquarters of the Victualling Board and it was this yard which supplied the other yards distributing food, rum, tobacco, medical supplies and clothing and bedding. To do so required large warehouses, abattoirs, pickling houses, brew houses, biscuit works, a cooperage, a rum distillery and mills. The Deptford yard closed in 1961.

The victualling yard at Stonehouse in Plymouth was known as the Royal William Yard and was the major victualling yard. It was constructed between 1826 and 1835 remaining in existence until 1992.

The victualling yard at Gibraltar (Rosia Harbour) was also of importance and was in operation by 1807. The yard is unique in that it had its own water supply reservoirs capable of keeping a whole fleet supplied for over a year.

Dockyard Police

The community around the naval dockyards was often a self-contained unit and encountered workplace crime such as theft of materials and cash, assault, sabotage and the like. To counteract such actions the Navy Board and Admiralty had their own police force (sometimes incorporated into county constabularies from about 1830 onwards).

66. Dockyard Police insignia.

Civilian workers were recruited from amongst the dockyard staff and the group was commanded by a Civilian Yard Warden who was usually a Royal Navy Lieutenant on half-pay. The police consisted of part time night watchmen and full time workers. Royal Marines were also employed as a military guard.

The standing dockyard police was established in 1834 and at that time included all the men who had previously been the wardens. This new force was full time and uniformed. The uniform usually included a cloak and a bowler hat making them distinguishable from other dockyard staff. In the larger yards the service was still backed up by Royal Marines.

In the 1860s much of the responsibility for policing the UK's Royal Dockyards passed to the Metropolitan Police with the men barracked in the dockyard itself. At this time the prime concern was the protection of property as at this time pilfering of copper and brass was at its height.

Royal Dockyard Corps

Lord Ellenborough, then First Lord of the Admiralty, mooted the idea of forming a 'militia' protecting the Royal Dockyards as early as 1846. The dockyard employees were to be its backbone. Seven dockyards began raising their battalions in the summer of 1847 and ultimately the force totaled around 10,500 men divided between an artillery force and an infantry force. A Colonel and Chief of Staff of the volunteers was appointed and was instructed to submit a plan for the re-organisation of the battalions. Financial difficulties and indifference at the Admiralty resulted in the disbanding in 1848. However this was not the end.

In 1846 permission was granted to establish another Defence Force known as the 'Dockyard Corps' to protect all Royal Dockyards. A pre-requisite to enrolment was that all the men had to be employed in these dockyards. Battalions of this Corps were formed in 1847 at principal Royal Dockyards. Those that appeared in the 1847 Army List were at Chatham, Woolwich, Sheerness, Portsmouth, Plymouth (Devonport) and Pembroke. They were granted Royal status a few months later becoming widely known as the Royal Dock Yard Corps comprising of both infantry and artillery units.

The officers were chosen locally from the heads of the various departments within the yards. In many cases the Corps instructors were retired Royal Marines, with serving Royal Marine Officers appointed as Adjutants. The many skills used in this dockyard made them versatile and all training was carried out after normal working hours Men received an attendance allowance on top of their normal wages.

Although controlled by the Navy department the Corps was actually under the auspices of the Army. Their special uniforms consisted of a double breasted tunic of blue cloth with a red collar and cuffs each having 16 quilt buttons in two rows down the front inscribed 'Royal Dock Yard Bttn.' around a fouled anchor and a cipher 'VR'. Their head dress was a spiked helmet. Officers wore a unique 31" sword bearing the inscription 'Royal Dock Yard Bttn.' and each man was issued with sword, bayonets and the French percussion musket.

The Royal Dock Yard Corps only lasted for about ten years. With the exception of the Malta Battalion (detailed above) it did not appear in the Army List after 1857. An attempt to reform the Corps in the early 1860s failed.

A small number of records survive and many details of an individual's service can be found in the dockyard records, albeit brief in content. The National Maritime Museum holds some appointment papers for the Chatham Dockyard Corps at its inception in 1848. Various records of individual commissions are held in applicable county record offices. Some information can be found in army personnel and pension papers. It is a matter of searching archive catalogues for information but comprehensive records have long since faded into oblivion.

Records of Dockyard Workers

The easiest records to search for any dockyard worker are the pay records which are organised by dockyard and for which you will need to know the following information: the name of the dockyard or victualling yard, name of person, period of employment or at least a possible year that the worker started work. To date the records are not searchable by name of person. Such records exist for the period 1660 to c.1868 although the records do not cover every yard in every year. There are also a different series of records for the dockyards, ropeyards and victualling yards.

There may be minor dockyards which are not shown in the above description and under which records are organised. You will also need to be aware that some dockyards changed or were known by different names during their existence.

Before searching it is important to know the difference between the 'Ordinary' and the 'Extraordinary'. Ordinary relates to those who were principally full time permanent employees and who were paid salaries and includes senior officers, clerks, foremen, artificers and labourers. Extraordinary relates to the payment of casual employees who were engaged as and when needed.

Dockyard Workers

In order to find information about your ancestor you should search under the name of the yard and by date of known employment. The main series for dockyard and ropeyard workers is series ADM 42, the records commonly known as yard books. There are yard books for the following dockyards: in the British Isles - Deal, Deptford (Royal Victoria), Royal William (Plymouth), Falmouth, Harwich, Kinsale, Leith, Pembroke, Portsmouth (Royal Clarence), Sheerness, Woolwich and Yarmouth; foreign yards - Antigua, Bermuda, Barbados, Canada, Africa, Flushing, Gibraltar, East Indies, Jamaica, Lisbon, Malta, Martinique, New York, Port Mahon, Port Royal, Prince of Wales Island, Rio de Janeiro, Sierra Leone and Tricomalee.

Before 1832 there were various classes of records which related to specific trades namely: shipwrights, coopers and labourers in series ADM 30, artificers in series ADM 106, rope makers, caulkers and coopers in series ADM 6. Not all years or employees in all yards are covered in the foregoing series.

There are also a series of records for the period post 1832 where employees received a pension. These are basically the same records as those who received Admiralty pensions from other branches of the service but of specific value for finding dockyard workers you should search series PMG 24 and 25 which run until c.1928/30.

If your search is unsuccessful it may also be necessary to search ships' musters in the classes ADM 33 and 36-38 and as a last resort the establishment books in ADM 7 as this latter series includes information on protection from the press (which dockyard workers were entitled to), the civil establishment and home yard salaries.

Some records of those who worked in dockyards between 1895 and the Second World War are retained by the Ministry of Defence and it is recommended that you use the facilities of the Veterans UK website to locate service details.

Victualling Yard Workers

Again it will be necessary to search under the name of the yard. There are two series of documents relating to victualling yard pay books series ADM 113 covers the period 1703 to 1857 and series ADM 224 covers 1712 to 1903. For the overlapping period it will be necessary to search in both series.

When researching dockyard workers it would also be useful to consult the records of dockyards held by the National Maritime Museum at Greenwich which holds a card index of senior dockyard officials up to 1832. This was originally compiled from classes ADM 6 and ADM 11 whose records are at The National Archives. Other records relating to individual yards include plans, manuscripts and other materials which will help put the 'flesh on the bones' of your ancestor's lives.

The National Maritime Museum is particularly important as a resource for the following records and you should refer to their archive catalogue for a breakdown of other documents held by them.

Chatham - letter books of correspondence between yard officials, the Admiralty and Navy Boards up to 1900, internal yard records (an extremely useful supplementary source of information) and a collection of plans dating from 1718-1867.

Pembroke - commissioners' and officers' letter books from 1783-1887.

Portsmouth - correspondence between yard officials, the Navy Board and the Admiralty from 1675 to 1899 in four groups, resident commissioner, admiral superintendent, the yard officers and miscellaneous.

Halifax - commissioners' and officers' letter books from 1783-1887.

Jamaica - various letter books.

There are a large number of plans for various years held by the museum for many of the dockyards.

Dockyard Workers awarded the Imperial Service Medal

67. Illustration Imperial Service Medal.

This medal was established in 1902 and was awarded to manual grade Civil Servants of the United Kingdom who completed 25 years of service upon their retirement. The medal is inscribed 'For Faithful Service'. It was not a medal earned of right but recipients had to be nominated by their heads of department after having shown outstanding service. Recipients are recorded in the honours section of the *London Gazette* supplements. Use **thegazette.co.uk** to locate your ancestor by searching in the advanced search section by date and under the exact phrase 'Imperial Service Medal'. In each section the PDF image will consist of more than one page with names organised alphabetically.

The Value of the Registers of the Dockyard Churches

Because the dockyards were in many cases their own communities and because every dockyard had its own churches which were used by both workers and servicemen for baptisms, marriages and burials of their families they are of value because such events are unlikely to be found in records of the civil ecclesiastical parishes. Some of the surviving registers are deposited at The National Archives and were detailed earlier in the section relating to genealogical sources, Other registers and records may be held locally in record offices alongside other parish records and are often catalogued or listed using their parochial names.

CHAPTER TWENTY-FOUR
Finding aids and online resources

M ost researchers today expect to be able to locate information quickly and where possible online. With the progression of digitisation of records there will be databases and records appearing on an almost daily basis whether on a commercial subscription site or on a website put together by enthusiasts. Many have been mentioned in the text of the book but a summary of available databases is given below (correct as of December 2013).

There are also many different finding aids available within the repositories and museum archives which will help locate information either on the men, the ships or the organisiation. The National Archives particularly has many finding aids available in the reading rooms to help locate document references and individuals some of which are gradually being incorporated onto Discovery.

Navy Dockyard Project

For some years now volunteers from the Naval Dockyard Society and TNA have been cataloguing some miscellaneous correspondence sent to the Navy Board. The date coverage is 1673-1789 but not all this is yet complete. The results include some correspondence held at the National Maritime Museum which comprises out-letters from the Navy Board to the Admiralty covering roughly the same period. Everybody wrote to the Board from the humblest seaman to the Admiral of the Red. They ask for more money, a superannuation, they report on the surveys of ships, offer solutions for the ravages of the worn or new cure-all medicines, they invent new technologies, ask for alterations to the ships, report on pressed men and arrange transports. All the naval world and administration is here and before the Industrial Revolution the Navy was the largest industry in the country. If you wish to access the results of the project it can be found using series ADM 106, ADM 354 and ADM 359 on TNA 'Discovery'.

Online data sources

Additional data sets are becoming available on a very frequent basis. It is recommended that if you subscribe to a commercial site you keep up to date with records and databases becoming available either by noting newsletter content or by keeping abreast of availability on such websites as Forebears or even Genuki.

The National Archives
www.nationalarchives.gov.uk
Royal Navy Ratings service records (ADM 139 and ADM 188) 1853-1923.
Trafalgar Muster Roll 1805.
Women's Royal Naval Service (WRNS) Service records - First World War.
Royal Naval Division service records - First World War.
Royal Navy Officers service record cards (ADM 340) c.1840-1920.
Royal Navy Officers service records (ADM 196) 1756-1931.
Royal Naval Reserve service records (BT 164) 1860 -1955.
Royal Naval Volunteer Reserve service records (ADM 337) 1905-1922.
Royal Naval Air Service officers' service records 1906-1956.
Next of Kin claims for pensions (ADM 45) 1830-1860.

Findmypast
www.findmypast.co.uk
Royal Naval Division casualties - First World War.
Royal Naval Division service records - First World War.
Royal Naval Volunteer Reserve Medal Roll - First World War.
Naval casualties - First World War.
Ships Lost at Sea (Royal Navy) - First World War.

Ancestry.co.uk
www.ancestry.co.uk
Royal Navy Surgeons Medical Journals 1817-1857.
Commissioned Sea officers of the Royal Navy 1660-1815.
Royal Navy War Graves Roll - First World War.
Navy Lists 1888-1970 (various with gaps).
Navy Medal and Award Rolls (ADM 171) 1793-1972.
British Navy Muster Rolls and Pay Lists (Canadian based ships) 1757-1836.
British Naval Biographical Dictionary.

Family Relatives
www.familyrelatives.com
Commissioned Sea Officers of the Royal Navy 1660-1815.
British Naval Biographical Dictionary.
Royal Naval College Dartmouth List 1920 and 1933.
Navy Lists (various years).
Minesweepers 1943.
Whitaker's Naval Directory 1898.

TheGenealogist
www.thegenealogist.co.uk
Navy Lists (various lists between 1822-1944.
Naval Despatches - First World War.
Royal Naval Memorial Register - First World War.

Forces War Records
www.forces-war-records.co.uk
Royal Naval Division Casualty Lists - First World War.
Royal Navy officers' Campaign Medals - First World War.
Royal Naval Volunteer Reserve Campaign Medals (Ratings) - First World War.
Gazette Awards and MIDs (Mentioned in Despatches).
Crimean War Naval (and Marines) Medal Roll.
Naval General Service Medal Roll.
Royal Navy Inter-war Roll of Honour 1919-1939.
Royal Navy Trafalgar Medal Roll.

Genes Reunited
www.genesreunited.co.uk
Royal Naval Division Service records - First World War.
Royal Naval Volunteer Reserve medal roll.

Other online data sets of interest for Royal Navy ancestors

The sites listed below are those which relate specifically to data of interest to family historians. There are of course may other enthusiasts' sites giving background information which have not been listed.

Ships of the Old Navy
www.ageofnelson.org
Complete histories of Navy ships (and those contracted to the Navy) up to about 1840 arranged alphabetically and giving names of captains and additional information about the life of the ship.

Royal Navy Officers 1939-1945
www.unithistoriies.com/officers/RN_officers
A database alphabetically listed of Royal Navy officers who served in World War Two. Some include photographs also birth and death dates, rank/rating with dates and seniority, decorations, career history including dates, name of ship, location etc. Database is heavily abbreviated but a key to abbreviations is included.

Naval History
www.pbenyon.plus.com/Naval.html
The site includes a comprehensive database and transcriptions of official directives, rules and regulations governing all branches of the Royal Navy. Some information on strategic locations of ships is also given. Covers mainly post 1840 period.

Shotley Burials
www.godfreydykes.info/GANGESANDSHOTLEYNAVAL
This is a small database of burials in the Ganges Burial Ground, mainly of the boys who trained there. Two lists are included, one organised under surname the other under burial date. The database includes name, rating, official number, death date and in some cases cause of death.

Ratings
www.rnranksand ratings.com
A comprehensive listing of the ratings divided into and covering various time periods.

20th Century Navy History
www.naval-history.net
This is an extremely comprehensive and informative website covering all aspects of naval history from the First World War to the present day. The various databases include information on ships, people, awards etc. The site is extremely useful for background information to the Royal Navy during both world wars and subsequent conflicts including the Falklands War. It is especially valuable for the section on ships' log books as it includes transcriptions and also links to digital images of the log books. The site is sometimes a little confusing to navigate but as you persevere it becomes more logical in the way it is organised.

Navy Lists

www.navylistresearch.co.uk

This website covers many of the published Navy Lists enabling research on Serving, Retired and Deceased Officers for the period 1827-2011. The site is the subject of a small annual subscription and can be researched by name, rank, ship, date of death etc.

Naval Biographical Database

www.navylist.org

This site details a biographical information database on those individuals who have served, or supported the Royal Navy since 1660, currently including Commission, Warrant and Yard Officers. It also identifies ships from 1660 to the early 19th century. Searches provide a listing of possible entries and include full name, rank etc. There is a charge for information required beyond that found in the listings.

Navy Records

www.navyrecordsonline.co.uk

An ever-expanding online subscription archive of miscellaneous British naval records and is the internet publishing arm of the Navy Records Society. The archive includes charts, portraits, cartoons, logs, letters, diaries, battle plans, sketchbooks, photograph albums and videos, much of which is unique.

Finding aids

The majority of those listed below relate to material currently available at The National Archives:

- Index to Captains Letters 1793-1815.
- Card Index of Courts martial 1680-1701.
- Widows' pensions 1846-1847.
- Royal Naval Chaplains Warrants 1698-1782.
- Commission and warrant Books index 1742-1846.
- Pursers' Nominal index from 1834 Survey.
- Card Index of out-patients for admission to Greenwich Hospital 1737-1840.
- Officers Widows pensions 1759-1819.
- Officers Marriage certificates index 1806-1866.
- Engineers' passing certificates 1863-1902.
- Midshipmen not achieving their Lieutenants exams 1801-1810.
- Effects papers index 1830-1860.
- Surgeons' qualifications 1700-1800.

Because 'Discovery' can be searched by name for many different records these indexes may at any time be superseded and no longer be available for reference.

Many documents referred to in this book incorporate their own indexes particularly those relating to classes ADM 1 and ADM 12.

Finding aids held by other repositories have not been included but if you intend to research it is worth searching research guides and online catalogues to find out what is available.

Museums with Information for Family Historians

National Maritime Museum
London SE10 9NF
Tel: 0208 858 4422
www.nmm.ac.uk

Royal Naval Museum
Portsmouth PO1 3NH
Tel: 02392 839766
www.royalnavalmuseum.org

Fleet Air Arm Museum
Yeovil BA22 8HT
Tel: 01953 840565
www.fleetairarm.com

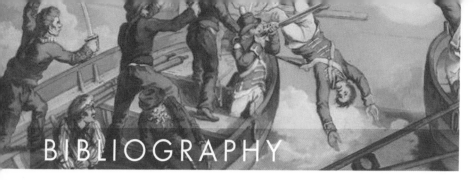

BIBLIOGRAPHY

Besides the sources mentioned in the foregoing text, the following are good reference books for more details relating to the history and records of the Royal Navy.

The Commissioned Sea Officers of the Royal Navy 1660-1815, Syrett & DiNardo, Published by Navy Records Society 1994.

Naval Biographical Dictionary (Commissioned officers alive in 1846), W R O'Byrne, Published London 1849.

An Illustrated History of the Royal Navy, A J Watts, Published by Brockhampton Press 1999.

Naval Records for Genealogists, N A M Rodger, published by The National Archives, 1998.

Various books on Naval Medals, K Douglas-Morris, published London 1982-1994.

The British Seaman, C Lloyd, Published by Collins 1968.

The Oxford Illustrated History of the Royal Navy, J R Hill, published by Oxford University Press 1995.

Battles and Honours of the Royal Navy, Arthur Dark, published by Hillingdon Family History Society 1998.

Britannia Rules - The Age of the Navy 1793-1815, C N Barkman, published by Book Club Associates 1977.

British Ships and Seamen, Grant Uden, published by Macmillan & Co. 1969.

Naval Courts Martial 1793-1815, John F Byrn, published by the Navy Records Society.

The Queen's Regulations and Admiralty Instructions for the Government of the Navy Service, Admiralty, published by HMSO 1862.

The Royal Naval Air Service, Brad King, published by Hikoki 1997.

Ships of the Royal Navy, James Colledge, published by Greenhill 1987.

Royal Navy Lieutenants' Passing Certificates 1691-1902, Bruno Pappalardo, published by the List and Index Society 2001.

Sea Power Ashore: 200 years of land based Royal Naval Operations, National Maritime Museum 2001.

The Navy in Transition 1814-1864 a Social History, Michael A Lewis, published by Hodder and Stoughton 1965.

A Guide to Naval Records in The National Archives of the UK, Randolph Cock, published by University of London Institute of Historical Research 2006.

About the SOCIETY OF GENEALOGISTS

Founded in 1911 the Society of Genealogists (SoG) is Britain's premier family history organisation. The Society maintains a splendid genealogical library and education centre in Clerkenwell.

The Society's collections are particularly valuable for research before the start of civil registration of births marriages and deaths in 1837 but there is plenty for the beginner too. Anyone starting their family history can use the online census indexes or look for entries in birth, death and marriage online indexes in the free open community access area.

The Library contains Britain's largest collection of parish register copies, indexes and transcripts and many nonconformist registers. Most cover the period from the 16th century to 1837. Along with registers, the library holds local histories, copies of churchyard gravestone inscriptions, poll books, trade directories, census indexes and a wealth of information about the parishes where our ancestors lived.

Unique indexes include Boyd's Marriage Index with more than seven million names compiled from 4300 churches between 1538-1837 and the Bernau Index with references to 4.5 million names in Chancery and other court proceedings. Also available are indexes of wills and marriage licences, and of apprentices and masters (1710-1774). Over the years the Society has rescued and made available records discarded by government departments and institutions but of great interest to family historians. These include records from the Bank of England, Trinity House and information on teachers and civil servants.

Boyd's and other unique databases are published online on **www.findmypast.com** and on the Society's own website **www.sog.org.uk**. There is free access to these and many other genealogical sites within the Library's Internet suite.

The Society is the ideal place to discover if a family history has already been researched with its huge collection of unique manuscript notes, extensive collections of past research and printed and unpublished family histories. If you expect to be carrying out family history research in the British Isles then membership is very worthwhile although non-members can use the library for a small search fee.

www.sog.org.uk

The Society of Genealogists is an educational charity. It holds study days, lectures, tutorials and evening classes and speakers from the Society regularly speak to groups around the country. The SoG runs workshops demonstrating computer programs of use to family historians. A diary of events and booking forms are available from the Society on 020 7553 3290 or on the website **www.sog.org.uk**.

Members enjoy free access to the Library, certain borrowing rights, free copies of the quarterly *Genealogists' Magazine* and various discounts of publications, courses, postal searches along with free access to data on the members' area of our website.

More details about the Society can be found on its extensive website at **www.sog.org.uk**

For a free Membership Pack contact the Society at:

14 Charterhouse Buildings,
Goswell Road,
London EC1M 7BA.
Telephone: 020 7553 3291
Fax: 020 7250 1800

The Society is always happy to help with enquiries and the following contacts may be of assistance.

Library & shop hours:

Monday	Closed
Tuesday	10am - 6pm
Wednesday	10am - 6pm
Thursday	10am - 8pm
Friday	Closed
Saturday	10am - 6pm
Sunday	Closed

Contacts:

Membership
Tel: 020 7553 3291
Email: membership@sog.org.uk

Lectures & courses
Tel: 020 7553 3290
Email: events@sog.org.uk

Family history advice line
Tel: 020 7490 8911
See website for availability

Society of Genealogists Publications

To view our full range of titles please visit:
www.sog.org.uk

Tel: +44 (0)20 7702 5483 | E-mail: sales@sog.org.uk